A Forgetful Nation

Ali Behdad

✤ A Forgetful Nation

On Immigration

and Cultural Identity

in the United States

Duke University Press

Durham & London

2005

© 2005 Duke University Press

All rights reserved.

Printed in the United States

of America on acid-free paper ⊗

Designed by CH Westmoreland

Typeset in Janson

by Tseng Information Systems, Inc.

Library of Congress Cataloging-

in-Publication Data

appear on the last printed page

of this book.

Frontispiece photograph by

courtesy of the Ellis Island

Immigration Museum.

For Hassan and Fatimeh

who gave me the courage to leave home,

And for Juliet, Roxana, and David

who showed me a way home

Contents

Preface

As I was writing this book, those who were familiar with my earlier work on nineteenth-century European travelers in the Middle East sometimes wondered about the disciplinary jump I was taking by writing about immigration and nationalism in the United States. Some were curious about the reason behind what they perceived to be a radical shift in my critical interest. Others expressed reservations about my authority, if not ability, to write about such complex and well-worn issues as immigration and national identity. Still others warned that I was committing academic suicide by moving from a familiar field to an unknown territory, and quite possibly perpetrating the crime of superficiality along the way. Disheartening though these queries were in the beginning, they helped me better understand what motivated my interest in the new topic and its connection with what I had written before.

Above all, what compelled me to pursue this project in spite of all the skepticism was something personal, the often disillusioning experiences and traumatic memories of being an Iranian immigrant in America. The topics of nineteenth-century European representations of the Middle East and immigration in the United States may seem unrelated critically, but for me they both raise important questions about identity, alterity, and culture. The writing of this book, like that of my first one, *Belated Travelers: Orientalism in the Age of Colonial Dissolution*, was a personal journey to make sense of my own experiences of immigration in the United States. While *Belated Travelers* was an attempt to engage the orientalist discourse that had construed me both as an exotic "oriental" and as a decadent "other," this book is an attempt to better grasp the immigrant history that has made me simultaneously a "model minority" and a threatening "alien" in America.

This book is the work of a first-generation immigrant who has survived the trauma of displacement and exile to become a "successful" citizen of the United States, only to realize that as a Middle Eastern subject I continue to be viewed as a threatening other.

In addition, on a theoretical level I began to realize, radical though the shift of my critical interest may have appeared to my skeptical friends and concerned colleagues, that I was actually working on a familiar topic. Immigration *is* an experience of traveling, of moving away from home to a new territory. It is not an accident that the first story of immigration to America, Crèvecoeur's *Letters from an American Farmer*, is also a travelogue by a Frenchman. Every immigrant tale is also a narrative of voyage. Immigration, like travel, is the encounter between at least two cultures. Although immigrating, unlike travel, is a permanent move, like traveling it demands an adventurous soul and entails the desire to encounter another reality, another culture, and often another language. And the immigrant, like a traveler who seeks renewal and enrichment by seeing other places and experiencing other cultures, leaves home to improve and enhance his or her situation in and through another place. The connection between traveling and immigration has become even more apparent in the age of globalization, as the immigrant experience is increasingly marked by a lifetime of traveling back and forth between old and new "homes." This book, then, is a continuation of my interest in the issue of travel and the ways the movement across national and cultural boundaries produces new identities and shapes cultures.

While building on the personal, historical, and theoretical findings of my earlier work, the focus of this book shifts from Europe to the United States of America and from orientalism and colonialism to immigration and nationalism. Though this shift demanded that I develop several new areas of research expertise, I chose this more difficult path because I was convinced, and remain so, that this area of inquiry has been unjustifiably neglected by postcolonial critics, and that it offers a much needed exploration of a critical subject too long overlooked. On the one hand, as Donald E. Pease has insightfully observed, in spite of their anamnestic readings of European colonial history by way of rethinking modernity, postcolonial critics have fallen into the ideological trap of American exceptionalism in concluding "that colonialism had little or nothing to do with the formation of the US national identity and that the study of the US culture will not affect their understanding of postcolonity."[1] Indeed, as Pease points out, not only did early settlers of North America collaborate "in the British Empire's colonial domination of the indigenous population," but also after independence, "the members of the US postcolony continued British colonial practices in their relations with native populations of neighboring territories and with migrants from other European colonies" (209). On the other hand, postcolonial theorists have ironically been forgetful of the neo-imperial context in which their works have been produced and received, evading for the most part the complex and powerful ways in which the United States has displaced European hegemony since the mid-twentieth century.[2] The historical rationale for a critical focus on Europe's cultural and political hegemony has been to produce the colonized's absent gaze and unwritten text, but these readings have rarely theorized the historical junctures that make the colonial encounter relevant to the neo-imperial condition today. Even more ironically, when postcolonial critics have broached such contemporary issues as globalization, transnationalism, and cultural hybridity, they have too often done so in a celebratory manner that views new configurations of power mostly in salutary terms. Disregarding the neo-imperial relations of power that continue to produce unequal developments throughout the world, Arjun Appadurai, for example, has coined the notion of "postnation" to describe the emergence of "strong alternative forms for organization of global traffic in resources, images, and ideas—forms that either contest the nation-state actively or constitute peaceful alternatives for large-scale political loyalties."[3] Similarly, Homi Bhabha, valorizing the redemptive power of postcolonial displacement, has suggested that postcolonial people "displace some of the great metropolitan narratives of progress and law and order and question the authority and authenticity of those narratives."[4]

Useful though concepts such as postnation and diaspora may be in locating the cultural implications of globalization, they nevertheless eclipse, if not fully dissimulate, neo-imperial relations of power. Postcolonial critics' inattentiveness to the continuing importance of nation and state is particularly problematic at this historical juncture, given the fortification of national borders in spite of the global flow of people across them, not to mention the forging of new partnerships between powerful states and global corporations. Especially since 9/11, not only has a new and powerful form of patriotism emerged in the United

States, but the tragic terrorist event has also enhanced the power of state apparatuses such as the FBI, the CIA, and the INS, linked and centrally organized now under the rubric of the new Department of Homeland Security. In addition, while national borders may no longer impede international trade and global economic transactions, they *do* nonetheless matter greatly when it comes to human subjects whose movements are now carefully regulated. As I will argue in the last chapter of this book, in the past thirty years an exclusionary and disciplinary form of state sovereignty has been solidified in the United States, as demonstrated, for example, by the expansion of the prison industry and the proliferation of the technologies of control at the border with Mexico. Similarly, the integration of Europe in the form of a union has also meant tougher restrictions on the movement of people to Europe from the Middle East, Africa, and most of Asia.

Arguing against the postnational positions of theorists like Appadurai and Bhabha, in the pages that follow I revisit the well-debated liberal tradition[5] of American nationalism by way of bringing it into a postcolonial problematic of nation and immigration. I argue that historical amnesia toward immigration is of paramount importance in the founding of the United States as a nation. As I use the term, the notion of amnesia is meant to signify a form of disavowal that entails a negative acknowledgment of what is historically and collectively repressed. Reading a broad range of discourses—from founding, and foundational, texts such as *Letters from an American Farmer* and *Democracy in America* to lesser-known works such as the writings of Know-Nothings and of public health officials at Ellis Island—I rely upon the idea of forgetting as a form of historical disavowal to guide my inquiry in several interrelated ways. First, I argue that the forgetful representation by the United States of its immigrant heritage is part of a broader form of historical amnesia about its violent formation. Both the benign discourse of democratic founding and the myth of immigrant America deny that nationhood has been achieved, at least in part, through the violent conquest of Native Americans, the brutal exploitation of enslaved Africans, and the colonialist annexations of French and Mexican territories. Second, I suggest that the myth of immigrant America is itself a forgetful narrative that disavows what I call the "economics of immigration," by which I mean not only issues such as the need for labor and the dynamics of supply and demand but also the political economy of immigration as a socio-legal phenomenon. Third, I use

the notion of amnesia to anchor my claim that the historical disavow-
als inherent in the nativist discourse of the United States are a crucial
component of its national culture. Often treated as an exception to the
prevailing myth of immigrant America, nativism has been overlooked
as a driving force behind much of the nation's immigration policy, as
well as a powerful force in defining citizenship and national identity
in ways that are both exclusionary and normalizing.

This book adopts the interdisciplinary approach of *Belated Travelers*,
building bridges among a variety of competing, but also complementary, academic domains and discourses: between the social sciences
and the humanities; between empirical knowledge and theoretical reflections; and between discourses of nationalism and practices of immigration. The issue of immigration has most often been treated empirically as a matter of politics and public policy in the United States,
and it has been studied almost exclusively by sociologists, historians,
political scientists, and legal scholars. *A Forgetful Nation*, while attentive to matters of policy, law, and history, formulates a theoretical understanding of immigration in the context of nationalism that
goes beyond compartmentalized approaches to these pressing issues
by considering the dynamic relation linking theoretical reflections on
national identity and immigration with the political and institutional
structures that produce them as concrete phenomena. As such, it not
only introduces a literary and cultural dimension into the traditionally
empirical fields of sociology and political science but also opens up a
new field of inquiry in the humanities by treating the question of immigration as a cultural phenomenon. At the same time, this book con-
tributes to cultural studies of nationalism by moving beyond celebratory theories of travel, instead bringing the study of national identity
into dialogue with legal discourses and social practices of immigration
that are often neglected by theorists of nationalism. And finally, in ex-
ploring the complex ways in which immigrants mediate such notions
as home, nation, and identity, *A Forgetful Nation* offers useful under-
standings of the predicaments of racial and cultural differences in the
United States.

Admittedly, my effort to cross discursive and disciplinary boundaries is neither critically comprehensive nor intellectually complete,
for it does push certain issues to the background by way of foreground-
ing others. To afford access and meaning to the central inquiry of
this book—the complex dynamics of forgetting in nation building—

the argument relegates other concerns to its textual margins. Among these issues is the predicament of gender. Although at select places in the text I point out the gendered nature of immigration and national discourse, I do not offer a substantial discussion of the role that gender plays in forming national identity, nor do I seriously engage the fact that immigration discourse has always been in part a gendered discourse in the United States. There are now several important studies that have explored the micro-mechanics of the gendering of national discourse, among which I wish to mention in passing Jacqueline Stevens's incisive and imaginative book *Reproducing the State*, in which she demonstrates the complex production of gender and sexual differences through membership practices of political societies, practices ranging from marriage laws that implicitly sanction sexual violence against women to citizenship laws that expatriate women who marry aliens.[6] Works such as Stevens's are a crucial complement to my own, and I hope that some of my insights about the productive role of forgetting may prove fructuous for theorists who seek to further develop our understanding of the interplay of gender, nationalism, and immigration.

Moreover, though I address the racialization of immigrants throughout this book, I provide neither a history nor a theory of race and racial formation in discussing immigrant America. There already exist many important empirical studies by sociologists, and theoretical works by ethnic studies scholars, which have contributed immensely to our understanding of racial formation in the United States and the role of immigration in it. Although *A Forgetful Nation* does not directly or critically engage the work of these scholars, its argument has benefited greatly from their critical insights. Michael Omi's and Howard Winnat's important work *Racial Formation in the United States*, in which they offer a substantial study of racism, racial theory, and the interplay of race, class, gender, and the nation since the civil rights movement, for example, constitutes an important intertext.[7] The problematic of nation and immigrant clearly demands a theoretical understanding of racial formation in the United States. In spite of the trans-historical scope of my argument, which unfortunately risks the impression of conflating not only various phases of immigration but also different types of immigrants, this book does not ignore the specific racial and ethnic markings of immigrants that complicate the story of immigrant America. As I move throughout the book between theoretical invocations of the immigrant and considerations of how particular immigrant groups are figured, I take great pains to include examples that are specified and historicized to demonstrate how new immigrants are racialized by different methods in different historical periods. For instance, in chapter 4 I contrast the rise of the Know-Nothings with the eugenics movement to differentiate the nation's horrendous treatment of Irish and German immigrants in the mid-nineteenth century from the nation's exclusionary and disciplinary processing of Jews and Italians at Ellis Island in the late nineteenth century. Similarly, in chapter 5 I address the particular ways in which negative representations of Latino and Middle Eastern immigrants in recent years have enabled a national politics of exclusion.

Discursively in dialogue with contemporary racial theory and empirical studies of immigration in the United States, this book makes a broader point about how racial and ethnic markings of immigrants complicate the story of immigrant America. The myth of immigrant America, I argue, not only obscures the ideological underpinning of national formation and the political economy of immigration but also disavows the importance of xenophobia in the founding of the United States. My argument concerns more specifically the predicament of racialization rather than the issue of race per se. I suggest that new immigrants are always racialized independently of their race and that the dynamics of racialization vary in different historical periods and contexts. My point parallels the argument made by ethnic scholars such as George Lipsitz that "political and cultural struggles over power have shaped the contours and dimensions of racism differently in different eras" and that the notion of race "tak[es] on different forms and serv[es] different social purposes in each time period."[8] Consider the maligning of the Irish and the Germans in the mid-nineteenth century, of Jews, Chinese, and Italians in the late nineteenth century, of Japanese and Germans during the Second World War, and of Mexican, Latin American, and Middle Eastern immigrants in the late twentieth century. In the United States, I suggest, there is no general theory of race; only particular practices of racialization. Moreover, race often matters in relation to the economics of immigration, by which I mean that immigrants' racialization is intertwined in complex ways with the issue of class and the political economy of social regulation. Even in the most racist movements, such as the eugenics war against eastern and southern European immigrants in the late nineteenth century and the early twentieth, the desire to exclude members of these groups from the American polity reflects socioeconomic concerns that these newcomers would become "public charges." Similarly, the passage of the Chinese Exclusion Act of 1882 may have been dictated as much by the economic crisis in western states as by the theory of Gobineau then current that human races are not equal. I hope that my broader argument, which pertains not so much to the specifics of race relations in America as to the general dynamics of projecting the immigrant other, will help to establish more clearly the connections among various accounts of race and racialization in theorizing national identity in the United States.

In the past few years, while pursuing this book project, I have had the opportunity to work with many wonderful students. I have learned a great deal from them, and their ideas and comments have influenced in important ways my thinking about immigration and nationalism. I wish to especially thank Mary Pat Brady, Linda Greenberg, James Hyung-Jin Lee, Nush Powell, and Erin Williams, all of whom directly contributed to this book as research assistants and without whose help this project would have taken even longer to complete.

Without the advice, friendship, and encouragement of Ross Chambers this book would have not been finished: his incredible generosity and sagacious comments on almost every page of this book are what ultimately enabled its realization. I also wish to express my gratitude to Bonnie Honig, Mark Seltzer, and Jenny Sharpe for their insightful criticism and incisive comments. Other colleagues at UCLA and elsewhere I wish to thank for many thoughtful and encouraging conversations, not to mention for their own scholarly contributions to my thinking: Zohreh Sullivan, James Clifford, Kitty Calavita, Françoise Lionnet, Joseph Boone, Eric Sundquist, Suvir Kaul, Efrain Kristal, Halleh Ghorashi, Kirstie McClure, John Michael, Chon Noriega, Mireille Rosello, Jinqi Ling, Khachig Tölölyan, John McCumber, Shu-mei Shih, Kenneth Reinhard, Dominick Thomas, Jennifer Fleissner, Timothy Brennan, Barbara Packer, Vincent Pecora, Rafael Perez-Torres, Ramon Gutierrez, Felicity Nussbaum, Thomas Wortham, George Van den Abbeele, Lisa Lowe, Elizabeth Mudimbe-Boyi, Rachel Lee, and Sangeeta Ray. There are many others I have not mentioned here to whom I am also grateful for support and inspiration along the way.

I wish to thank the park rangers at both Ellis Island and Angel Island, especially Barry Moreno and Ellen Loring, for giving me informed tours of these immigrant stations and for providing me with useful information about how immigrants were inspected at these gates of entry.

I owe special thanks to Ken Wissoker for being a superb and supportive editor, to Fred Kameny and Courtney Berger for their editorial help, and to the anonymous readers at Duke University Press for their extremely helpful comments on the manuscript. My immense gratitude also goes to my family and many friends who kept encouraging me to go on in moments of personal and intellectual crisis; I wish to especially thank Amir and Hamid Behdad, Wendy Belcher, Jeanette Gilkison, Houman Mortazavi, Masoud Ghandehari, Nicholas Mellen, Elham Gheytanchi, Masood Jelokhani-Niaraki, Morteza Mostafavi, Shahrzad Talieh, Sophie McClaren, Michael Seabaugh, and David and Jackie Louie. And finally, I am infinitely indebted to Juliet Williams, who in taking a powerful stand for critical integrity and intellectual passion, not to forget being a clearing for love, made the completion of this book not only possible but enjoyable.

Several research grants from UCLA's academic senate, a resident fellowship at the Humanities Research Institute at UC Irvine, and a UC President's Fellowship facilitated the completion of this book by providing me with cherished time to ruminate and write, and I wish to express my indebtedness to those who supported this project at various stages of its development.

Introduction

Nation and Immigration

"We're ignorant about how we started." — Lee Iacocca[1]

A few months after the passage of the Immigration Act of 1891, which established the first federal immigration agency, Ellis Island was formally opened on 1 January 1892 to become the main port of entry to the United States.[2] Over 70 percent of those who came to this country from 1892 until 1924 were processed there.[3] A self-contained station with a work force that eventually numbered over seven hundred, Ellis Island was essential to the development of the country's immigration policy and to the rise of the Immigration and Naturalization Service (INS) as a powerful state apparatus.[4] For it was there that the newly born Immigration Bureau developed, refined, and formalized its regulatory practices and other immigration procedures, while the federal government used the example of Ellis Island to elaborate and institute its exclusionary policies of immigration. And yet, if you visited the Ellis Island Museum of Immigration — which opened in September 1990 to commemorate the nation's immigrant tradition — you would not find any reference to the INS, nor would you learn much about how the federal government's experiments there helped to usher in a new era of immigration control.[5] In spite of a few passing references to its having been an "Isle of Tears" for "a few unfortunate" immigrants who were rejected or detained, the historical Ellis Island is mostly celebrated as an "Isle of Hope," America's "front doors to freedom."[6] A symbolic repository of the nation's "immigrant heritage," the museum aims to enable its visitors to retrace the steps of their ancestors in a welcoming fashion that erases most evidence of the island's original disciplinary function. The museum devotes only a small exhibit, titled "Public Servants," to the doctors, nurses, inspectors, interpreters, matrons, stenographers, and clerks who often worked twelve hours a day, seven days a week, during the peak immigration years. And discussion of the nation's anti-immigrant tendency is confined to a small exhibition called "The Closing Door" that deals mostly with the restrictive legislation of the early twentieth century, thus relegating to a distant past any negative sentiment toward immigrants or the state's exclusionary practices of immigration control. Transforming the disciplinary institution into a national monument that celebrates America's immigrant tradition, the museum obscures the very historical and political significance of Ellis Island.

When I asked an informed park ranger about this historical amnesia, he admitted that the museum's planning committee, headed by Lee Iacocca, for the most part had to erase the unpleasant aspects of immigration control at the island in order to turn it into the symbol of America's immigrant heritage. "The organizers and sponsors romanticized Ellis Island for fund raising,"[7] he pointed out; "they wanted to create a positive image of America's immigrant history."[8] The pragmatic decision to leave out most of the history of immigration control in the island reflects the forgetful way in which the museum represents the country's immigrant tradition. In the celebratory and patriotic exhibitions of the Ellis Island Museum, "memory is not reclaimed" but officially invented, as Barbara Kirshenblatt-Gimblett observes.[9] The museum's representation of America's immigrant heritage is an "invented tradition," in which romanticized images of the past inculcate patriotic values in the viewer.[10] In explaining the function of the Ellis Island Museum, Iacocca describes it as an "ethnic Williamsburg" created to make "people feel that this is a great country, that they have a heritage to be proud of" (Smith, "A Leader for Liberty," 30). Funded by the private sector and built, ironically, in the wake of a new era of immigration restriction in the 1980s, the museum therefore not only marginalizes the disciplinary practices and exclusionary policies of the original immigration center but also chooses to ignore the complexities of the nation's immigration history, by making those "who passed through the facility become prototypes for all arrivals to America no matter what their point of origin, port of entry, time of arrival, or circumstances" (Kirshenblatt-Gimblett, *Destination Culture*, 180). The museum's monolithic and patriotic narrative of immigrant heritage, in sum, eclipses both the violent history that characterizes the peopling of America and the actualities of the nation's immigration policies that continue to regulate, discipline, and exclude certain "aliens" to this day.

I begin my discussion of immigration and cultural identity in the United States with the resurrection of Ellis Island as a national monument, because it provides a cogent example of what I explore in this book: how the liberal myth of immigrant America denies the actual history of immigration in the United States, a denial that I argue is paramount to the imagining of a national culture. The Ellis Island Immigration Museum is but the most recent articulation of the myth of immigrant America upon which the nation is founded. Indeed, beginning with J. Hector St. John de Crèvecoeur's invocation of America as "every person's country" in 1782, through the celebration of the country as a "nation of many nations" in the poetry of Walt Whitman in the nineteenth century, to John F. Kennedy's portrayal of the United States as a "nation of immigrants" in the twentieth century, the official archive of the nation is replete with examples of a founding myth that defines immigration as a form of national hospitality. Like these earlier articulations of the founding myth, the nation's monument dedicated to commemorating its immigrant heritage is a forgetful reinvention that suppresses historical knowledge about the economics of immigration,[11] while producing a pseudo-historical consciousness about what it means to be an American. Dedicated to recounting "America's immigration story," the museum, like other cultural iterations of the founding myth, constitutes a "retrospective illusion" that disregards how the nation's open-door immigration was born of a colonialist will to power and a capitalist desire for economic expansion.[12]

Modes of Forgetting

Historical amnesia toward immigration, I argue in this book, is paramount in the founding of the United States as a nation.[13] But before I elaborate my argument about the productive function of amnesia in imagining the nation and its cultural and political implications, let me take a short theoretical detour to distinguish my usage of the concept of forgetting. I use the notion of amnesia throughout my discussion to mean a form of cultural disavowal that simultaneously denies certain historical facts and produces a pseudo-historical consciousness of the present. Forgetting in this case does not entail mnemonic foreclosure—what Freud called *Verwerfung*—but negation, or *Verneinung*, to use the language of psychoanalysis.[14] In other words, the historical amnesia that I elaborate here is not to be equated with the kind of repression in which an ideational representative (*Vorstellungsrepräsentanz*) is kept completely out of our collective consciousness. Repression as foreclosure, Freud reminds us, "cannot occur until a sharp distinction has been established between what is conscious and what is unconscious: that *the essence of repression lies simply in the function of rejecting and keeping something out of consciousness*" (*General Psychological Theory*, 105; emphasis in original). Foreclosure is an emotional defense mechanism against certain internal instinctual impulses that are distressing or disturbing to us and that we therefore unconsciously wish to banish from our consciousness.

The kind of historical forgetting that I thematize throughout my discussion is closer to the Freudian notion of negation, "a repudiation, by means of projection, of an association that has just emerged" (*General Psychological Theory*, 213). In contrast to foreclosure, in which an ideational representative has no access to our consciousness because we have unconsciously repressed it, in negation "the subject-matter of a repressed image or thought can make its way into consciousness on condition that it is *denied*" (213–14; emphasis in original). Negation, Freud explains, "is actually a removal of the repression, though not, of course, an acceptance of what is repressed" (214). In negation, one may acknowledge an event, but the subject either denies its significance or refuses to take responsibility for it. As such, disavowal is a split perception of what constitutes our reality, a perception vacillating between denial and a supplementary acknowledgment. The notion of historical amnesia that I elaborate in this book entails a negative acknowledgment of what ultimately is historically and collectively suppressed. Forgetting here is a form of disavowal in which one consciously decides to keep certain knowledge at bay. "To deny something in one's judgment," as Freud remarks, "is at the bottom the same thing as to say: 'That is something that I would rather repress'" (214).

Disavowal, as the psychoanalyst John Steiner further elaborates, can take two forms: it can be either "turning a blind eye" or a "retreat from truth to omnipotence."[15] On the one hand, disavowal can be a nonsystematic need to be innocent of a troubling recognition, a kind of vague awareness "that we choose not to look at the facts without being conscious of what it is we are evading" ("Turning a Blind Eye," 161). In this form of denial, Steiner suggests, "we seem to have access to reality but choose to ignore it because it proves convenient to do so" (161). The average citizen, for instance, may have a vague idea of the violent acts committed by the U.S. military in Iraq, but he or she disregards them by way of supporting the American troops and being patriotic. On the other hand, disavowal can be a more systematic form of denial in which the subject takes a self-righteous position, acknowledging what happened but refusing to take responsibility and yet feeling guilty for having done something. While this form of denial, like turning a blind eye, marks an ambiguous relation to knowledge, it involves conscious "distortions and misrepresentations of truth" (233). Throughout the second Iraq war, for example, the defense secretary Donald Rumsfeld and other members of the Bush administration denied any responsibility for the killing of innocent civilians, blaming Saddam Hussein for using them as human shields to muster opposition toward the American invasion. In this form of denial, the subject often projects his or her guilt onto others by blaming them for what has occurred, attempting thus to hide the implications of his or her own actions. Disavowal, as a retreat from truth to omnipotence, entails deception and a deliberate attempt to cover up records and memories of the past. This form of denial, as Ross Chambers remarks, "ensures a perpetually renewable state of cultural innocence, but it does so at the cost of inevitably betraying some knowledge of the injustice, the guilt, or the pain that the act of denial fails (or refuses) to acknowledge, and of which it is, therefore, as Freud taught us, a symptom."[16]

As will become clear in the chapters that follow, by describing the United States as a forgetful nation I wish to make several interrelated points about the history of its national culture. First, I suggest that the nation's forgetful representation of its immigrant heritage is part of a broader form of historical amnesia about the formation of the United States as an imagined community. Theorists of the nation form, from Ernest Renan to Étienne Balibar, have demonstrated the importance of forgetting to the political project of founding a nation.[17] Histories of nations, they argue, are always presented as triumphant narratives that repress the means of brutality through which national unity is achieved. The will to imagine a unified community entails an originary violence that must be elided in the official history to legitimize the nation's founding. The United States is no exception, for as I discuss in chapter 1, it too is an amnesiac nation that persistently disavows its violent beginnings to fashion an imagined democratic community. In the official history of the nation, we are told, the United States was founded by a distinguished community of pilgrims whose love of freedom and equality of conditions enabled them to form a democratic society: "The emigrants who fixed themselves on the shores of America in the beginning of the seventeenth century severed the democratic principle from all the principles which repressed it in the old communities of Europe, and transplanted it unalloyed to the New World."[18] This benign myth of democratic founding refuses to acknowledge how the formation of the American polity was achieved through the violent conquest of Native Americans, the brutal exploitation of enslaved Africans, and the colonialist annexations of French and Mexican territories. It is not that the official history of the nation denies the occurrence of these violent acts; rather, it denies responsibility for them and ignores their historical implications for how the nation was founded, by considering them aberrations from America's exceptionalist path.[19] Historical disavowal here takes the form of a retreat from truth to omnipotence, in which the nation does not deny the gradual destruction of the indigenous population but refuses to take responsibility for it or feel guilty about it. As I will show in chapter 2, for example, Tocqueville acknowledges that the annihilation of the native peoples of North America "began from the day when Europeans landed on their shores," but then denies that their genocide and the dispossession of their land by European colonizers enabled the founding and expansion of the nation, as he quickly adds that the Native Americans' "implacable prejudices, their uncontrolled passions, their vices, and still more perhaps their savage virtues, consigned them to inevitable destruction" (27–28). Even when there is a recognition of certain guilt and an assumption of responsibility, say in the case of slavery, one encounters a kind of cultural deletion, according to which the nation undercuts or diminishes the implications of past events by claiming that they happened a long time ago and therefore must be laid to rest. Doing so ultimately makes possible a pseudo-historical consciousness toward the situation of African Americans today, a consciousness that in deflecting attention from the nation's racial history blames them for the violence and poverty so prevalent in America's inner cities.

The disavowal of such originary forms of violence in the nation's founding is necessary in making the United States the fulfillment of a democratic project that was naturally devised by a community of enlightened Europeans who were destined to transform the "wild forests of the New World" into a "great nation," to use Tocqueville's words again (26, 28). "Project and destiny," Balibar remarks, "are the two symmetrical figures of the illusion of national identity" (338). Unmindful of the means of brutality through which the nation was formed, we as a nation believe that we are collectively connected to the pilgrims and that our imagined community is the destined outcome of their vision of a democratic polity. The project of democratic founding, I will demonstrate in this book, is a forgetful narrative, producing the retrospective illusion that freedom and equality, not brutality and conquest, were the principles upon which the nation was founded, principles whose repetitive invocation in the official discourse of founding continues to support the imaginary singularity of national culture in the United States.

Second, I call the United States a forgetful nation to draw attention to the complex ways in which the myth of immigrant America is itself a forgetful narrative, as it is frequently called upon to displace the historical origins of nation building in the United States and to shore up a sense of national pride and patriotism. The myth of immigrant America, as the liberal historian Hans Kohn characteristically remarks, is synonymous with American national identity: "The character of the United States as a land with open gateways, a nation of many nations, became as important for American nationalism as its identification with the idea of individual liberty and its federal character."[20] Whether liberal or conservative, historians and politicians, as I will elaborate in chapter 3, have frequently conjured up this founding myth for the national project of self-renewal. That we are an immigrant nation, hospitable to the huddled masses, makes us feel good about ourselves, regenerating in us a profound sense of national pride. Even Ronald Reagan, whose conservative administration tightened the nation's borders and criminalized undocumented immigrants by approving the Immigration Reform and Control Act (IRCA) of 1986, polemically asked in 1980 when accepting his party's nomination: "Can we doubt that only a Divine Providence placed this land, this island of freedom here as a refuge for all those people in the world who yearn to breathe freely, Jews and Christians enduring persecution behind the Iron Curtain, the boat people of Southeast Asia, of Cuba and Haiti, victims of drought and famine in Africa?"[21] As this comment makes evident, the myth of immigrant America as the self-manifestation of national character embodies the symmetrical figures of project and destiny: the narrative consists in believing that every generation has embraced and passed on to the next the invariant idea of the United States as an asylum for the oppressed, and that the realization of such a project is the inevitable destiny of the nation.

And yet, as an illusory retrospective narrative, the myth of immigrant America needs to deny the historical context of its formation while ignoring the horrendous disciplining and criminalizing of aliens that is happening around us today. Reagan's comment brings into focus how the myth of immigrant America obscures the historical fact that Jewish, Catholic, Haitian, and Asian immigrants have been figured as threatening others in different periods, including the time when Reagan gave his acceptance speech. The myth of the United States as a refuge for the oppressed of all nations, as I will propose in chapters 1 and 3, fails to acknowledge many historical facts about the nation's past, most importantly that its open-door immigration throughout the nineteenth century was motivated not by hospitality but by a colonialist will to appropriate the land and by a capitalist desire for expansion.[22] Jefferson's Republican vision of westward expansion demanded lax immigration and naturalization laws to populate the newly acquired territories with white Europeans and to help the nation's agrarian economy, but in a speech delivered in 1801 he too used the discourse of hospitality to justify an open-door policy, thereby masking the strategic interest with lofty and beneficent ideology. But since the very founding of the nation, legislative debates about immigration have rarely revolved around human rights or helping the needy of the globe; instead they have focused on such issues as national security, the social costs of immigration, and the economic advantages and disadvantages of foreign labor. These pragmatic concerns and interests are never admitted into the celebratory narrative of immigrant America, however—a narrative that relies on such lofty ideas as hospitality, liberty, and democracy to explain the nation's desirability to foreigners. In the second chapter of *A Nation of Immigrants*, titled "Why They Came," John F. Kennedy maintains that the driving forces behind immigration are religious freedom, political liberty, and economic opportunity, while he represents immigrants as heroic people "who dared to explore new frontiers, people eager to build lives for themselves in a spacious society that did not restrict their freedom of choice and action" (2). To recuperate immigrants for the project of national founding and renewal, the nation's economic and political needs that motivated its open-door policy must be disregarded. In addition, the celebratory myth of immigrant America represents immigrants as adventurous heroes in search of liberty, obscuring the fact that most of those who came to this country in the nineteenth century were economic refugees and indentured laborers for whom immigration meant servitude, not freedom. The liberal narrative of immigration, as I demonstrate in chapter 3, is a repetitive discourse of self-legitimation that to shore up national pride and patriotism constantly reproduces in a recuperative fashion the narrative of America as a hospitable nation and immigrants as oppressed masses.

The myth of immigrant America also entails what Stanley Cohen calls "contemporary denial," in which a "perceptual filter is placed over reality, and some knowledge is shut out."[23] The pretense that the United States is a hospitable nation eclipses not only the economic dimensions of immigration but also the disciplining of its aliens by such state apparatuses as the FBI, the INS, and the Border Patrol, institutions whose genealogy goes back to the Immigration Act of 1891, by means of which the federal government began to build the administrative machinery to regulate and control immigration at Ellis Island. As I will demonstrate in chapter 5, the nation's treatment of its immigrants, as exemplified by its conduct along the border with Mexico, is marked by violence and militarization, surveillance and discipline, all to produce a docile and cheap labor force, while also normalizing and assuring the illusive exercise of disciplinary power over immigrants, and increasingly over the general citizenry. The rhetoric of illegality and transgression at the border, coupled with the fear of terrorism, has broadened and legitimized the extent of the federal government's disciplinary power. Brown-skinned immigrants and citizens are now routinely subjected to surveillance, interrogation, incarceration, and deportation as the perception of the foreigner as a threat to democracy has been rapidly codified into such discriminatory laws as the USA Patriot Act (signed into law on 26 October 2001). Today there is no literal denial of these exclusionary and disciplinary practices, but we are constantly invited to ignore most of their implications. We tend to overlook how the surveillance of the terrorist foreigner has made everyone the potential subject and object of the state's disciplinary gaze. The state's juridical and administrative rationality, enthusiastically embraced by the general public—mostly because of the dissemination by the news media of alarmist information about terrorists and their activities—plays an important role in producing a popular form of vigilantism while depriving average citizens of their basic civil liberties.

Third, I use the notion of forgetfulness to describe the historical disavowal inherent in nativism as a crucial component of national culture. The myth of America as an asylum obscures the ideological underpinnings of the state and the political economy of immigration, as well as the importance of xenophobia in the founding of the United States. The phenomenon of nativism, by which I mean "an intense opposition to an internal minority on the grounds of its foreign (i.e., 'un-American') connections,"[24] is not completely repressed in the official history of the nation, but its significance as a powerful component of national identity is consistently denied. Often treated as an exception to the prevailing myth of immigrant America, nativism is almost never acknowledged as a driving force behind much of the nation's immigration policy, one that continues to define citizenship and national identity in exclusionary terms and in a normalizing fashion. Historically, however, xenophobia has been central to the national imaginary, present even in the discourses of liberal thinkers and politicians. Jefferson, who carried the pro-immigration banner, often spoke disparagingly about the immigrant "mobs of great cities in the East" and German settlers in the Midwest who preserved "their own languages, habits, and principles of government."[25] Nativism, I argue in this book, does not contradict the national myth of asylum; rather, it is the culmination of what the myth disavows.

The American national culture, as I will illustrate in chapter 4, has always embodied a nativist or anti-foreign component to manufacture an imagined sense of community. In contrast to the Jeffersonian Republican vision that advocated an open-door immigration policy to enable the nascent nation's westward expansion, the Federalists' valorization of the "native" born as the ideal citizen made many Americans oppose free immigration.[26] As reflected in the short-lived Alien and Sedition Act of 1798, imposed by the Federalist administration of John Adams, the representation of the foreigner as a political and social menace has been a fundamental element of American nationalism since the founding. To possess "the genuine character of true Americans," as John Adams claimed, was to "have no attachments or exclusive friendship for any foreign nation" (Grant and Davison, *Founders of the Republic*, 6). To be an immigrant implies by definition a certain attachment to another country, an attachment consequently marked as "un-American." The figure of the "alien" as a menacing source of sedition, discontent, insurrection, and resistance provides a differential other whose perpetual presence is necessary in order to manufacture a homogeneous national identity.

America's "other" does not remain the same, however, for every historical epoch demands a new representation of the seditious foreigner, a representation that is shaped by different cultural conditions, economic needs, political exigencies, and social conflicts. The late-eighteenth-century fear of foreign radicals that helped to secure the passage of the Alien and Sedition Acts has been continuously reinvented in new forms at moments of national crisis: in the mid-nineteenth century the Know-Nothings scapegoated the Irish and other Catholic immigrants, considering them disloyal and thus unsuitable for citizenship; in the late nineteenth century flourishing anti-Chinese sentiment in the West eventually led to the passage of the Chinese Exclusion Act of 1882, which barred Asian immigrants from entering the country until 1965; in the early twentieth century the eugenics movement constructed Jewish and other immigrants from eastern and southern European countries as racially inferior, a perception that helped bring about the passage of the racist quota laws of the 1920s, which also remained on the books until 1965; in the 1980s the association of Mexican and Latin American immigrants with illegality enabled the passage of the Immigration and Nationality Act (1986) and Proposition 187 in California, which denied to undocumented aliens education, medical care, and other social services; and since 9/11 the association of Middle Eastern immigrants with terrorism has given rise to discriminatory laws that deny them entry and subject those already living in the United States to interrogation, detention, or deportation, all without legal counsel. My aim in enumerating these cases of anti-alien sentiment and their subsequent codification into exclusionary laws is not to ignore their rather different and complex contexts but to point out the prevalence of xenophobia throughout American history and its productive function in the national imaginary. What we encounter in every anti-immigrant claim is a differential mode of national and cultural identification that posits

a fundamental difference between the patriotic citizen and the menacing alien. The project of imagining a homogeneous nation is never
complete. It requires the continual presence of the immigrant as other,
through whom citizenship and cultural belonging are rearticulated.

Immigrants are useful to the political project of national identity,
through an exclusionary logic that defines them as differential others
and also through inclusive means of identification that recuperate
them as figures of cultural conformism, exceptionalism, and regeneration. Assimilation as a more subtle denial of difference has been
integral to how the United States has imagined itself as an immigrant
nation. Since the founding, the notion of cultural and political assimilation has always accompanied the myth of immigrant America,
as newcomers have been "domesticated" and forced to lose their old
national "skins" to become American citizens. John Quincy Adams
stated bluntly that the immigrants "come to a life of independence,
but to a life of labor—and, if they cannot accommodate themselves to
the character, moral, political and physical, of this country with all its
compensating balances of good and evil, the Atlantic is always open
to them to return to the land of their nativity and their fathers . . .
They must cast off the European skin never to resume it."[27] As Adams's
statement illustrates, the dissolution of difference has been deeply embedded in the national culture since the earliest days of the nation:
to be accepted as immigrants and to be eligible for citizenship, newcomers have had to forsake their ethnic identities and relinquish their
political and cultural differences.[28] In the early twentieth century, the
popular notion of the "melting pot," forgetfully celebrated as a description of America's cultural diversity, further normalized the gradual dissolution or domestication of difference and diversity as a vital
part of national culture. Cultural and ethnic differences were toler-
ated only to the extent that they could be melted into a single national
form. Even multiculturalism, as a new cultural politics of difference
displacing the notion of the melting pot after the civil rights era, was
not able to transform alterity into an American civic reality, as it too
was recuperated by the dominant culture as a sign of its power of ab-
sorption. Today the notion of difference remains an abstract liberal
ideal, masking the economic and social inequalities that belie the uni-
versal language of American inclusiveness. Lisa Lowe is to the point
in arguing, " 'Multiculturalism' supplements abstract political citizenship where the unrealizability of the political claims to equality be-

come apparent: it is the national cultural form that seeks to unify the diversity of the United States through the integration of differences as *cultural* equivalents abstracted from the histories of racial inequality unresolved in the economic and political domains."[29] The discourse of national identity in the United States is a linear narrative that begins with difference but ends in sameness, thus reaffirming the thesis of American exceptionalism. As Bonnie Honig remarks, "the exceptionalist account normatively privileges one particular trajectory to citizenship: from immigrant (to ethnic, as in Walzer but not in Tocqueville) to citizen."[30]

On the other hand, the recuperation of the immigrant as a "supercitizen" provides the nation with a powerful cultural trope to reaffirm the nation's capitalist values and nationalist norms. As blatantly revealed by the subtitle of Joel Millman's *The Other Americans*, "How Immigrants Renew Our Country, Our Economy, and Our Values," the figure of the immigrant other can be recuperated by liberal thinkers in a seemingly positive and benevolent fashion by being transformed into an agent of national renewal. In *Democracy and the Foreigner*, Honig insightfully discusses such uses of immigrants in the political project of American nationalism. The idealized immigrant, she argues, not only "solves" America's democratic problems of legitimacy and consent but is also the "agent of national reenchantment" (74). In contrast to the threatening other whose alterity is deployed to define a homogeneous, imagined community, the model immigrant is held out as the proof of America's exceptionalism. In this case, she remarks, the successful immigrant is an "object of identification," acting as "the screen onto which we project our idealized selves" (78). Successful immigrants are strategically deployed by both liberals and conservatives to reaffirm the nation's principles of capitalism, communalism, liberalism, and the traditional family (77). Francis Fukuyama, to cite an example, offers a passionate defense of "Third World" immigrants, arguing that their "stronger family structures and moral inhibitions" and "their work ethic and willingness to defer to traditional sources of authority" make them ideal citizens and also the solution to the "decay of basic social relationships evident in American inner cities."[31] Immigrants' economic success helps sustain the belief that capitalism is a meritocratic system, while their traditional values position them so as "to have and to foster the social, civic, and familial ties that the social democracy presupposes" (Honig, *Democracy and the Foreigner*, 82). A source of national pride, the good immigrant thus reinvigorates national culture and shores up a sense of patriotism among citizens.[32] At the same time, as Fukuyama's remarks symptomatically indicate, the archetype of the successful immigrant is rallied to shame and discipline the internal minorities, such as African Americans, Native Americans, and Latinos, and in so doing to shift the locus of culpability from the dominant majority to subjected classes. Indeed, as ethnic scholars have also argued, the "immigrant analogy" so prevalent among the adherents of the ethnicity paradigm is mobilized to blame African Americans and Native Americans for their economic and social plight by neglecting the nation's racial history and the radical differences that separate their experiences from those of white European immigrants.[33]

Hospitality and National Ambivalence

The myth of immigrant America, I have been suggesting, uses the model of hospitality to describe the nation's relationship with its immigrants, a model that obscures how the economics of immigration and the history of racial formation in America have delimited the boundaries of hospitality.[34] That we are a forgetful nation is a function of how we treat immigration as a matter of national hospitality, instead of rising to the moral challenge that we need immigrants in such ways as to renew our democratic polity, our weakened economy, and our civic values. In the remaining pages of my introduction, I wish to discuss the cultural and political implications of what it means to define immigration as a matter of national hospitality. Jacques Derrida has theorized the structure of hospitality as one of antinomy: "an insoluble antinomy, a non-dialectizable antinomy between, on the one hand, *The* law of unlimited hospitality (to give the new arrival all of one's home and oneself, to give him or her one's own, our own, without asking a name, or compensation, or the fulfillment of even the smallest condition), and on the other hand, the law*s* (in the small plural), those rights and duties that are always conditioned and conditional, as they are defined by the Greco-Roman tradition and even the Judeo-Christian one, by all of law and all philosophy of law up to Kant and Hegel in particular, across the family, civil society, and the state."[35]

The law of hospitality constitutes an aporia in which the claim of absolute hospitality—to offer to the other one's home and resources without asking anything in return—clashes with hospitality by right, that is, a more conditional form of hospitality in which the alien other is subjected to a broad range of immigration laws and forced to adhere to our cultural norms and social values. The relationship between the host and the guest, Derrida states, is paradoxical because it is governed by "two regimes of a law of hospitality: the unconditional or hyperbolic on the one hand, and the conditional and juridico-political, even the ethical, on the other" (136-37). The incommensurable difference between juridico-political laws of hospitality and the absolute law of unlimited hospitality renders the relation between the host and the guest undecidable, making it constantly teeter between xenophilia and xenophobia, reception and rejection, inclusion and exclusion.

Derrida's remarks about two regimes of hospitality provide a useful theoretical distinction with which to consider the cultural and political implications of the nation's founding myth. The myth of immigrant America as a narrative of hospitality maintains competing perceptions of national identity, perceptions that I further argue can coexist and form an insoluble antinomy through historical amnesia. Hospitality cannot be affirmed without forgetting our hostility toward immigrants, nor can we impose on our guest restrictive and disciplinary laws of immigration without suspending, at least momentarily, our belief in being a hospitable nation. *The* law of unlimited hospitality, on which the myth of immigrant America is founded, denies both hostility toward immigrants and the laws of immigration that inform the relationship between citizen and alien. The law of absolute hospitality, as Derrida points out, is incommensurable with the hospitality by right that regulates the actual relation between the citizen and the immigrant other (25). In fact, as I will discuss in chapter 5, the laws and procedures of immigration in the United States are anything but "hospitable" toward immigrants, since they regulate and control their practices of everyday life on a micro-mechanical level. While an ethical and unlimited claim of hospitality has been central to liberal articulations of national identity, the state has constantly imposed normative and prescriptive laws of hospitality that regulate the daily practices of immigrants and foreigners. The laws of immigration rigorously delimit the boundaries of citizenship as cultural and political enfranchisement, making hospitality conditional and conditioned by our economic needs, cultural demands, and political desires as a nation.

In addition, hospitality necessitates hostility toward new arrivals to mark the exteriority of the immigrant in relation to national citizenship. The notion of hospitality assumes a differential relation between the citizen as host-native and the immigrant as guest-foreigner. For the guest to be offered hospitality, he or she must first be treated as an outsider, a stranger who does not fully belong. Hence the ambivalent form of identification that grounds national culture and civic identity in the United States: our self-image as a nation of immigrants makes us offer unlimited hospitality to strangers who land on our shores; at the same time, as native citizens, we treat them as aliens who must abide by our rules and adopt our social norms.

That the nation vacillates between hospitality and hostility, xenophilia and xenophobia, because there are competing paradigms of cultural identity in the United States is obvious to anyone familiar with its history of nationalism and immigration. Many political theorists and historians have argued that the American polity tolerates and legitimizes opposite perceptions of nationality and citizenship because it is a democratic regime. "The genius of American society," Martin Lipset and Earl Raab state, "is that it has legitimized ambiguity."[36] The embracing of opposite notions of citizenship and nationality, according to these scholars, paradoxical though it may seem, is an enabling factor, for the very idea of democracy means the coexistence of antithetical values. Even more recent theorists who have critically engaged the dynamic of ambivalence have overlooked the insolubility of difference, by attributing it either to particular parties (Walzer)[37] or to certain traditions (Smith).[38] In addition, economists and legal scholars have elaborated the contradictory ways in which the nation's laws and policies have been articulated. Elizabeth Hull, for example, has maintained that American immigration laws have always been incongruous, demonstrating a great deal of uncertainty about the country's mission: "Should the United States be a refuge for the 'tired and the poor,' or an outpost, properly off-limits to the 'wretched refuse' of the world?"[39] Other scholars, such as the sociologists Wayne Cornelius and Jorge Bustamante, have further explained that the nation's contradictory reception of its immigrants is motivated by economic factors.[40] America's immigration policies, they argue, constitute a schizophrenic pattern, welcoming immigrants when labor is in short supply and turning against them when there is an economic slump.

Although these views are partly right, the ambivalent mode of immigration that I elaborate in this book is neither about democratic ambiguity nor reducible to a cyclical economic phenomenon. The opposing perceptions of immigration do not form a dialectical relation à la Hegel either, for they also do not arise out of each other, nor do they ever transcend into a unity. Rather, I use the notion of ambivalence to theorize a productive and irreconcilable difference between competing perceptions of national identity, which instead of undoing or undermining one another coexist and reinforce one another through historical amnesia. Forgetting ensures a continual vacillation between hospitality and hostility, between a claim of total acceptance of foreigners and the laws that regulate and restrict their reception. The incommensurable difference between America as a hospitable haven and America as a xenophobic outpost is a function of what these opposing myths perpetually disavow, a disavowal that enables their continual repetition as new economic and social crises emerge. Contrary to the commonsensical perception of immigration as a cyclical, democratic phenomenon, the continual coexistence of hostility and hospitality does not amount to a contradiction but an insoluble antinomy, for the two coexist, albeit through equivocation, as necessary partners in defining national culture. Immigrants as others have a productive function in national culture, for they simultaneously shore up the mythical view of the United States as a cradle of democracy and the view of it as a threatened asylum. The nation's ambivalent hospitality thus provides an important site of ideological contestation where concepts of nationality as citizenship, and of state as sovereignty, can be rearticulated and reaffirmed. The insolubility of immigration as hospitality suggests that American national consciousness is always articulated through and dependent on a binary logic of cultural and political identification. Whether a corrupter of our principled prosperity or the enabler of our democratic capitalism, the immigrant is at once a critical supplement and a threatening other through whom American identity is imagined and reproduced. The different views of immigration constitute an ambivalent form of national culture that simultaneously acknowledges the nation's immigrant formation and denies its cultural and social effects. My aim in this book is to disclose the performative and productive effects of this ambivalence, inviting us to explore our cultural and political attachments to the undecidability of immigration.

Furthermore, I use the notion of an ambivalent mode of cultural

identification throughout this book to underscore the general split between hospitality and hostility, xenophobia and xenophilia, and also
the particular ways in which the competing notions of American identity are themselves ambivalently articulated. As I will demonstrate regarding liberal valorization of immigrant America in chapter 3 and
the discourses of nativism in chapter 4, every articulation of American cultural identity espouses opposite views of citizenship and community. Historical forgetting in each instance allows for an ideologically unsettled response to the question of "Who is an American?"
The narrator of Crèvecoeur's *Letters from an American Farmer*, for example, vacillates between a colonialist will to power and a humanist
attitude toward the indigenous and enslaved populations, thus representing the emerging nation simultaneously as an idyllic and heterogeneous nation and as a violent and racially segregated one. Similarly,
Tocqueville's description of national culture in *Democracy in America*
teeters between a religious idea of America as a providential gift to a
chosen people and a secular one of a superior human race transforming a hostile wilderness into an earthly paradise. These ideological ambivalences, I show, are a function of how the nation treats its immigration as a matter of hospitality informed by the ethics, instead of the
economics, of reception.

Ambivalent hospitality, I further argue, operates not only in a cultural sphere but also in a politico-legal sphere where the laws of citizenship and belonging are more concretely defined. As legal historians have argued, American immigration laws and policies, in being
perpetually rearticulated and re-formed, have demonstrated a great
deal of ambivalence in vacillating between reception and rejection,
amnesty and exclusion. Indeed the ideological split between the Jeffersonian Republican vision of open immigration and the Federalist
championing of a "nativist" polity has been recapitulated in every immigration act. For example, the National Origins Acts of 1921 and
1924, while attempting to restrict the number of "undesirable" aliens
to restore an "optimal" ethnic configuration by imposing a strict quota
system, established no quota for Mexican and other Latin American
immigrants: this exception facilitated the migratory movement of a
large body of farm workers, which has continued to this day. Similarly,
the Immigration and Nationality Act of 1965 eliminated the racial and
ethnic biases of previous acts in a gesture of unlimited hospitality,
but created instead a new system of visa allocation that gave prefer-

ence to a professional class of aliens and radically limited the number of immigrants from Mexico, Latin America, and U.S. colonies.
And finally, the IRCA of 1986 attempted to control the flow of undocumented immigrants by expanding border enforcement efforts and
sanctions against employers who hired "illegal aliens," while at the
same time offering an extensive amnesty and legalization program for
over three million undocumented immigrants. My aim in listing these
different immigration acts is to point out how the state's ambivalence
about controlling immigration parallels the national culture's split reaction toward immigrants, a parallel that attests to the circulatory relation between the state's apparatus of immigration control and the
nation's ambivalent mode of cultural identity.

The regulation of the immigration crisis by the state, I wish to suggest, is at once responsive to the nation's concern about the intruding
other and productive of a differential form of cultural identification.
The way the nation relates to the state, as Balibar remarks, has been
conventionally viewed in terms of "reflecting": either the state creates
the nation in response to political and economic constraints, or the nation constitutes the state "as a way of fulfilling the needs of its collective consciousness, or of pursuing its material interests" (332). I posit
that on the issue of immigration the relationship is in fact circular, in
consonance with Balibar's insight that "a state always is implied in the
historic framework of a national formation" (331). The relation should
not be reduced to one of causality, for state and nation are mutually
implicated in each other, though remaining conceptually and socially
distinct.

The history of immigration law in the United States offers a compelling context in which to consider how the nation, as an imagined community, and the state, as a web of politico-legal apparatuses, work in
tandem to produce the nation's "laws of hospitality." The state solicits
the nation's consent in regulating immigration while contributing to
the popular perception of immigration as a national crisis, leading to a
national consensus that the crisis must be solved by imposing restrictions and limits. Consider the immigration acts of the early twentieth
century. Based on the findings of the Dillingham Commission of 1910
and in response to intense political pressure from nativist citizens who
embraced the eugenics movement, as well as from labor organizations
on the West Coast, the Immigration Act of 1917 made passing a literacy test a requirement for immigration and excluded laborers who

originated in the "Asiatic Barred Zone," while the National Origins Acts of 1921 and 1924 provided a quota system that limited the annual number of immigrants from each admissible nationality to 3 percent of the landed immigrants of that nationality currently resident in the United States based on the census of 1910, privileging in this way western European immigrants over all other immigrants. These acts radically limited the nation's hospitality toward new arrivals by establishing a policy of restriction based on a racially hierarchical order of eligibility. These laws, as Walter Benn Michaels has argued, also marked the displacement of an ideological notion of American identity—which defined belonging as a status that can be achieved through actions, such as immigration and naturalization—in favor of a cultural notion of national identity, defined in terms of family and racial inheritance.[41]

The passage of these racially exclusionary laws underscores the consensual character of the state's regulatory practices. For the quota laws were adopted in response to the importuning of such civic organizations as the American Federation of Labor, as well as to demands by racial nativists to restrict the flow of new immigrants from eastern and southern Europe to maintain racial homogeneity. The state, in other words, did not simply act in a repressive way by catering to the interests of capitalists and employers whose need for cheap labor made them supportive of lax immigration laws. Instead, it yielded to a broader public demand for federal control of immigration. However, caught between the demands of organized labor to curtail the flow of immigration and the needs of employers and capitalists for cheap labor, the state proved more ambivalent in its enactment of immigration laws. A series of statutes were included in these acts that exempted Mexicans and other Latin American immigrants from both the literacy test and the quota system. Responding to pressure from southwestern agricultural growers, the state acknowledged their demands, enacting laws that were at once restrictive and accommodating. The immigration acts of 1917–24 satisfied both the white nation's desire to maintain its racial superiority and the capitalists' need for cheap labor.

We encounter a similar split reaction to the nation's immigration dilemma with the passage of the IRCA in 1986. In response to widespread public pressure to curtail the flow of undocumented workers across the border from Mexico, the new act included an employer sanctions measure that for the first time made hiring undocumented workers illegal and punishable. And yet, as Kitty Calavita observes, "concerned not to 'harass' employers, Congress crafted employer sanctions that were largely symbolic."[42] Not only did the law include provisions for categories such as Special Agricultural Worker and Replenishment Agricultural Worker that made it possible for growers to employ temporary Mexican workers, it also included an "affirmative defense" clause that "protects employers from prosecution as long as they request documentation from workers, regardless of the validity of the documents presented" (Calavita, *Inside the State*, 169). Like the immigration acts of 1917–24, the IRCA responded to a vigilant public's demand to restrict the flow of immigration across the southern border, thus acting against the interests of agricultural and service employers, while at the same time paying attention to the employers' lobbying for sanctions not so onerous as to disrupt their businesses. Once again the state did not merely serve the interests of the ruling class, nor did it simply impose legislation from above on the general public. Rather, the state's restrictive laws of hospitality were instituted in response to contradictory demands from the national community and the capitalist class, and with the consent of both.

By Way of Conclusion?

Elaborating on the immigration deal forged between the Clinton administration and Congress to ease the passage of the Immigration Act of 1996, Rahm Emanuel, the White House senior political advisor, remarked, "We're a nation of immigrants and a nation of laws, and this agreement respects both those ideas."[43] Emanuel's comment, aimed at capturing the political compromise between a Democratic White House and a Republican-dominated Congress, offers a symptomatic expression of how the nation's ambivalent form of cultural identity informs the state's laws and practices of immigration. We claim to be a nation of immigrants, governed by the law of unlimited hospitality; and we are a nation of laws with which we control our immigrants. The "laws" in this case, if we were to follow the propositions of the bill, are all aimed to limit the nation's hospitality toward new arrivals: doubling the Border Patrol, installing fences and barriers along the border with Mexico, streamlining the deportation process, creating pilot projects to verify the immigration status of job applicants, and imposing tougher penalties on smugglers of immigrants.

That Emanuel invokes Kennedy's liberal statement about our being a nation of immigrants at a historical juncture when some of the most exclusionary practices of immigration control are being codified into laws reflects, above all, how the myth of immigrant America is often deployed equivocally to obscure the state's violent treatment of immigrants. The narrative of America as a hospitable asylum provides a powerful and enduring form of cultural equivocation, one that is perennially mobilized to mask the exclusionary and regulatory practices of immigration throughout the nation's history.

Emanuel's paradoxical statement, moreover, speaks to how the politics of immigration in the United States perpetually defer confrontation with the core contradiction of national culture, a deferral that allows the mobilization of immigrants to manage the nation's political, economic, and cultural predicaments. The acknowledgment that we are a nation of immigrants, while repeating the myth of immigrant founding, also points to a veiled recognition of the state's inability to control the flow of immigrants, a recognition necessitating the regulatory practices that the state legislates: "they" keep coming and we have to keep regulating them. This is appealing, and useful, precisely because it holds in reserve a criminalizable class, much like the in-and-out-of-prison population, to be targeted as such whenever doing so is politically or economically expedient. As a result, the politics of immigration strive for closure through legislation, but always remain ambivalent, open-ended, and unsettled, a condition that both accommodates the nation's new economic and political needs and recuperates recalcitrant and oppositional forces that cultural hegemony engenders. Located at the interstices of national consciousness and state apparatuses, immigration's ambivalences make the concept of "nation-state" imaginable in America. For while the figure of the "alien" provides a signifier of otherness through which the nation defines itself as an imagined community, the juridical and administrative regulation of immigration, produced in collaborative ways with the nation's political and economic exigencies, helps to construe the collective sovereignty of the modern state. Immigration, in short, is both a necessary mechanism of social control to legitimate state apparatuses and an essential contribution to the formation of national culture—paradoxically, since it is so often cast as a threat to national culture.

1

Imagining America

Forgetful Fathers and the Founding

Myths of the Nation

In his seminal lecture "What Is a Nation?," delivered on 11 March 1882 at the Sorbonne, Ernest Renan spoke of the importance of amnesia in the act of founding a nation. "Forgetting," he remarked, "is a crucial factor in the creation of a nation, which is why progress in historical studies often constitutes a danger for [the principle of] nationality" (11). Renan argued that the political project of founding a nation often entails forgetting the originary violence, forgetting that the sense of national unity was achieved initially by means of brutality. To create a homogeneous community, dissidence and dissent must be eliminated, but such a violent eradication is never remembered: "every French citizen has to have forgotten the massacre of Saint Bartholomew, or the massacres that took place in the Midi in the thirteenth century" (11). Though made in the context of France, Renan's argument offers powerful insight into how Americans have historically defined their national identity. The United States, I want to argue in this chapter, is an amnesiac nation that disremembers its violent beginnings to fashion itself as a unified imagined community. More particularly, my critical aim here is to consider the specific historical acts of forgetting that mark the ambivalent form of nation building in the United States. In the first part of my discussion, I will consider how the founding fathers' debate about immigration brings to the fore the nation's constitutive amnesia, while in the second part I will elaborate the theoretical and historical implications of forgetting by reading Crèvecoeur's *Letters From an American Farmer* (1782) as a foundational account of the nation's ambivalent civic identity.

*The Benevolent Father
and the Forgetting of Violence*

A historically revealing example of how amnesia is paramount to the founding of the nation is the debate over immigration between two of the founding fathers, Thomas Jefferson and Alexander Hamilton, in the beginning of the nineteenth century. In his First Annual Message to Congress in 1801, Jefferson wrote, "I cannot omit recommending a revisal of the laws on the subject of naturalization. Considering the ordinary chances of human life, a denial of citizenship under a residence of fourteen years is a denial to a great proportion of those who ask it, and controls a policy pursued from their first settlement by many of these States, and still believed of consequence to their prosperity. And shall we refuse the unhappy fugitives from distress that hospitality which the savages of the wilderness extended to our fathers arriving in this land? Shall oppressed humanity find no asylum on this globe?"[1] Jefferson's benevolent attitude toward new immigrants, as expressed in his rhetorical questions, is forgetful of many things. But before we recover these, let us first look at what his political rival, Alexander Hamilton, remembered by way of exposing the president's amnesia in his policy recommendation. The misrepresentation of the encounter between Native Americans and pilgrims as one of hospitality gave Hamilton ample ammunition to attack the president's deceptive benevolence toward immigrants. During the winter of 1801–2 he published a series of eighteen articles entitled "The Examination" in the *New York Evening Post* to refute Jefferson's annual message. In the seventh of these articles, he remembered Jefferson's own *Notes on Virginia*, in which he had claimed that populating the nation with immigrants would compromise the nation's homogeneity. There Jefferson had argued that immigrants would "bring with them the principles of the governments they leave, imbibed in their early youth; or, if able to throw it off, it will be in exchange for an unbounded licentiousness, passing, as is usual, from one extreme to another. It would be a miracle were they to stop precisely at the point of temperate liberty. In proportion to their numbers, they will share with us the legislation. They will infuse into it their spirit, warp and bias its directions, and render it a heterogeneous, incoherent, distracted mass" (108).

In his presidential address Jefferson seems peculiarly forgetful of this earlier statement against lax immigration. In the *Notes* he had advocated a narrow, nationalist idea of homogeneity that rejected the naturalization of immigrant and indentured workers (that is, the Virginia model of immigration); in his speech, he calls for a humanist notion of a heterogeneous community that is accepting of all oppressed masses of humanity (the Pennsylvania model of immigration).[2] To critique Jefferson's contradictory position toward immigration, Hamilton reminded him of the moment of the pilgrims' arrival. I quote at length from Hamilton's seventh article to reach the broader implications of Jefferson's amnesia:

> It might be asked in return, does the right to *asylum* or *hospitality* carry with it the right to suffrage and sovereignty? And what indeed was the courteous reception which was given to our forefathers, by the savages of the wilderness? When did these humane and philanthropic savages exercise the policy of incorporating strangers among themselves, on their first arrival in the country? When did they admit them into their huts, to make them part of their families, and when did they distinguish them by making them their sachems? Our histories and traditions have been more than apocryphal, if any thing like this kind, and gentle treatment was really lavished by the much-belied savages upon our thankless forefathers. But the remark occurs, had it all been true, prudence inclines to trace the history farther, and ask what has become of the nations of savages who exercised this policy? And who now occupies the territory which they had inhabited? Perhaps a useful lesson might be drawn from this very reflection.[3]

Hamilton is of course right about Jefferson's having misrepresented the reception accorded to the pilgrims as one of acceptance and hospitality. Jefferson recast the violent encounter between Native Americans and early British colonizers as a convivial occasion, disregarding both the pilgrims' sense of alienation in the New World and the genocide of Native Americans in various Indian wars, not to mention his own earlier characterization of Native Americans in the Declaration of Independence as "merciless . . . savages, whose rule of warfare is an undistinguished destruction of all ages, sexes & conditions." Ignoring all these facts helped Jefferson rhetorically in arguing for a pro-immigration position. Hamilton was quite perceptive to have critiqued Jefferson's rhetoric, for even if Jefferson's narrative of friendly reception had been true, the outcome could hardly have justified his stance toward immigration. The dislocation of Native Americans speaks to the failure of a liberal immigration policy, not to its success.

What Jefferson's rhetoric also obscures is the economic dimension of immigration, since he discusses the issue of naturalization in purely political terms. The desire for a more prosperous life in America that pulled European immigrants here is represented as a desire for political freedom, while the need for cheap immigrant labor that fueled the pro-immigration stance is couched as national hospitality. Such a misrepresentation reaffirms America's ideology of exceptionalism, the idea that the United States is a free country, free of political oppression and religious persecution. The buried reference to the "prosperity" that states enjoy by accepting immigrants is the only acknowledgment that immigrants economically enabled the nation. It is worth remembering that Jefferson had in fact made the issue of immigration a charge against George III by accusing him in the Declaration of Independence of having prevented the growth of the colonies by "obstructing the laws of naturalization of foreigners; [and] refusing to pass others to encourage their migrations hither; & raising the conditions of new appropriations of lands." In the nation's official discourse, the question of immigration gradually loses its economic dimension as it is recast in humanitarian terms—we claim to be a democratic and hospitable community helping the oppressed masses of humanity, instead of acknowledging that immigrants are helping the nation's territorial expansion and economic growth.

Jefferson's forgetfulness was not so much contradictory, which is what Hamilton thought, as politically expedient. Jefferson's failure to discuss the economics of immigration reflects his desire to disavow, in the Freudian sense that I described in the Introduction, two important issues: the actual condition of immigrants at the time and the political utility of unrestricted European immigration to expand the nation territorially. The myth of immigrant America and the idea of American exceptionalism have made us think of early immigrants as adventurers and heroes in search of an ideal life of liberty and religious freedom, forgetting that most immigrants well into the nineteenth century were economic refugees. To pay for their passage to America, many immigrants had to enter into exploitative contracts with ship captains or agencies as "indentured servants" or "redemptioners," which deprived them of their basic freedom as human subjects for at least four years, until they were able to pay off the cost of their passage to America. The horrendous conditions of indentured labor, vividly described by the English traveler Henry Bradshaw Fearon in his *Sketches of America* (1818), offer many examples of how, contrary to what Jefferson claimed, immigration to America for many poor Europeans meant servitude, not freedom. Indeed the working conditions of many immigrants were so harsh that some states, such as Maryland and Pennsylvania, passed laws to protect newcomers from "cruel and oppressive impositions by masters of the vessels in which they arrive and likewise by those to whom they become servants."[4]

Jefferson's humanist picture of America as an asylum for the oppressed also draws attention to the political expediency of encouraging immigration to populate the ever-expanding nation with white European settlers who also, as Smith points out, "felt more affinity for the partisans of small farmers and democratization than for mercantile and financial elites" (*Civic Ideals*, 139). Jefferson's amnesia is a convenient move to justify pushing Native Americans westward and populating new territories with white European immigrants who embraced the Jeffersonian Republican vision of an agrarian society. The narrative of the Native Americans' warm welcome to pilgrims provides the benevolent president with a rhetorical tool: the expansionist interest of the nation in attracting immigrants who can claim land and increase capital is represented as hospitality toward the oppressed of the globe. Here benevolence toward one community means brutality and violence toward another. In Jefferson's narrative, however, European immigrants are the beneficiaries of American liberty and freedom, not the unwitting enablers of the nation's expansion and participants in the slow destruction of the indigenous population.

Of course Jefferson had good reasons to sidestep his earlier argument: since he wrote the *Notes*, the burgeoning nation's expansion westward through the Treaty of Paris in 1783 and the forthcoming Louisiana Purchase of 1803 necessitated a faster population growth than he had predicted earlier. The annexation of new territories taken and purchased from Native Americans and European countries made a constant flow of immigration from Europe indispensable to building a powerful nation. But the nation's need for labor was, and as I will show later *is*, often couched as a desire for liberty and prosperity. It is significant that Jefferson focused solely on the "push" factor of immigration in his speech (political and religious oppression in Europe was, according to him, the force behind immigration), marginalizing the "pull" factor at work in the late eighteenth century and throughout the nineteenth. By "pull" I do not mean the mythologized attractions of America as a haven of liberty and prosperity, but rather the deliberate practice of boosterism that the original colonies and later the western states pursued in Europe. Since the late eighteenth century, immigration agents were employed by ship owners, land speculators, and state agents throughout European cities to stimulate a desire to come to America. These agents told workers of an abundance of well-paying jobs and advertised the country as a prosperous and free land, disseminating handbills and posting placards in every public place.

In addition to these methods of recruitment, a substantial body of literature promoted the virtues of the New World. Crèvecoeur's *Letters* and Morris Birkbeck's less famous *Letters from Illinois* (1818), for example, were instrumental in generating the myth of America as a promised land of economic opportunity. These texts, as I will discuss below, mediated the immigrant's desire for America, a desire born of the need for labor and economic necessity, and not just the love of liberty. Enthusiastic immigration success stories translated the economic need for labor into a political desire for liberty and an individual ambition for prosperity. In its representations of the pioneer life, this literature emphasized the "pull" factors of immigration and thus obscured the colonialist drive to populate the continent with white settlers and the expansionist tendency of the country's immigration policy. Far from benevolently accepting the oppressed, the nation, through its chauvinistic literature and practices, produced a desire for immigration in Europe by actively pursuing a policy of "pull." But the creation of this desire is always masked by the mythical discourse of immigration in the United States. In the nation's official history, immigration is always cloaked in the garb of national hospitality, an altruistic act to help the oppressed that covers what was surely a politically motivated project of territorial and economic expansion.

*The Conservative Father
and the Forgetting of National Trauma*

While Jefferson's annual message offers an example of political disavowal to build a nation, Hamilton's response demonstrates a personal form of negation to imagine a patriotic American identity. Ironically, Hamilton, who was able to remember the colonial occupation of America, was forgetful of the pilgrims' dislocation, that they were once a community of strangers and exiles in a new land. Hamilton viewed the early colonists as the true native population, constructing them as a superior race in danger of extinction by the arrival of new immigrants from Europe whom he viewed as the "Grecian horse," corrupting and invading the democratic polity of New England Puritans. Hamilton's rhetoric disavows not only the fact that the "natives" were once immigrants themselves, but also his own immigrant history: Hamilton was a naturalized alien, and to cast himself as a native he had to mask his original status as a foreigner.

Hamilton's biography provides an interesting context for understanding how his personal amnesia contributed to his overzealous patriotism. Born out of wedlock to an outcast European couple, and marked by indigence and shame in the island of Nevis in the West Indies, his own exilic history compelled him to be forgetfully nativist.[5] Hamilton was abandoned in his early youth by his father, whose incompetence at business had estranged him from his family, and raised on the island of St. Kitts by his mother, who had the reputation of having "whored with everyone." His desire to move to North America at the age of seventeen was his way of casting off the shameful history that haunted him in the Caribbean. Immigration to America enabled him to forget this alienation. In the context of his painful personal history, Hamilton's obsessive anti-immigrant stance was a form of "acting out," symptomatically repeating the trauma of his own exilic past. For him, forgetting through repetition seems to have functioned like a defense mechanism that helped him to transcend the pain of his dislocation and sense of cultural and personal alienation, and to fashion a new identity as an American hero. How else can we account for the compulsive rejection of anything foreign by a foreigner? Or Hamilton's passionate patriotism in fighting against the British colonizer on behalf of a community he had recently joined? It strains credulity to believe that his hypernationalism did not mask a deeper ambivalence. Hamilton's amnesia is emblematic and productive of a patriotic form of national identity in which the denial of one's own "foreignness" is the requisite for being an American. He was able to become a great patriotic champion in America because he was able so successfully to forget where he came from.[6]

The debate between Hamilton and Jefferson about immigration points to two forms of amnesia in the founding of the nation. The conscious silence about the violent origin of American nationality and the actual aims of a lax immigration policy function to imagine a welcoming and benevolent nation and thus unconsciously to negate the nation's immigrant roots and fashion a patriotic national identity. My argument that the disavowed history of colonial America is a critical component of American national identity is in keeping with Renan's idea that nation building is an act of forgetting the originary and constitutive violence. The nation must disremember its deeds of violence and its heterogeneous immigrant roots to imagine itself as a homogeneous community. This national amnesia is evident in the founding fathers' debate. Jefferson expediently overlooked the brutality of the country's English forefathers toward the country's indigenous people so as to posit the myth of America as a democratic nation hospitable to its newcomers. Hamilton, who remembered the inhospitable encounter between the pilgrims and the Native Americans, is forgetful of the immigrant status of the "natives" and his own alienness, an amnesia that enables him to advocate a nativist position and to maintain the nation's imaginary homogeneity and coherence. Lost in both narratives is the uprooting of communities—in one case, the indigenous population of North America and in the other, pilgrims and European immigrants—a precondition for the formation of national consciousness. Exile and displacement are not only the simple opposite of nationalism, as cultural critics have consistently claimed,[7] but also the necessary requisites to imagining a national community in the United States. Uprooted from their national communities, the pilgrims reenacted their own trauma of dislocation by brutally displacing Native Americans, a violence that marked the very origin politically of our nation. "Unity," as Renan observes, "is always effected by means of brutality" (11). In the nation's historical memory, or its foundational myth of immigrant America, Europeans' experience of exile and the violence involved in establishing their polity are always disremembered. To become a nation, the early European settlers had to suppress their own experiences of exile and those of the population that they dislodged from the land. The displacement of the indigenous people is what enabled pilgrims to build a nation; the suppression of their own alienation as exiles helped them to imagine a national identity.

But what can we learn from the forgetfulness of our nation's founding fathers? What should we remember of their debate if we are to understand better the birth of national consciousness in the United

States? The politically expedient denial of immigration's actual aims (Jefferson) and of the nation's immigrant roots (Hamilton) have produced an ambivalent form of national identity in the United States. The historical amnesia about immigration makes Americans, as a national community, simultaneously maintain opposite attitudes toward immigrants, continuously vacillating between xenophilia and xenophobia, hospitality and hostility. On the one hand is Jeffersonian expedient hospitality toward the oppressed masses; on the other is Hamiltonian reactionary xenophobia toward newcomers. Since its very founding, the United States has embraced contradictory notions of community, and has incessantly fluctuated between insecurity and confidence, vigilantism and hospitality, xenophobia and xenophilia, because the actual aims of its immigration policies and "laws of hospitality" are incompatible with the nation's claim of unlimited hospitality.

As I have suggested in my introduction, many scholars have already pointed out that the history of nationalism and immigration in the United States is marked by ambiguity and uncertainty. Some have attempted to explain the nation's contradictory views about immigration on political grounds, by claiming that the American polity must tolerate and legitimize opposite political views to remain a democratic nation. The very idea of democracy as the rule of majority, they suggest, implies opposite views and antithetical values. Other scholars have further tried to explain the nation's ambivalence in economic terms. Citing historical examples of periods of receptivity followed by periods of exclusion, they have argued that the nation's economic condition dictates a cyclical reaction against immigrants. While political scientists view the nation's ambivalence as an ideological necessity, sociologists and economists consider it a purely reactive phenomenon. The economic slump of the 1880s, for example, is seen as having inaugurated a period of restriction after a century of an "open-door" policy. Or the nation's swollen unemployment rate of the early 1950s is blamed for "Operation Wetback" of 1954, which scapegoated Mexicans and sanctioned the mass deportation of farm workers after a long period during which the political refugees of the Second World War were admitted. The nation's ambivalence toward its immigrants is viewed here as part of a duplicitous pattern of welcoming immigrants when the nation needs them for its economic growth and turning against them when there is economic hardship.

In contrast to these views, I use the notion of ambivalence to theorize a *productive* difference between competing notions of national identity. The "genius" of American society is not that it has legitimized ambiguity, as Lipset and Raab have argued, but that it has been able to manufacture a powerful form of cultural equivocation, which can obscure differences by rhetorical practices and allow the citizenry to have it both ways. The opposing poles of identification, in other words, not only coexist as in an antinomy but also reproduce and reinforce one another, ensuring a continual fluctuation between the myth of immigrant America and its nativist opposite. The incommensurable difference between America as an immigrant haven and America as an anti-immigrant outpost is a function of what these opposing myths negate, a negation that necessitates their repetition as new historical and social crises appear. Contrary to the commonsensical view of immigration as a cyclical phenomenon, immigration is a practice and discourse of exclusion that has always accompanied the myth of an immigrant America. Even during the so-called era of the open door in the nineteenth century, when the United States maintained a lenient immigration policy, the nation was awash with anti-foreign sentiment and every group of newcomers was portrayed as unassimilable and alien, unable or unwilling to embrace the democratic principles of the nation. But the continual coexistence of hostility and hospitality does not constitute a contradictory response to immigration, as is commonly argued. Rather, hospitality and hostility, as the effects of competing myths of America, are partners in the production of national identity in the United States.[8] These countervailing dispositions—one reviling the foreigner and another embracing the immigrant—lay bare an irreconcilable difference at the core of civic identity in America.

To discover the historical roots of the nation's ambivalent discourse of hospitality, I wish to consider in the remaining section of this chapter a seminal account of life in colonial America, Crèvecoeur's *Letters*. In the official historiography of the nation, the Revolution has always been constructed as a moment of radical rupture with its colonial past. But Crèvecoeur's text is a powerful reminder that the shift from colonial to Republican America, though it inaugurated a general transformation of political relations, involved a great deal of continuity and repetition between the pre- and post-revolutionary eras. The book displays the competing ideologies through which the United States originally fashioned its cultural identity, while inventing the myth

of immigrant America that encouraged Europeans to seek their for-
tunes in the New World. Heavily cited by the liberal founding fathers
such as Washington and Jefferson, and highly popular in immigrant-
exporting cities of Europe, Crèvecoeur's text offers important historical insights into the ideological underpinnings of nation building in
America and the opposing discourses that informed the construction
of its civic identity.

Home Abroad:
The Immigrant and the Traveler

It is interesting, if obvious, that one of the founding texts of American
literature, a key document of American national identity, was written
by a recently arrived immigrant. J. Hector St. John de Crèvecoeur, an
Anglophile French Jesuit who had traveled extensively in the colonies
as a salesman and land surveyor and gained a name for himself as a
lieutenant in the French regiment in Canada, finally decided to settle
in New York in 1769.[9] He became a naturalized British subject, bought
a large farm, and married an American woman with whom he had
three children. Though he returned to France in 1778 after the War
of Independence broke out, he later took up residence in the United
States after the war as the official representative of Louis XVI. Surprisingly, Crèvecoeur's *Letters*, which he first published in England,
attained only a moderate fame in America in the half-century after its
publication before being recognized as a canonical piece of American
literature. By contrast, the book immediately achieved great success
in Europe, where it was translated into several languages and succes-
sively marketed in various immigrant-exporting cities.[10] The irony of
the book's initial reception is a sign above all of the nation's ability
to imagine a new identity by inventing a desire for itself in Europe.
Crèvecoeur's work was a celebratory American text unwittingly meant
for a European audience. As an account of the prosperous lives of
colonial Americans, it sold the idea of immigration to many Europeans, enticing them to leave their old homes and search for a new
identity in the New World.[11] In the oft-cited third letter, for example,
the narrator describes how upon arrival, the newcomer experiences a
sense of "national pride" as "he beholds fair cities, substantial villages,
extensive fields, an immense country filled with decent houses, good

roads, orchards, meadows, and bridges."[12] By describing America in such salutary terms, Crèvecoeur's *Letters* mediated and perpetuated in Europe the desire for America, a desire that was at the origin of the will to imagine a nation. I say at the origin because the book's seductive power played a central role in the nation's geographical and economic growth by advancing its policy of populating the newly acquired territories with white European immigrants. It is worth noting that Jefferson borrowed extensively from Crèvecoeur's text and from his own correspondence with the author, using his description of America as "the asylum of freedom; as the cradle of future nations, and the refuge of distressed Europeans" to posit the myth of immigrant America in his first annual speech (7). Crèvecoeur's text confirms that before a national identity could be articulated in the United States, a desire for it had to be invented in Europe. It is perhaps for this reason that the book was a successful piece of promotional travel literature in Europe before it was recognized in the United States as a book about American civic identity.

But what made this text so popular in Europe? How did it articulate the desire for America? And what role did this desire play in imagining a nation in the United States? A starting point to answer these questions is the generic ambivalence of the text. By generic ambivalence I mean that the book is both the epistolary narrative of an ordinary American and the travelogue of an erudite European. The generic split between autobiography and travelogue in Crèvecoeur's text, I want to argue, is symptomatic of the ambivalent way in which American national identity is historically articulated as both settled and mobile, unassuming and ambitious, and individualistic and communal. James, whose individual identity represents the collective American self, is both a humble farmer who lives a sedentary and unalloyed life and an aspiring traveler who transforms himself into a sophisticated man of letters through his promontory observation of the American landscape and its occupants.

Scholars of early American literature have often treated the *Letters* as an anomalous text, arguing that it contradictorily vacillates between the "inherited conventions of autobiography and the philosophical letter," to use the words of one critic.[13] Nonetheless, Crèvecoeur's text has been uniformly considered a quintessential articulation of an emerging American identity: from D. H. Lawrence, who described the *Letters* as the "emotional . . . prototype of the American," to a contemporary reader, Stephen Fender, who has argued that the text "gave America its first moral geography," almost every critic has read the text as a founding narrative of American cultural identity, disregarding the fact that much of the book is actually the account of an enlightened traveler's journey across America.[14] While the first three letters recount James's euphoric pleasures of living in America as a colonial settler, the next nine are the observations of an adventurer who explores and describes the other parts of America to his European interlocutor, Mr. F. B., a European traveler himself. Like the Greek *theoros*, James travels throughout America to observe the rituals and practices of a polis different from his own to provide his European readers with a *theoria* of "what is an American." Even when James stays at home, he engages in short excursions to visit new settlements, "on purpose to observe the different steps each settler takes, the gradual improvements, the different tempers of each family, on which their prosperity in a great measure depends" (62). Using such tropes as navigation, touring, and exploration, the letters also thematize the notion of travel to theorize America and its civic culture, as I will discuss below. That the American farmer is also a traveler demonstrates how the imagining of national consciousness in the United States is a product of travel, of cultural and geographical displacement. To become an American, one leaves home and experiences displacement. Identity, Crèvecoeur's text demonstrates, is not self-conferred but must be imagined differentially, through first knowing the identity of another. It is ironic that the nomadic native peoples of America were for that very reason excluded from the nation's future, as I will discuss in the next chapter.

The immigrant's dislocation and sense of disorientation as a foreigner in a new land, however, make him or her culturally ambivalent and philosophically divided. James constantly vacillates between his past European self, which he must forget, and his future American identity, which he must imagine. The tension between Europe, which represents the narrator's past, and America, which symbolizes his future, is evident from the very beginning of Crèvecoeur's narrative. In the introductory letter, in which James contemplates the idea of writing his impressions of America, his wife warns him about his inability to relate anything of significance to his interlocutor, the "great European man, who hath lived abundance of time in that big house called Cambridge; where, they say, that worldly learning is so abundant, that people get it only by breathing the air of the place"

(12). Although the village minister would ultimately persuade the ordinary farmer to write his observations of America, throughout the narrative James remains self-conscious about his European audience, always comparing the European with the American and forever feeling intellectually inferior to his European counterpart. As the preposition "from" in the title of the book also indicates, the letters are addressed to European readers, and Europe, as the ultimate destination of James's letters, remains central to how an American identity is imagined. The Old World, however, plays a dual role in the birth of national consciousness in America: it acts as the other that mediates the invention of an American identity while it provides the immigrant with the intellectual and practical tools to succeed in the New World. To understand the productive tension between Europe and America in the text, let us consider these poles of identification more closely.

In its first role, Europe is something to forget. The Old World is the place from which the immigrant departs, and consequently it is associated with cultural and political difference, just as the European is figured as the differential other of the American self. As the point of departure, Europe represents America's past, the past that must be abandoned or negated in order for the America of the future to emerge. The geographical move to America entails a temporal passage, thus denying to Europe "coevalness" with the New World. As the minister initially tells James, in America "every thing is modern, peaceful, and benign," and this makes Americans "strangers" to Europe, where "feudal institutions" and "revolutions, desolations, and plagues" have enslaved its people (15). Throughout the narrative, James continues to associate Europe with servitude and dependence, chaos and poverty, while he represents America in contrast as "the asylum of freedom; as the cradle of future nations, and the refuge of distressed Europeans" (7). The trajectory of becoming an American as a narrative of progress is therefore defined as a process of renouncing one's European past, "the former servitude and dependence," the "mechanism of subordination, that servility of disposition, which poverty had taught him" (58–59). The American is a propulsive figure whose imagination, instead of focusing on the past, "wisely spring[s] forward to the anticipated fields of future cultivation and improvement, to the future extent of those generations which are to replenish and embellish this boundless content" (15).

To become an American, one must disavow the European other in oneself, a disavowal that is both intellectual and practical. It is intellectual because it means believing in a new and abstract system of political ideals and values. Americanization involves an ideological departure from European *moeurs*, the general body of intellectual views, moral beliefs, cultural values, and social manners. According to Crèvecoeur, "He is an American, who, leaving behind him all his ancient prejudices and manners, receives new ones from the new mode of life he has embraced" (44). Such a view anticipates the Federalist vision of John Quincy Adams, who demanded that the immigrants cast off their European skin, more than it does the liberal tradition that celebrated America's ethnic diversity. The immigrant's disavowal is also practical, because it means adopting and developing new practices of everyday life that are consistent with the new natural and social environment. In the *Letters* the European is represented as a differential figure whose sophistication and leisure bring into focus the value of James's simplicity and hard work. Unlike his European counterpart, who "can live upon what they call bank notes, without working," the American is a "simple farmer" who toils wearily on his land, cutting down trees, making fences, and buying and clothing his slaves (21, 23). The immigrant must leave behind the Old World's leisurely and decadent mode of life to be able to succeed in America as a hard-working farmer.

And yet in its second role, Europe is something to retain and even emulate. The introductory letter begins with an acknowledgment of James's intellectual debt to his interlocutor, who gives him a quick tour of Europe's intellectual landscape to prepare him for his journey: "I gave you nothing more than what common hospitality dictated; but could any other guest have instructed me as you did? You conducted me, on the map, from one European Country to another; told me many extraordinary things of our famed mother-country, of which I knew very little; of its internal navigation, agriculture, arts, manufactures and trade: you guided me through an extensive maze, and I abundantly profited by the journey; the contrast therefore proves the debt of gratitude to be on my side" (11).

James's expression of gratitude is of course meant to draw attention to the radical difference between the humble American farmer and the sophisticated European. But that he needs the discursive tour of a European gentleman before embarking on his own journey across the New World indicates the mediated nature of his vision of America and its cultural identity. For James to provide his Euro-

pean audience with a discursive voyage to America, he must first take
a similar journey to Europe and become intellectually competent as a
traveler-narrator. Whereas elsewhere in his narrative James describes
the American differentially as "a new man, who acts upon new principles" and "must therefore entertain new ideas and form new opinions," here and throughout his narrative he emphasizes that the new
immigrant "retraces many of his own country manners . . . [and] hears
the names of families and towns with which he is acquainted" (44, 56).
Americanization therefore entails a mimetic form of identification in
which the immigrant's European heritage provides the cultural condition for his unique individuality. As Nancy Ruttenburg remarks, "Far
from celebrating self-invention, the *Letters* insist that the legitimate
renewal of self in America requires scrupulous 'tracing' of a (narrative) line already established by father, fatherland, or Nature."[15] Indeed, Europe always remains with and in James, for it provides him
with both the cultural capital that makes him successful in America
and the philosophical tradition that informs his narrative. It is suggestive that when James advocates the need to forget one's European
past, he is careful to warn the prospective immigrant against the danger of "passing from one extreme to the other" by "forget[ting] it too
much" (59).

Forgetting is always a selective process in Crèvecoeur. James com-
pares the experience of immigrating with navigation to demonstrate
the importance of coming to America prepared. "Landing on this
great continent," he points out, "is like going to sea, they must have
a compass, some friendly directing needle; or else they will uselessly
err and wander for a long time, even with a fair wind" (68). Like a sea
voyage, immigration entails unexpected vicissitude and hardship, re-
quiring thus intellectual, cultural, and economic readiness acquired in
Europe. According to the narrator, what distinguishes the successful
immigrant is the "national genius" that he brings with him from his
native country, the knowledge of how to cultivate the land and how
to survive as a "frontier-man" in the wilderness. The cultural and real
capital brought from his European fatherland is paramount to the immigrant's survival in the New World. James attributes his own prosperity in America to his father's having given him "the art of reading
and writing" as well as "a good farm and his experience" (25). These
are the "sort[s] of materials" that the village priest reminds James to
recognize within himself if he is to succeed as a writer and farmer (17).

The knowledge and experience that have been passed on to James are what guarantee his prosperity as an immigrant as much as they authorize him as a narrator.

More important is the role of the philosophical baggage that James carries with him from Europe. Of course, as I will elaborate upon briefly, this intellectual capital is not always acknowledged as such by the narrator, who actively underplays the role of Europe in his cultural development by way of distinguishing himself as an American. A reference to his philosophical culture appears in the introductory letter, however, where James mentions, "My father left me a few musty books, which *his* father brought from England with him" (12). Though he does not tell us which books these were, his intellectual reflections in the text reveal the philosophical ideas and ideals that he carries with him from Europe. Indeed, as scholars of early American literature have pointed out, Crèvecoeur's work is indebted to a broad range of intellectual traditions in Europe, ranging from the pastoral conception of society to Enlightenment philosophy.[16] As a result, the book portrays America at once as the realization of the *philosophes'* vision of an agrarian democracy in which order, progress, and intelligibility prevail and as the pastoral ideal of pre-industrial society, not to mention as the romantically wild and prelapsarian paradise discovered by benevolent Europeans and transformed into a cultivated garden. Similarly, James, the typical American, acts both as a rational settler who views the European colonization of the New World as a progressive move and as a romantic traveler who marvels at the primitive beauty of its landscape and the pastoral simplicity of its people.

The philosophical baggage that James brings with him from Europe, however, remains thematically absent in Crèvecoeur's *Letters*, an absence (or forgetting) that I would argue is central to the understanding of his cultural ambivalence as an American. That the books are musty suggests that they have not been read in a long time, thus symbolizing the narrator's renunciation of his European intellectual tradition and his embrace of the humble and non-intellectual life of a farmer. In the very beginning of the book, the narrator reminds his interlocutor, "You well know that I am neither a philosopher, politician, divine, or naturalist, but a simple farmer" (22–23). Indeed there is a strong anti-intellectualism throughout Crèvecoeur's text, even though in taking up writing "James will ally himself with the 'cunning folks,' those who don't engage in physical labor but traffic instead in forms of absence or

immateriality," as Ruttenburg points out (279). Given his contradictory stance toward intellectual work, it should come as no surprise that
the letters are presented as the spontaneous impressions of an ordinary
person, not the philosophic reflections of an intellectual. The narrator, we are told in the beginning, is "dressed in [his] simple American
garb," not "clad in all the gowns of Cambridge" (19). For the American
farmer, his plow is his pen, the instrument through which he thinks
and lives.

But the thematic anti-intellectualism of Crèvecoeur's *Letters* obscures the important ways in which Europe's intellectual traditions inform the narrator's representation of America and his definition of
national identity. James's forgetfulness makes him embrace competing notions of history and community: while the works of Enlightenment philosophers help him to posit the notions of human progress
and the pursuit of self-interest as effective means to found an ideal
society, eighteenth-century ideas of the pastoral and nature enable
him to market America as an "asylum" and a "retreat, a place to re-
tire to away from the complexity, anxiety, and oppression of European
society," to use the words of Leo Marx (*The Machine in the Garden*,
87). The narrator's philosophical ambivalence allows him to espouse
simultaneously a utopian vision of America that romanticizes its natural and primitive beauty and a rationalist view of the emerging nation
that valorizes the idea of social and economic progress, represented by
the "chain of settlements which embellish these extended shores" (40).
The passage in which the narrator describes "the true and the only
philosophy of the American farmer" offers an important example that
makes it possible to discern the ideological utility of the American's
intellectual ambivalence (27):

> What should we American farmers be without the distinct possession
> of that soil? It feeds, it clothes us: from it we draw even a great exuber-
> ancy, our best meat, our richest drink; the very honey of our bees comes
> from this privileged spot. No wonder we should thus cherish its posses-
> sion: no wonder that so many Europeans, who have never been able to
> say that such portion of the land was theirs, cross the Atlantic to realize
> that happiness! This formerly rude soil has been converted by my father
> into a pleasant farm, and, in return, it has established all our rights. On
> it is founded our rank, our freedom, our power, as citizens. (27)

The blurring of the words "soil" and "land" in this passage brings
into focus the ambivalent nature of the American farmer's agrarian

philosophy. James oscillates between a romanticized (apolitical?) notion of soil in which the man and the earth are organically connected and a rational (political?) understanding of settlement as a colonial possession of the land claimed through labor. The organic soil is valorized as the natural source of man's subsistence and happiness. In this narrative, America is represented as a fertile land, nature's garden, where every immigrant can grow. The narrator often uses natural elements as metaphors to describe the situation of the immigrant: he is like a "plant," a "seed," or a "sprout growing at the foot of a great tree" (45, 175, 55). The American's naturally benign relationship with the plenteous land enables him to grow and "become a tree bearing fruit" (55). The closer the immigrant is to his environment and the more he learns about it, the more he will prosper. In this romantically apolitical vision of America, cultural identity is articulated as an organic and benevolent phenomenon, the product of a natural link between the humble farmer and the soil. Far from a colonial settler, the American is a "farmer of feelings," "an humble . . . planter, a simple cultivator of the earth" whose sincere motives allow him to maintain a peaceful relationship with the rich earth (7).

And yet the references to the European desire for possessing a piece of land and his father's conversion of the "rude soil" into a "pleasant farm" suggest an opposite, Lockean notion of what constitutes being an American. In this sense the American identity is associated with property and a willful appropriation of the soil, through which it becomes land. Following Locke's *Second Treatise of Government*, the American claims the land as his property by mixing his labor with it. In this narrative, America is not a paradise found but a wild and primitive stretch of earth in need of cultivation. The soil is now described as infertile and rude, and it is the farmer's labor, cultivation, and therefore rightful possession of the land that constitute his freedom and power. The owning of the land through his labor liberates the European immigrant from servitude and subordination and makes him a free man in control of his own destiny.

The notion of land as something to possess in order to achieve individual freedom is however born of a colonialist will to power that must disremember both the "Indians" who have been pushed beyond the frontier and the slaves whose labor is exploited to cultivate the land. Far from being a simple, peace-loving cultivator, the American farmer is a sophisticated and calculating colonizer who appropriates the land from the "noble savage" and uses the slave as a convenient

Lockean prosthesis to cultivate it for his own benefit. The movement from European subjectivity to American identity, in other words, entails willful acts of colonizing the land and exploiting the slave's labor. Remembering, or rather forgetting, that what reduced him to servitude in Europe was his having "owned not a single foot of the extensive surface of the planet," the naturalized American realizes his desire for freedom and happiness through colonialist possession of the land and slave labor (42). While in the pastoral discourse an organic relationship to nature defines the American, in the rationalist discourse it is mastery over it that constitutes his identity and claim to citizenship.

The ideological implications of the narrator's philosophical ambivalence, his teetering between the rational and the pastoral, become acute as he explores the dark and wild sides of America, the slavery in the South and the frontier life in the West. These parts of the narrative, as criticism of Crèvecoeur's text has shown, offer a dystopic vision of the emerging nation, representing the cultural and social predicaments of these settlements as the disillusionment of America's idyllic image.[17] Here the American farmer, turned enlightened traveler, tries to provide answers to the question "Would you prefer the state of men in the woods to that of men in a more improved situation?" (163). He visits Charles-Town (Charleston, South Carolina) and explores the western frontier to provide his audience with some answers to this important question. Slavery in the South and frontier life in the West are symbolically important because they represent the two opposites of the American agrarian utopia. One has moved too far from nature, the other too close to it. In each case the traveler's reflections point to a philosophical split between the romantically naïve and the soberly rational views of America, an ambivalence, I argue, that inadvertently exposes the ideological limits of the principles upon which the nation is founded.

In Charles-Town James faces the social limits of the idea of progress and the notion of self-interest as the basis of liberal democracy. Though the city is the capital of one of the richest provinces, "the center of our beau monde," with "inhabitants [who] are the gayest in America," it has become a place of decadence and human misery (151): "While all is joy, festivity, and happiness, in Charles-Town, would you imagine that scenes of misery overspread in the country? Their ears, by habit, are become deaf, their hearts are hardened; they neither see, hear, nor feel for, the woes of their poor slaves, from whose painful labours all their wealth proceeds. Here the horrors of slavery, the hardship of incessant toils, are unseen; and no one thinks with compassion of those showers of sweat and of tears which from the bodies of Africans daily drop, and moisten the ground they till" (153).

Not surprisingly, Crèvecoeur accounts for this decadence in contradictory terms: his position is both essentialist, blaming the hot "climate [that] renders excesses of all kinds very dangerous," and constructionist, suggesting that commerce and its degenerative effects of greed, luxury, and slothfulness have led to the decline of civilization (152). Instead of the modest farmer, the inhabitants of Charles-Town are "lawyers, planters, and merchants" who "have reached the *ne-plus-ultra* of worldly felicity," but at the cost of moral degeneration, including enslaving blacks and living immoral lives (152). As a benevolent humanist, James devotes much of his discussion of the region's moral corruption to the issue of slavery, describing the horrendous conditions of plantation labor and the gruesome torture of a rebellious slave. The narrator's extensive description of the horrors of slavery is at once the abolitionist discourse of a romantic and the pragmatic critique of a rationalist. The narrator is critical of the mistreatment of slaves in the South because the denial of liberty is against human nature (romantic or emotional view) and because the mistreatment of slaves does nothing but "sow the seeds of inveterate resentment, and nourish a wish of perpetual revenge" (pragmatic or rational view) (157).[18]

In Charles-Town the rational, enlightened society of agrarians has reached the limits of what constitutes progress. There slave work has replaced free labor and commerce has succeeded farming, producing a corrupt and unequal social structure and a decadent and immoral culture. The more economically successful the society has become, the further it has moved from what is "natural to mankind," namely liberty, prosperity, and the pursuit of happiness, values that are meant to define the ideal American identity. The shadow of slavery taints the economic success and social progress of its white inhabitants, exposing the dark sides of the will to power and the pursuit of happiness. Although Crèvecoeur does not quite broach the predicament of slave labor as a contradiction in the Lockean theory of property, his negative portrayal of Charles-Town unwittingly reveals the dubiety of agrarian democracy. Crèvecoeur's discussion of the town's mode of production unintentionally makes clear that the principles of self-interest and progress upon which liberal democracy is founded would ultimately lead every colony to the moral and cultural decay that has overtaken the South. If according to the Enlightenment narrative of progress commerce is to follow agriculture, it will not take long for the virtuous community of Nantucket to suffer the fate of Charles-Town.

While the southern planters have drifted so far away from nature that they have become decadent, the frontier people have moved so close to it that they have become primitive and savage. Whereas slavery points to the social limits of progress, the alienation of the frontier man brings into focus the cultural limits of romanticizing nature and primitive culture. Predictably, the life of the frontier man is narrated ambivalently, as the narrator's philosophic division makes him view nature in opposite ways. The experience of living in wild nature is both liberating and alienating. A primitive lifestyle does offer the immigrant "the most perfect freedom, the ease of living, the absence of those cares and corroding solicitudes which so often prevail with us" (202). Witnessing the hazardous effects of commerce in Charles-Town, the narrator begins his last letter with the escapist fantasy of living in an Indian village: "I wish for a change of place; the hour is come at last that I must fly from my house and abandon my farm!" (187). There is always something primordially "bewitching" and "indelible" in primitive nature that pulls the European toward it, especially after observing the degenerative consequences of commercial activity. It is for this reason that according to the narrator thousands of Europeans have joined aboriginal communities, because they find the "social bond" of these communities "far superior to any thing to be boasted of among us" (202).

But as the title of the last letter, "Distresses of a Frontier-man," indicates, there is another side to living in the wilderness. Unlike the quaint, pastoral life of the simple farmer, the life of the frontier man is characterized by distress and alienation. While the vastness of the land condemns him to a life of solitude and alienation, his fear of the wilderness prevents him from enjoying his meal and deprives him of a peaceful sleep. Here raw and wild nature, far from being a benevolent provider, is the source of calamities and misery, making "self-preservation" instead of hospitality the cultural norm. The closer the frontier man gets to nature, the more primitive he becomes. Primitivism, in other words, marks the cultural limit of the romantic idea of nature in America. In the wilderness, there is no community or cultural bond; and "what is man when no longer connected with society?" (187). The frontier man is thus represented as an alienated and solitary individual whose violated feelings and "erratic thought" distance him far from the principles of enlightened inquiry and rationality (197).

What are the ideological implications of the narrator's philosophical ambivalence? And what conclusions can we draw from the book's generic amalgam? To begin, the generic split between a settler's epistolary discourse and a European travelogue speaks to the "dialogical imagination" of the *Letters*, making the book into an inclusive narrative that simultaneously captures the points of view of the prospective European immigrant and the American citizen.[19] The knowledge of Europe and the experience of living in America "dialogizes" the narrative's point of view, enabling the narrator to valorize the experience of immigration as progress while mythologizing the civic virtues of American society. Consider how he markets the idea of immigration to his European audience in the following passage:

> A country [i.e., Europe] that had no bread for him; whose fields procured him no harvest; who met with nothing but the frowns of the rich, the severity of the laws, with jails and punishments; who owned not a single foot of the extensive surface of this planet. No! Urged by a variety of motives here they came. Every thing has tended to regenerate them. New laws, a new mode of living, a new social system. Here they are become men. In Europe they were as so many useless plants, wanting vegetative mould and refreshing showers. They withered; and were mowed down by want, hunger, and war; but now, by the power of transplantation, like all other plants, they have taken root and flourished! (42–43)

The narrator's knowledge of the predicaments of living in Europe helps him rhetorically to posit America as a utopian place to live. As someone who is both a settler and traveler, he is endowed with a double vision, able to compare the oppressive condition of Europeans with the prosperous one of Americans in such a way as to lure new immigrants, while reinvigorating the communal bond among the settlers by reminding them of what a great life they are having in America. The farmer's organic relation with the land gives him the metaphoric language in which to boast about American liberty and prosperity, while the comparative perspective allows him to construct the move from Europe to America as a trajectory of progress. As the narrator himself remarks, the move to America makes oppressed Europeans human again. Immigration can thus be described "objectively" as a process of regeneration and rebirth and America as the land of freedom and opportunity.

Moreover, on a thematic level the narrator's philosophical ambivalences also made his representation of the New World appealing to a plurality of audiences. As Christine Holbo observes, "Expressing opinions which range from conservative Whig to political Lockean, James is everything to every reader" (55). The varied and versatile representation in the *Letters* of the American landscape construed the nation as a desirable destination for everyone. Crèvecoeur's text is not contradictory but dispersed: its philosophical ambivalences render it a polyvalent text, embracing competing notions of identity and culture. Its romanticized narrative of the American wilderness made the country seductive to those solitary readers in search of adventure and novelty, while its representation of the enlightened, agrarian society made it attractive to those in search of a communal and pastoral life. America could be both a primitive place for the adventurous traveler to explore and a highly civilized society for the economic refugee to settle. It is for this reason that the book was embraced so enthusiastically by followers of Coleridge and Rousseau, who admired its romantic imagination, while it enjoyed a great deal of popularity among rationalists and physiocrats, who were seduced by its portrayal of agrarian democracy.

That Crèvecoeur's work has also become canonical in the United States and is taught throughout its educational system as one of the founding documents of the nation further testifies to how powerfully indispensable ideological antinomy is to imagining an American civic identity. Crèvecoeur's book suggests that in America, slavery and freedom, colonialism and liberty, individuality and community, nature and culture are not logically incongruous but constitute insoluble antinomies in which antithetical positions, paradoxical ideologies, and conflicting values maintain complementary relations and form ideological continuities. For in America the communal bond is founded on the principle of self-interest, freedom is acquired by enslaving others, and progress is achieved through colonial expansion. As Ruttenburg also argues, "The lesson that James learns and that he promotes to newly arrived immigrants as the blueprint of authentic selfhood, both personal and national, is that true freedom entails confinement, true novelty entails repetition, true individuality entails conformity: all of which guarantee that in America appearances will coincide with essence" (*Democratic Personality*, 281). Here differences are divested of their potential for conflict and made to produce cultural conformity. In America any difference in belief or blood that would have clashed anywhere else "burns away in the open air, and consumes without effect" (51). Cultural, racial, and ideological differences, according to the narrator, "wear out" in the New World, as "individuals of all nations are melted into a new race of men," while "religious indifference is imperceptibly disseminated from one end of the continent to the other" (44, 48, 50–51). Crèvecoeur illustrates that American national identity is the site of a productive *in-difference* that neutralizes the tension between competing notions of culture, politics, and subjectivity. Differences, in short, are made to make no difference.

2

Historicizing America

Tocqueville and the Ideology of Exceptionalism

"To be able to write about America without quoting Tocqueville," Joseph Epstein observes in his introduction to Tocqueville's *Democracy in America*, "has become no easy task, so de rigueur, so indispensable has his thought become to the consideration of nearly every aspect of American life."[1] I begin my discussion of Tocqueville with this statement to acknowledge that in a book which contends that America has a forgetful relation with its (immigrant) past, it seems imperative to focus attention on a well-trodden text such as *Democracy in America*, since it offers an early and enduring effort to characterize America's democratic self-understanding. Epstein's claim provides a point of departure for my argument here as a *symptomatic* statement of the popularity that Tocqueville's text has historically enjoyed in furnishing the United States with what has been claimed to be *the* theory of its democratic formation. As Dominick Lacapra has pointed out, "In *Democracy in America*, Tocqueville is often understood as providing 'us' in North America with a self-image—a way to read ourselves."[2] Expediently canonized by politicians and political scientists as a thesis of American exceptionalism, *Democracy in America* has stood for generations of Americans as an ur-text through which to understand and interpret their political culture in new ways. At the same time, Tocqueville's text has been instrumental as a discursive vehicle for the nation, driving its rituals of self-renewal. Indeed, as Donald Pease has remarked, "Historians, political scientists, literary theorists, philosophers, and citizens alike have invested Tocqueville's works with a metahistorical knowingness about U.S. democratic culture," allowing it to be deployed as a pedagogical and political tool to reassert, in a celebratory and mythologized fashion, the nation's claim to liberal democracy and the ideology of American exceptionalism.[3] It should come as no surprise that one thing which has remained constant in various readings of Tocqueville's text, and in its reception, has been its privileging of the principle of democracy rather than the specificity of its historical context. *Democracy in America* has always been viewed as a trans-historical treatise on the unique birth and formation of democracy in the United States rather than a historically specific description by a French aristocrat of an early-nineteenth-century civil society and its micro-mechanical principles of governmentality. Interestingly, Tocqueville himself privileged the notion of "democracy" over the "America" that he viewed as the "framework" for his argument. The French title, *De la démocratie en Amerique*, more accurately translated as "Concerning democracy in America," emphasizes that what Tocqueville wished to elaborate was a political theory of democracy, not a description of American democratic exceptionalism. My aim in this chapter is to subject the staple assumptions about the birth of democracy in America to critical analysis in order to expose the ambivalent and forgetful ways in which democratic power and national identity have been historically articulated in the United States.

Recently political theorists and cultural critics have reconsidered the many uncritical and politically expedient interpretations of *Democracy in America*, those which have so often been deployed to refurbish the nation's ideology of exceptionalism. William E. Connolly, for example, has argued that Tocqueville's "democratic ethos of pluralization" entails limits and exclusion, pointing out how the text problematically espouses an "un-Rousseauian" form of diversity in which the extermination of the native population and the colonization of their land are rationalized as necessary to the realization of a "civic-territorial complex."[4] Claude Lefort, in a similar vein, has noted Tocqueville's contradictory representation of American democratic subjectivity, arguing that he inconsistently vacillates between an aristocratic model of civil society "organized in terms of multiple networks of personal dependency" and a liberal bourgeois model that relies on notions of independence and autonomy: this oscillation ultimately prevents him from recognizing that "the experience of political and individual freedom, and the advent of a new idea of power and right, coincide with a new experience of knowledge, with the advent of a new idea of truth."[5]

While Connolly and Lefort elaborate the internal contradictions of *Democracy in America*, Pease draws critical attention to how the scholarly and popular revival of Tocqueville in recent years has enabled the ideology of American exceptionalism, mobilizing once again a differential form of political and civic identification through which U.S. citizens can define their unique national identity. Just as cold war historians such as Louis Hartz and Henry Steele Commager "adapted Tocqueville's description of U.S. exceptionality to construct a mythology of national uniqueness out of whose narrative themes U.S. citizens constructed imaginary relations to the cold war state," the Tocqueville revival today, Pease points out, speaks to a recurrent form of democratic imaginary that is based on "the logic of antagonistic differences," now articulated in relation to Islamic states such as Iran and Iraq ("After the Tocqueville Revival," 95). A return to Tocqueville, he further argues, "might be conceptualized as a symbolic compensation for the absence of an adequate conclusion to the cold war" (99).

In keeping with these insights, in what follows I elaborate two ways in which my own concept of forgetting encourages us to reread *Democracy in America* against both its authorial intentions and the problematic history of its reception in the United States. As a general point, I contend that a critical sensitivity to the notion of historical amnesia guides us to the margins of the text, away from the more familiar themes of democracy, equality, and freedom which have been seized upon by politicians and traditional historians to perpetuate the ideology of American exceptionalism. In the first two sections of this chapter, I argue that Tocqueville produces an archetype of a forgetful historiography which has been appropriated as a reference point in the construction of the myth of immigrant America. In the last part of the chapter, I shift my focus to Tocqueville's discussion of democratic self-governance, arguing that Foucault's concept of governmentality enables us to see how the author of *Democracy in America* lays the ground for forgetting just how pervasive and coercive the American state truly is, a state whose regulatory mechanisms are vital in disciplining immigrant others, as I will show in chapter 5.[6] My reading of Tocqueville aims not merely to question Tocqueville's own political and cultural assumptions about the birth of democracy in the United States. Rather, my goal in subjecting these assumptions to critical analysis is to make a broader argument about the ambivalent ways in which democratic power and national identity have been historically articulated. My discussion of *Democracy in America* therefore involves a contrapuntal analysis, in which I consider the text against its critical margins, reading the general and synthetic theory of democracy against the text's supplements—marginal discussions of slavery, the pushing away of the native population to annihilation, the control of population, and the micro-mechanics of property laws upon which citizenship and cultural identity in the United States rest. Although my contrapuntal approach here precludes reliance on linear argumentation, I hope to demonstrate the dynamic relation among monumentalizing historiography (in the first section), the political economy of race (in the second), and techniques of governmentality (in the last).

Above all, what made Tocqueville a "friend" to Americans, I want to suggest, is not the political theory of democracy that he gave them but a canonized history of how their nation-state was imagined in an "exceptional" way by pilgrims. I say canonized because the archive that Tocqueville used while writing his book in France was one consisting of the dominant discourses of the nation, including official documents such as historical and legislative records of various states as well as such foundational texts as Jefferson's *Notes on Virginia*, Nathaniel Morton's *New England's Memorial*, and *The Federalist*. Ironically, readers of *Democracy in America* have consistently privileged the role of Tocqueville's first-hand observation of America's political and civic institutions in coming up with his theory of democracy. Sheldon Wolin, for instance, has argued that if Tocqueville was able to theorize democracy, bringing it into focus for the first time as the central subject of modern western political thought, it was because he traveled extensively in America.[7] In contrast to this view, I wish to address the role of discursive mediation in Tocqueville's act of theorizing, by showing how much his vision of America was indebted not only to the official archive of the nation that he consulted during his American residency but also to the large body of European travelogues of the New World that he read before and after embarking on his journey. The detour through earlier descriptions of America triangulated the relation between observation and theory. As an enlightened European keen on systematizing what he read and discovered in America, Tocqueville synthesized a plurality of official discourses that he had collected and studied during his nine-month stay in 1831–32, in order to write a monumentalizing history purporting to show how a new political system was founded in the United States on the principle of democracy by European settlers.

Such a history, produced from the official archive of the nation and

European travelogues of North America, I will argue, *forgetfully* recounts the founding of the nation by mythologizing the "accidental and providential" elements that enabled the Anglo-Saxon pilgrims to create a free and democratic nation based on the principle of equality. Tocqueville's text is written from the dominant perspective of Puritan New Englanders as a quest for democracy, pushing the violent facts of the nation's historical beginning—slavery, expansionist wars, and the destruction of the Native population—to the margins of the story. An example of Freudian negation, *Democracy in America* does not entail a complete mnemonic foreclosure but embodies a structure of disavowal that undermines the significance of the nation's originary and constitutive violence through ideological and ideational projection. The nation is therefore mythologized as the realization of a political desire for liberty and equality, and this act of mythologizing obscures how it is also a nation-state born of specific practices of conquest and government. As I will elaborate below, Tocqueville brings in his discussion of slavery and the condition of Native Americans belatedly in the last chapter of the first volume, after he has already summarized his argument and effectively ended his book in the previous chapter. The official history of the nation that he reconstructs is a celebratory and monumentalizing account of national identity in the United States, one that in neglecting the violent beginning of the nation as well as its own discursive contradictions lends itself trans-historically to ideological appropriation as the ur-text of American exceptionalism. But Tocqueville was able to write the thesis of American exceptionalism only by ignoring how the United States was founded on genocide and slavery, annexation and war, conquest and colonialism.

Whereas the official archive of the nation helped Tocqueville to compose his history of nation building in the United States, his studies of the American penal laws, court records, and penitentiary system nonetheless enabled him to provide an interesting account of how the principle of governmentality was developed. The ostensible and official reason for Tocqueville's travel to America was a study of its penitentiary system (like his travel companion Gustave de Beaumont, Tocqueville was a public prosecutor), and his exploration of the micromechanics of state regulations led him to understand how the principle of governmentality was elaborated and exercised in the United States. Beneath the history of nation building that Tocqueville recounts is an important discussion of how a new science of government based on techniques of population control and political economy was founded, a science rooted in micro-mechanical practices of the average citizen instead of general theories of sovereignty. In America the art of government does not concern the sovereign figure of a monarch, but is defined as a multifarious and dispersed form of power that concerns every citizen and every new arrival.[8] Such a description of governmentality in the United States, though marginalized in the text by Tocqueville's general theory of democracy, reveals the mechanisms of governing in America that are vital to manufacturing national consensus through discipline and micro-regulation—mechanisms, I argue, that continue to operate to this day in the United States in defining the boundaries of citizenship and cultural identity. The lack of critical attention to this aspect of *Democracy in America* reflects a forgetful liberal tradition of historiography in the United States which leaves out the micro-mechanics of power that constitute the notion of democracy, a term whose broader historical and political implications are often taken for granted. Like Tocqueville himself, even radical political theorists like Wolin have tended to describe American democracy as a political ideology shaped by culture instead of power, principles instead of techniques. In contrast, my discussion in this chapter looks at the margins of Tocqueville's study of democracy for the historical traces of how the science of governing, concerned with specific issues of population, security, property, and self-regulation, is developed in the United States. The principle of governmentality, I argue, belies the narrative of American exceptionalism and the myth of immigrant America.

The History of Nation Building in America

The key to understanding Tocqueville's forgetful history of nation building in the United States appears toward the end of the first volume, in chapter 17, where he summarizes the argument of his book by listing the major factors that enabled pilgrims to establish a democratic republic in the New World. "All the causes which contribute to the maintenance of the democratic republic in the United States," he writes, "are reducible to three heads: I. The peculiar and accidental situation in which providence has placed the Americans. II. The laws. III. The manners and customs of the people" (332). Split as he is between the accidental and the intentional, nature and culture, Tocqueville above all emphasizes the geographical specificity of the American republic that facilitated the rise and maintenance of democracy, while claiming that the legal and sociocultural particularities of its European inhabitants enabled them to establish a government based on democratic principles. Throughout *Democracy in America*, he attempts to reconcile the accidental factors (geography) and the intentional ones (culture) that made democracy uniquely possible and successful in the United States. Polemically successful though Tocqueville may have been in achieving this goal, I want to suggest that his discursive oscillation between the accidental and religious on the one hand and the intentional and secular on the other indicates more importantly a fundamental paradox in the official discourse of national identity in the United States. In the dominant discourse of the nation, the story of its birth is told in contradictory terms, as both a providential accident and the intentional human construction of a superior race, a "chosen people" *choosing* a new and unique form of democratic government. Before I elaborate upon the implications of such a contradiction in enabling the ideology of American exceptionalism crucial to the fashioning of national identity in the United States, let us consider these two notions of beginning in *Democracy in America* to understand how the story of nation building is recounted in the official discourses of the nation from which Tocqueville draws in his research.

A well-informed traveler, familiar with the large archive of European travelogues of the New World, such as Volney's *Tableau des États-Unis* (from which he often quotes), Crèvecoeur's *Letters*, and Chateaubriand's *Voyage en Amérique*, Tocqueville first discusses the geography of the United States. Like his precursors, he was most struck by the unique landscape of North America. His description of America, like a travelogue, therefore begins with a promontory description of North America's physical features instead of the democratic ideology of its inhabitants:

North America presents in its external form certain general features which it is easy to discriminate at the first glance. A sort of methodological order seems to have regulated the separation of land and water, mountains and valleys. A simple, but grand, arrangement is discoverable amidst its confusion of objects and the prodigious variety of scenes. This continent is divided, almost equally, into two vast regions, one of which is bounded on the north by the Arctic Pole, and by the two great oceans on the east and west. It stretches towards the south, forming a triangle whose irregular sides meet at terminates, and includes all the remainder of the continent. The one slopes gently towards the Pole, the other towards the Equator. (19)

In this panoramic view of North America's geography, Tocqueville observes an orderly landscape, systematically divided and providentially gifted. The first chapter of *Democracy in America* following this passage consists of a general description of North America's geographical situation to familiarize the reader with the particular environmental or "natural" factors that contributed to the birth of a nation. As the text of an enlightened European traveler heavily mediated by the observations of earlier travelers such as Chateaubriand, Darby, Humboldt, Volney, and Warden,[9] it symptomatically represents North America in opposite terms. Like these earlier descriptions of America, *Democracy in America* portrays North America contradictorily as fertile and barren, hospitable and hostile, empty and occupied, contradictions, I suggest, that are discursively necessary because they cater to both the religious idea of America as a providential gift to a chosen people and the secular idea of a superior human race transforming a hostile wilderness into an earthly paradise. In the official archive of North American historiography and European travel literature, from which Tocqueville constructs his description of America, there are no references to the occupation of the New World by Europeans; nor is there an interest in an in-depth study of the prior histories of native Americans, but only sketchy references to "some wandering tribes [who] had been for ages scattered among the forest shades or the green pastures of the prairie" (24). In short, as an instance of discursive negation, the text is a nexus of historical denial and a grudging form of acknowledgment.

Like Crèvecoeur, Tocqueville is in part able to cover over this contradiction by espousing a Lockean notion of property and arguing that land in the New World was unclaimed before the arrival of Europeans whose "labor" gave them the right to claim it. The original inhabitants of North America, according to him, "seem to have been placed by Providence amidst the riches of the New World to enjoy them for a season, and then surrender them," thus never claiming the land as their property (28). Following Locke's discussion of the emergence of private property in the *Second Treatise of Government*, Tocqueville makes a distinction between land and soil to justify the occupation of the New

World as an act of civilization. "It is by agricultural labor," he reasons, "that man appropriates the soil, and the early inhabitants of North America lived by the produce of the chase" (27). The land, in other words, appears as a providential gift given to the chosen and enlightened community of Anglo-Saxon pilgrims to establish an ideal, democratic nation through their hard work and cultivation of the soil. In this manner, Tocqueville is able to simultaneously adopt a religious view of the nation, representing it as a divine gift to the "chosen people," while maintaining a secular view of it as the historical product of human occupation and the cultivation of land.

To underscore the higher status of European emigrants in the Enlightenment narrative of progress, moreover, the providential gift must also be contradictorily portrayed as arid and wild to emphasize their superior civilization: the ability and industry of New England Puritans to cultivate the soil makes them the legitimate owners of North American land. Whereas, for example, in his description of Mississippi prairies Tocqueville observes that "nature displays an inexhaustible fertility," when he describes North America at the time of the pilgrims the landscape is portrayed as utterly wild and inhospitable. The Atlantic shore, "the cradle" of the English colonies, is a chaotic and empty coast where "the fall of a tree overthrown by age, the rushing torrent of a cataract, the lowing of buffalo, and the howling of the wind were the only sounds which broke the silence of nature" (22, 24). Such a "grave, serious, and solemn" space, he suggests, nevertheless "seemed created to be the domain of intelligence" (23). Throughout his discussion of American geography, Tocqueville upholds the Enlightenment idealization of agrarian democracy as the superior social order. "In that land," he maintains, "the great experiment was to be made, by civilized man, of the attempt to construct society upon a new base; and it was there, for the first time, that theories hitherto unknown, or deemed impracticable, were to exhibit a spectacle for which the world had not been prepared by the history of the past" (28). Although the passive structure of the sentence betrays a religious view of American democracy, there is still an emphasis on the work and intelligence of civilized man in cultivating the land with which the democratic nation begins. Here the United States is an experiment by a "superior" race to form a new democratic society in the New World, a society that exhibits the most enlightened aspects of human civilization, such as order, intelligibility, and democratic government.

The contradictory representations of the North American landscape as both fertile and arid in Tocqueville make the birth of the nation at once an inevitable act of Providence and the intentional work of a chosen race. Caught between a religious view of America and a secular view of the United States, Tocqueville's text demonstrates the productive ways in which paradoxical representations of North America facilitate the democratic myth of the nation as a providential *and* human exception: the nation is narrated as both a unique manifestation of divine direction and a great social experiment by an exceptional race. Tocqueville's contradictory representations of America and its geography reflect a broader discursive ambivalence in his text and in the work of its liberal readers between a deterministic view of American society and a constructionist representation of its democratic state. Tocqueville attributes the birth of a democratic nation in North America at once to exceptional geography and material resources and to the unique ideas, manners, and customs of its enlightened citizens.

That Tocqueville begins his text with the physical description of North America suggests how well he understood the importance of geography and the natural resources of North America to the imagining of a democratic nation.[10] The religious notion of land as a divine gift to the chosen people highlights the very importance of geography in the nation's growth and prosperity. Several times in *Democracy in America* Tocqueville returns in passing to the unique physical situation of the nascent republic, underscoring the effects of nature on the culture of democracy:

> The chief circumstance which has favored the establishment and the maintenance of a democratic republic in the United States is the nature of the territory which the Americans inhabit. Their ancestors gave them the love of equality and of freedom, but God himself gave them the means of remaining equal and free, by placing them upon a boundless continent, which is open to their exertions. . . . The physical causes, independent of the laws, which contribute to promote general prosperity, are more numerous in America than they have ever been in any country in the world, at any other period of history. In the United States not only is legislation democratic, but nature herself favors the cause of the people. (225–26)

In this exemplary passage, Tocqueville uses a religious discourse to underscore the great significance of the wealth of the new continent and its unique geographical position in establishing and maintaining a democratic nation. What enables the birth of democracy in America is above all that the "Continent still presents, as it did in the primeval time, rivers which rise from never-failing sources, green and moist solitudes, and fields which the ploughshare of the husband-man has ever turned" (336). Forgetful of his earlier claims about the inhospitable and infertile land upon which pilgrims landed, Tocqueville now acknowledges that the incredible resources of the vast continent helped to create and sustain the democratic nation. Providentially bestowed, the physical prosperity of the United States, he thus suggests, is what influences both the opinions and the physical actions of Americans (343). In this narrative of nation building, culture is determined by nature, and a rich ecology is the precondition of a democratic society. The continent's natural wealth guarantees the nation's economic success, and in doing so makes democracy possible. Several times in his text Tocqueville mentions that the country is strategically protected by vast oceans in the East and the West, and that "Americans have no neighbors, and consequently they have no great wars, or financial crises, or inroads, or conquest to dread" (333). The material conditions of North America, he insistently observes, are fundamental to the growth and prosperity of the nation and to the maintenance of democracy.

And yet, in spite of this deterministic view of a democratic polity, Tocqueville's enlightened account of American democracy advances an ideological theory of nation building in the United States according to which the laws, manners, ideas, and customs of its citizens account for its democratic form of self-definition. In chapter 2 Tocqueville embraces a constructionist view of America, attributing the birth of the democratic nation to the powerful tradition brought to the New World by a culturally superior community of Europeans. On several occasions, he suggests that the growth of the United States bears clear marks of its "enlightened" origin, what he calls its "national character" (30). At the origin of the United States is the particular race of Anglo-Saxon Puritans who shared characteristics of a superior culture:

> At the period when the people of Europe landed in the New World their national characteristics were already completely formed; each of them had a physiognomy of its own; and as they had already attained the stage of civilization at which men are led to study themselves, they have transmitted to us a faithful picture of their opinions, their manners, and their laws. (30)

These men had, however, certain features in common, and they were
all placed in an analogous situation. The tie of language was perhaps
the most durable that can unite mankind. All the emigrants spoke the
same tongue; they were all offsets from the same people. Born in a country which had been agitated for centuries by the struggles of faction,
and in which all parties had been obliged in their turn to place themselves under the protection of the laws, their political education had
been perfected in this rude school, and they were more conversant with
the notions of right and the principles of true freedom than the greater
part of their European contemporaries. At the period of their first emi-
grations the parish system, that fruitful germ of free institutions, was
deeply rooted in the habits of the English; and with it the doctrine of
the sovereignty of the people had been introduced into the bosom of
the monarchy of the House of Tudor. (31)

What is privileged in this narrative of nation building in the United
States is the commonalities of European emigrants and the uniquely
superior culture that constituted the birth and growth of a unique
nation. Tocqueville lists five factors—racial homogeneity, linguistic
uniformity, equal social status, a democratic political ideology, and
a socially organized religion—to distinguish the particular national
character of Americans. As suggested by the reference in the second
passage to European emigrants being "offsets from the same people,"
Tocqueville viewed the homogeneity of race as central to the imagining of the nation, a racialist view, needless to say, that overlooks the
other two major "races" in America as well as the ethnic differences
within the European immigrant community itself—differences which
at that time were perceived as *racial* differences. Such a racially homogeneous body has a common language that unites it into a durable
imagined community, durable because the population can transmit
and communicate its ideas, laws, and cultural manners. Following the
Enlightenment's theory of human progress, Tocqueville represents
these emigrants as having achieved the highest level of civilization because of their turbulent history in Europe, a "rude school" in which
they were politically educated about notions of rights and the principles of liberty and freedom. In addition, the Puritan parish system
of maintaining a self-governing form of moral and religious order was
internalized and shared by these emigrants, providing them with the
very notion of the sovereignty of the people upon which democracy
is founded. The Puritanism of the pilgrims, he points out, was not

merely a "religious doctrine, but it corresponded in many points with the most absolute democratic and republic theories" (35). Thus Puritanism was not a simple religious order but an ideological paradigm, helpful in organizing and maintaining civil society and community. Once the pilgrims were in America, their "analogous situation," a reference to the presumed fact of their equal social status in the New World, further gave them an organic and practical appreciation of the principle of equality upon which their form of government was founded. "The emigrants," he elaborates, "had in general no notion of superiority over one another" (32), and their equal status made them form an equal civil and political society, claims that deny class and economic differences among early settlers.

Constructed from the dominant archive of the nation—works such as Cotton Mather's *Magnalia Christi Americana, or the Ecclesiastical History of New England, 1620–1698* and Nathaniel Morton's *New England Memorial—Democracy in America* tells what became the official story of nation building in the United States, a forgetful history that denies differences as well as the limits and exclusions of the democratic ethos of pluralization, as Connolly insightfully observes. In this story the agency of a superior and homogeneous race of Anglo-Saxon Puritans is what engenders the exceptional birth of democracy in America. Here polity displaces Providence, and politics dislocates geography: what made democracy possible are the sociopolitical intentions of an enlightened community, not the divine accident of America's nature. Early emigrants, Tocqueville recounts, neither were "obliged by necessity to leave their country," "nor did they cross the Atlantic to improve their situation or to increase their wealth" (35). Forgetful of the ambitious desires of early European colonizers and the large mass of immigrants who crossed the Atlantic precisely to improve their situation and increase their wealth, he claims that "the call which summoned them from the comforts of their homes was purely intellectual; and in facing the inevitable sufferings of exile their object was the triumph of an idea," namely the founding of a democratic nation (35). Tocqueville's rhetorical claim about the political intention of the nation's founders belongs to a celebratory and monumentalizing discourse of national identity as exception, which views the United States in purely ideological terms and denies the economic factors that enabled the birth and expansion of the nation. Through discursive negation, the early emigrants' will to colonize and their economic ambition to establish colonies are narrated as a call for democracy and the benevolent desire to establish an equal society. By claiming that the nation was founded on abstract ideas of democracy and liberty, Tocqueville fails to acknowledge early settlers' concrete goals of establishing economically profitable colonies.

The shift from a religious and deterministic to a secular and constructionist view of America thus privileges an ideological notion of American exceptionalism, according to which the colonial conditions and the economic forces that enabled the establishment of a nation are marginalized by general theories of equality and liberty. In Tocqueville's text and in the liberal tradition of its reception, the United States is viewed as an idealist construct, produced by the will of an enlightened community and its lofty "idea" of democracy. Culture, not nature; politics, not geography; and democratic principles, not capitalist ambitions constitute the key words in this liberal tradition of national identity.

The Political Economy of Race in America

Such a forgetful history of nation building in the United States obscures many historical facts about the origins of the nation, among which are the economic factors that contributed to its rise, the issue of slavery, the destruction of the native inhabitants of North America, and the imperialist policies of expansion and annexation. Recent critics of Tocqueville, as I mentioned above, have already pointed out some of these historical lacunae in *Democracy in America*. Lacapra, to cite another example, has mentioned both the deficiency of economic analysis and the cursory treatment of the other two races in the United States, American Indians and blacks. Tocqueville, he argues, did not "elaborate a theoretically informed discussion of industrialization and the relation of capital and labour in a capitalist, industrialized economy," as his contemporary Marx did (111). Moreover, Lacapra contends that the last chapter of *Democracy in America*, in which Tocqueville addresses both "the present and probable future condition of the Indian tribes" and the "situation of the black population in the United States," assumes a racist view of the nation. "A pronounced sense of Western superiority," Lacapra argues, "is blatant in Tocqueville's treatment of both American Indians and African-Americans in

Democracy in America" (95). While Tocqueville was against the bio-logical racism of Gobineau, his rhetoric betrays "a cultural or 'moral' racism closely bound up with a theory of stages of civilization" (94).[11]

Although I agree with Lacapra's critique of Tocqueville, I want to suggest that in spite of its racist assumptions and lack of economic analysis, the margins of *Democracy in America* can actually be studied as an elaboration of America's political economy, addressing such critical factors as the role of population and the importance of land in estab-lishing a democratic republic in the United States. The last chapter of the book, afterthought though it is, reflects not just the moral racism of an enlightened philosopher but also the concerns of a pragmatic, perhaps utilitarian, observer who considers racial dynamics a function of political economy. Here as elsewhere in his text where he speaks of blacks and American Indians, Tocqueville analyzes the predicament of race relations in the contexts of population and land.

Let us consider more closely Tocqueville's supplementary chapter by way of showing how the issue of race is addressed as a pragmatic concern of democratic governing. The last chapter of *Democracy in America* appears on the surface as the statement of a resolute and reli-gious abolitionist who opposes slavery and views American Indians as free, independent "noble savages." Tocqueville speaks of the du-plicitous policies of state and federal governments toward American Indians while renouncing the institution of slavery for degrading the black population and corrupting white people. Beneath this liberal view of America's "other" races, however, we encounter a descrip-tion of America's racial configuration in the context of such utilitar-ian concerns as population, property, and land. The title of the chap-ter, "The Present and Probable Future Condition of the Three Races Which Inhabit the Territory of the United States," underlines that what Tocqueville offers is not a representation of race relations per se but of how different racial populations inhabit as well as populate and cultivate the land. The distinction between unclaimed land and culti-vated soil in Tocqueville points to the political economy of race rela-tions in America that will determine and affect the viability of a suc-cessful nation-state in North America.[12]

As for American Indians, Tocqueville cites an anonymous "official document" to argue that that they, like "the noble of the Middle Ages in his castle," consider only "war and hunting . . . worthy to be the occupations of a man," an observation that allows him to account for the decline in their population since the Europeans brought with them the useful knowledge of agriculture. Native Americans, in his view, could never fashion a civil society, the autonomous and self-regulating polity that enabled modern man to move beyond the state of nature. In Tocqueville's romantic view of the native population of North America, a community of noble savages living in a Rousseauian natural society has unfortunately come into contact with a "superior" race of human beings who have achieved a higher form of civilization by developing agriculture and inventing industry. This violent and destructive encounter is partially blamed on European colonizers, a backhanded acknowledgment that undermines his dismissal of violence in the act of nation founding. For example, Tocqueville mentions that American Indians both received disingenuous promises from Europeans and were subjected to their corrupting influences. He even elaborates on the systematic and "legal" ejection of the indigenous population by "importunate whites," and the tricking of American Indians by "firearms, woolen garments, kegs of brandy, glass necklaces, bracelets of tinsel, earrings, and looking glasses" (394–95).

And yet, in spite of these perceptive observations, Tocqueville ultimately attributes the destruction of the native population to its lack of agricultural knowledge and refusal to cultivate the land, adopting thus an implicatory mode of disavowal—what Steiner calls "a retreat from truth to omnipotence"—that blames it for its own annihilation. Denying them coevalness, Tocqueville claims that Native Americans occupy an earlier stage of human civilization and therefore cannot withstand the compelling forces of European progress. He uses his distinction between land and soil to argue that human progress requires both territorial fixity and the cultivation of soil. Because the American Indians were a nomadic people unaccustomed to agriculture, they could not establish a viable civilization in America. "Men who have once abandoned themselves to the restless and adventurous life of the hunter," he claims, "feel an insurmountable disgust for the constant and regular labor which tillage requires" (397). As "noble savages," they lived harmoniously in nature, while wandering the rich continent. Though Tocqueville critiques Europeans' failure to "civilize" these people by teaching them how "to cultivate the soil," he retreats from truth to omnipotence by blaming the American Indians' own "indolence" and perception of labor as "evil" for the "gradual disappearance of native tribes" (396–97).

Constructed from the romantic travelogues of North America by European travelers of the eighteenth century while also philosophically relying on the Enlightenment narrative of the stages of human development that denies coevalness to Native Americans, Tocqueville's text regards the destruction of the indigenous North Americans as an unfortunate consequence of their inability to assimilate into the political economy of white civilization. What destroyed the native population, according to him, was neither racism nor war but the incommensurable differences between Native Americans' natural society and nomadic economy on the one hand and the civil society and sedentary economy of European settlers on the other. The situation of American Indians could have been utterly different, he speculates, had they known agriculture or had the European introduced them to the cultivation of soil. This perception of the relation between American Indians and European immigrants speaks to the concerns of a utilitarian philosopher, because although it acknowledges in a superficial fashion the unfortunate dislocation of the American Indians, it nonetheless minimizes their genocide at the hands of European colonizers by attributing it to the failure of the indigenous population to cultivate the land. In this narrative, the economic relation of people to land displaces the violent facts of race relations and territorial expansion. While before the "age of discovery" the native population could happily thrive "in the freedom of the woods," with the arrival of white Europeans it began to decline because of the incompatibility of an economy of hunting and gathering with the agricultural economy of the emigrants (401). What Tocqueville forgets about the discussion in Congress of the fate of the American Indians, from which he often cites, is the systematic way in which European emigrants were able to reduce the indigenous population through both territorial expansion and the introduction of an agricultural economy, depriving the native inhabitants of natural resources necessary to their survival. Disavowal therefore makes possible the exceptionalist narrative of America's founding. While as a humanist Tocqueville regretted that "the Indians will perish in the same isolated condition in which they have lived," as a pragmatist he viewed such a catastrophic event as the inevitable consequence of human progress, thus excusing the barbarism that accompanied European civilization in North America and the founding of the nation.

This wavering between the romantic and the rational is also characteristic of how Tocqueville viewed the issue of slavery in America. As with the indigenous population, Tocqueville addressed the situation of the nation's blacks from the perspective of a rationalist while maintaining a critical abolitionist view of how white colonizers reintroduced slavery in the Americas. What concerned Tocqueville the most was not the degraded conditions of blacks in America but the system of slavery, which he considered antithetical to both the nation's liberal ideology and its political economy. "Attacked by Christianity as unjust, and by political economy as prejudicial," slavery was "the most formidable of all the ills which threaten the future existence of the Union" (440, 411). Although Tocqueville "execrates" those Europeans "who, after a thousand years of freedom, brought back slavery into the world once more," his discussion of the topic, as the title of this section of the book indicates, was about "the dangers with which its presence threatens the whites" (440). Tocqueville discussed the predicament of slavery mostly from an economic perspective, by comparing the prosperity of the northern states, where it had been abolished, to the poverty of the southern states, where it remained in existence. Although Tocqueville's economic argument is less prominent, and hence has received less critical attention than his moral case against slavery, I would not be inclined to consider his economic objection mere rhetoric, for it seems expressive of his deeply pragmatic approach to social problems in America. My point in highlighting the importance of Tocqueville's economic objection to slavery is not to suggest that he was insensitive to the profoundly immoral nature of slavery, as some readers have argued, but rather to draw attention to his belief in the congruity between the moral and the economic.

Contrasting the economic conditions in two states, Tocqueville first of all observed striking differences in population: "the population of Ohio exceeds that of Kentucky by two hundred and fifty thousand souls," though Ohio was established twelve years later (418). He explained this discrepancy by positing that slavery discouraged new immigrants from settling in the South, a region they found inhospitable and economically disadvantageous. "European emigration," he pointed out, "is exclusively directed to the free states; for what would be the fate of a poor emigrant who crosses the Atlantic in search of ease and happiness if he were to land in a country where labor is stigmatized as degrading?" (425). Secondly, because slavery degrades labor and makes the worker unmotivated, southern states were less prosperous and more decadent. While in Ohio "the fields are covered with abundant harvest" and "the man appears to be in the enjoyment of that wealth and contentment which is the reward of labor," in Kentucky "the society seems to be asleep, [and] the man to be idle" (418). Thirdly, Ohio was more prosperous because the free workman "does his work quicker than the slave" and because "the expense of a [slave's] maintenance is perpetual" (419). Slavery, in other words, was not simply oppressive toward blacks but, more importantly, economically disadvantageous to the white population. Historically, Tocqueville thus argued, "the colonies in which there were no slaves became more populous and richer than those in which slavery flourished. The more progress was made, the more it was shown that slavery, which is so cruel to the slave, is prejudicial to the master" (417).

Tocqueville, to use his own words, attacked slavery "in the name of the master," an attack in which "interest is reconciled with morality" (421). Whereas Christianity aimed to abolish slavery "by advocating the claims of the slave," in the rational discourse of a utilitarian like him slavery was to be rejected on economic grounds: the interests of the master, not the claims of the slave, were what made slavery unacceptable and inefficient in the democratic nation. In such a discourse, humanism is combined with rationalism, morality with interest, to elaborate the incompatibility of slavery with democracy.

The economic critique of slavery, however, relegates the predicament of race relations and the violence that constitutes it to the margin of democracy, belittling not only the contribution of blacks to the founding of the nation but also the historical conditions that rendered them unequal to whites in the first place. *Democracy in America* blames slavery for the unequal situation of blacks in the United States and the economic ills of the South, but slights the historical and legal reasons that have excluded a whole race from equal citizenship. Tocqueville utterly avoids, for example, the plantation economy upon which southern states were founded and mentions only in passing the condition of emancipated blacks, disregarding the overbearing legal obstacles (such as blacks' inability to own property and their consequent exclusion from political participation), economic policies (for example, an open-door policy of immigration to increase the supply of free, white labor), and the white population's racial prejudices, all of which have led to and perpetuated the black's "wretched and precarious existence" in America (425). In short, the economic view of slavery obscures the complexities of race relations and the racial ideology that accompanies democracy as it tries to account for the unequal conditions of races in the United States.

Everyday Practices of Self-Governing in the United States

While economic rationality provided Tocqueville with a convenient theory with which to push America's racial inequalities to the margins of *Democracy in America*, it also furnished to him a political paradigm with which to study some of the micro-mechanical practices of democratic government—practices that played an important part in defining the boundaries of citizenship and cultural identity in the United States. Earlier I argued that a structure of disavowal informs Tocqueville's treatment of America's racialized others; in the remainder of this chapter I consider the dynamic of forgetting in the context of his study of the practices of democratic self-governance. More specifically, in what follows I consider how Tocqueville analyzed the American legal and legislative system by elaborating the ways in which a new form of government arose out of specific practices of self-regulation—practices which, one may add, exclude the other races on a local level while imposing a normative notion of citizenship on new immigrants. It is these practices that tend to be forgotten in liberal-minded accounts of American democracy as an application of the principles of liberty and equality, and it is this sort of forgetting that facilitates the elevation of *Democracy in America* as the canonical thesis of American exceptionalism.

To account for the novelty of American democracy, Tocqueville begins his discussion of democratic government with the original laws of the British colonies, which he argues were the foundation on which the Union was built. Tocqueville notices legal and legislative links between white emigrants and "the land of their forefathers in England," an observation at odds with his earlier claim that the political ideals of Anglo-Saxon Puritans were the product of their education in the "rude school" of political and religious persecutions which compelled them to emigrate to North America (41). Reading the earliest historical and legislative records of New England, he points out that white emigrants were able to adopt and implement a form of self-governing based on their English legal tradition and institutions. Tocqueville locates two sets of legal and legislative practices in various codes of the New England colonies, practices that he claims were crucial in enabling a democratic form of self-governing in America. First, he observes the importance of Puritan penal laws in the constructions of colonial communities, providing the example of the Code of 1650 in Connecticut. In this document Tocqueville notices an affinity between the penal laws of the state and the biblical tradition on which Puritan juridical laws are based. The laws, which above all punished blasphemy, sorcery, adultery, and rape, were "copied verbatim from the books of Exodus, Leviticus, and Deuteronomy" (42). But the preventive measures that these laws imposed went beyond such religious generalities and touched every aspect of civil society. For example, the code punished "idleness and drunkenness with severity" as well as "intercourse between unmarried persons," and prohibited "the use of tobacco" (43). The aim of such penal laws, Tocqueville observes, "was the maintenance of orderly conduct and good morals in the community" (42). That is, the penal codes, though religious in origin, had the secular aim of maintaining social and civil order. That they were more disciplinary than repressive—in minutely regulating the everyday behavior of the community for the seeming benefit of everyone—meant that they also enabled a normalized notion of civic identity, one useful in regulating the practices of immigrants and racial minorities.

In contrast to the biblical legal tradition, however, these laws were not handed down as if from a higher authority. Rather, "they were freely voted by all the persons interested" (42). The laws were therefore not repressive but constituted instead a form of self-regulation to create an orderly community: their aims were to enable a harmonious civil order, not to prevent individual liberty. The Code of 1650 offers Tocqueville an original example of how penal laws of the United States were established, as well as a primary document for locating the legislative rationality of American democracy. In this document Tocqueville finds an advanced theory of government attentive to the welfare of the community on a micro-mechanical level. As an early example of the legislative foundations on which American civic identity is based, the Code of 1650 shows European emigrants' "remarkable acquaintance with the science of government and the advanced theory of legislation" (45). What makes this theory so advanced is that it maintains a rational approach to how government relates to civil society. Citing the various parts of the code, Tocqueville points out how the multifarious concerns of legislation in the United States cover every aspect of civil society: "In the States of New England, from the first, the condition of the poor was provided for; strict measures were taken for maintenance of roads, and surveyors were appointed to attend to them; registers were established in every parish, in which the results of public deliberations, and the births, deaths, and marriages of citizens were entered; clerks were directed to keep these registers; officers were charged with the administration of vacant inheritances, and with the arbitration of litigated landmarks; and many others were created whose chief functions were the maintenance of public order in the community" (45–46).

Born out of a utilitarian theory of government that sanctions a form of moral rule to produce utility for all people, such laws concern every aspect of civil society as "the law enters into a thousand useful provisions for a number of social wants" (46). Like penal codes, they work on a detailed level and are concerned with pragmatic issues of security and civic order. The aim of legislation in American society is to establish not a sovereign and hierarchical notion of power over the community but a stable social order, by attending to the welfare of society on a micro level. Following the theoretical insights of liberal political economists such as Adam Smith and Jeremy Bentham, Tocqueville saw in America a new form of modern government in which state policies sought to encourage political efficiency and economic prosperity without seeming oppressive or regulatory, at least not toward the white population. Problems of population, public order, arbitration of land are privileged, as government becomes a regime of multiple civil regulations instead of a monolithic structure of power. Although the points of application in American legislation are plural and their functions diverse, their common aim is always to empower white citizens politically and encourage their economic prosperity, not to regulate their lives or take away their liberty. Because the laws are not founded on a principle of sovereignty, they are not repressive but disciplinary and rational, for they aim to maintain social order and security through surveillance of the population and regulation of its everyday activities. The aim of these laws is to enable a productive relation among white citizens while maintaining their political hegemony over others. If the government monitors the rate of population growth, regulates the division of land, or establishes a police force, it does not do so to impose its power over the white population but to generate social order and economic prosperity through the knowledge of its citizens and their ordinary activities. In this manner, the laws posit a normalized sense of civic identity that can be deployed to regulate and control various racialized groups as well as new immigrants.

Such a multiple and detailed regime of civil regulation demands an informed community of citizens who can actively participate in the everyday practices of the government, becoming its agents as much as the points of its application. To function efficiently, democratic power relies on the principle of making everyone interested in willingly performing his or her civic and political duties. It is for this reason that the Code of 1650 pays special attention to public education, a focus which Tocqueville considers the most "original character of American civilization" (46). Claiming that "one chief project of Satan [is] to keep men from the knowledge of the Scripture," the Code introduces "clauses establishing schools in every township and obliging the inhabitants, under pain of heavy fines, to support them" (46). Tocqueville notes that education in America serves a disciplinary aim by providing citizens with the tools to become active participants in self-governing and by achieving "civil freedom" through the observance of divine and human laws. Education makes Americans interested in the "welfare of their country" by making them "partakers in the Government" (280). Pedagogy turns Americans into patriotic citizens who will effectively perform their civic duties. "Everyone," he points out, "takes as zealous an interest in the affairs of his township, his country, and of the whole state, as if they were his own, because everyone, in his sphere, takes an active part in the government of society" (281). Thus pedagogy founds its authority in a tradition of praxis. As such, education helps citizens to internalize rational state policies, effectively and efficiently performing their civil and political duties without feeling the exorbitant power of the state. Because that education is only available to white citizens, it also maintains their cultural and political hegemony.

The micro-mechanical nature of laws in the United States thus introduces a new notion of patriotism or "national pride" that "resorts to a thousand artifices" (281). Sovereignty and patriotism are founded on the ideas of "common good" and common interest: citizens obey the law, perform the tasks expected of them, and respect the established civil order, not out of obligation to a higher power but out of self-interest. Legislative government, in short, to use Foucault's words, "is a question not of imposing law on men, but of disposing things: that is to say, of employing tactics rather than laws, and even of using laws themselves as tactics."[13]

The micro-mechanical nature of penal codes and legislation that "descend to the details of public business" suggests a tactical notion of power that is established from below (313). Tocqueville locates the origin of American democracy in the code's attention to the details of everyday life and its dispersion of authority into minute practices of self-regulation. "In the laws of Connecticut, as well as in all those of New England," he argues, "we find the germ and gradual development of that township independence which is the life and mainspring of American liberty at the present day" (44). Whereas in Europe, political power "commenced in the superior ranks of society, and was gradually and imperfectly communicated to the different members of the social body," in the United States power emanates from below on an ascending order: "In America, on the other hand, it may be said that the township was organized before the country, the country before the State, and the State before the Union" (44–45). In such an ascending structure of power the township becomes "the agent of the Government," because it is able to mobilize the community to participate in the disciplinary practices of political authority on a micro-mechanical level:

> The township serves as a center for the desire of public esteem, the want of exciting interests, and the taste for authority and popularity, in the midst of the ordinary relations of life; and the passions which commonly embroil society change their characters when they find a vent so near the domestic hearth and the family circle.
>
> In the American States power has been disseminated with admirable skill for the purpose of interesting the greatest possible number of persons in the common weal." (74)

In contrast to the tendency to centralize authority in European monarchical systems of government, in America, political power is dispersed and disseminated, allowing the average white citizen to participate in it through the ordinary practices of his or her domestic life. Every citizen, Tocqueville remarks, "practices the art of government in the small sphere within his reach" (76). Power is brought down to the family circle and domestic hearth, implicating everyone by making each citizen at once its agent and its point of application.

In such a system of power relations, authority is strengthened and re-spected because it is viewed as beneficial and advantageous to the inter-est of every white citizen. What secures the average citizen's "affec-tion" toward the government and active participation in its affairs is "the well-being it affords him" (75–76). Unlike the European, the aver-age white American citizen is concerned about "the condition of his village, the police of his street, [and] the repairs of the church or of the parsonage" because he finds these issues connected with himself and affecting his own welfare (103). In the United States citizenship is thus not an abstract construct but a concrete act performed so as to link the citizen to the governing of society, making him or her take "as zealous an interest in the affairs of his township, his country, and of the whole state, as if they were his own" (281). What Tocqueville fails to observe, and what we may add by way of contextualizing his discus-sion of democratic self-governing, is that such a normalized notion of civic identity also maintains white hegemony over racialized and im-migrant communities by establishing structures that encourage and enable what Lipsitz calls "a possessive investment in whiteness."[14]

Such a normalized notion of citizenship also allows governmen-tal power to be exercised tactically and sparingly. Tocqueville points out that although the United States has a much weaker criminal po-lice force than European countries and fewer magistrates and public prosecutors, crime is much more efficiently punished here than any-where else. "The reason [for this anomaly] is, that every one conceives himself to be interested in furnishing evidence of the act committed, and in stopping the delinquent" (106). What makes governmental power economically efficient and politically more effective is the inter-nalization of authority by the average citizen. In America the commu-nity assumes responsibility for the constraints of governmental power on an individual level, as every citizen becomes an agent. The volun-tary inscription of citizens in governmental relations of power reduces the number of people who exercise it, while making the exercise of disciplinary power more efficient by extending its applications on a local level.

This normalization of disciplinary power is most importantly strengthened by the republican principle of trial by jury. Tocqueville devotes a substantial part of his discussion of democracy to this topic because he finds in the jury the ultimate democratic institution. Trial by jury, he points out, "places the real direction of society in the hands of the governed, . . . instead of leaving it under the authority of the Government" (326). Such an institution disperses power and empowers the average, albeit white, citizen within a democratic framework. Tocqueville views the "jury as a political institution" since it inscribes the average citizen in a tactical fashion within relations of power by raising him "to the bench of judicial authority" (325, 327). What makes trial by jury particularly useful to the exercise of power is not only its disciplinary effect on the average citizen, as discussed above, but also its pedagogic function. Because jury trial is not merely reserved for criminal offences but extended to civil causes as well, it becomes a "gratuitous public school" in which every citizen is educated about civic responsibility and public duty (329). The institution introduces the average citizen to the laws of the country because it "communicate[s] the spirit of the judges to the minds of all the citizens," thus preparing them to participate in and contribute to the nation's "free institutions" (329). The aim of such a political education is twofold: self-discipline and vigilantism. On the one hand "the jury teaches every man not to recoil before the responsibility of his own actions," thereby introducing the average citizen to the principle of self-disciplining that is necessary to an economically efficient form of governmental power. If in the United States crime is punished more effectively in spite of a weak police force, it is because the average citizen has already internalized the disciplinary principles that make him or her a responsible and law-abiding subject. Jury duty, Tocqueville states, "makes [citizens] feel the duties which they are bound to discharge towards society, and the part which they take in the Government" (329). In short, it makes the individual a dutiful subject who takes responsibility for his or her own actions. On the other hand, through the experience of trial by jury, "every man learns to judge his neighbor as he would himself be judged" (329). Jury duty furnishes the citizen with the knowledge and "practical intelligence" to judge others, transforming the average citizen into a voluntary agent responsible for others' actions as well.

To sum up, Tocqueville's discussion of the original penal codes and civil legislation of the United States demonstrates that at the origin of the nation are the everyday practices of self-governing, not the general principles of equality and liberty. The foundations of nation building in the United States are therefore not merely ideological or strictly political, as liberal thinkers have suggested, but utilitarian and pragmatic.[15] "The spirit of Americans," Tocqueville argues, "is averse to general ideas; and it does not seek theoretical discoveries" (363). Americans, unlike their European counterparts, "hold practice in more honor than theory" (343). The emphasis on practice instead of theory suggests that the nation is not born out of lofty political ideals, as is commonly claimed by liberal theorists, but imagined from below as a utilitarian construct to attend to and promote the welfare and happiness of its white citizens. The polity is not imposed from above by a centralized federal government but begins with the micro-societies of townships and the everyday practices of ordinary white citizens. Throughout his text, Tocqueville stresses that "the Union is an ideal nation which only exists in the mind," and that the power of the federal government is always limited by the authority of individual states (188). In such a nonsovereign and ambiguous notion of national community, the government appears invisible because it is simultaneously everywhere and nowhere: "Nothing is more striking to an European traveller in the United States than the absence of what we term the Government, or the Administration. Written laws exist in America, and one sees that they are daily executed; but although everything is in motion, the hand which gives the impulse to the social machine can nowhere be discovered" (77).

Because the laws of the United States are tactical and concern minute details of civic society, and because they are applied and practiced by average citizens, the regulatory practices of the government, or administrative bureaucracy, are invisible, though they permeate every aspect of people's daily lives. The influence of a centralized, bureaucratic authority is actually undermined in the United States as the government "distribut[es] the exercise of its privileges in various hands, and in multiplying functionaries, to each of whom the degree of power necessary for him to perform his duty is entrusted" (78). The distribution of governmental power, its dissemination in the details of social fabric, renders it both more effective and less visible—more effective because its application is all-encompassing and plural, less visible because its practice "demands the daily exercise of a considerable share of discretion on the part of those it governs" (188). In the United States legislation penetrates the very core of civil society as the law descends to the minutest details of citizens' lives. What distinguishes the American polity is the web of relatively invisible, micro-mechanical techniques of governing as opposed to the macro-political ideologies of liberty and equality of which everyone is aware. The nation, in sum, is founded on a governmental rationality that designates a dispersed form of authority, invisibly legislating and thus tactically regulating the lives of those it governs by implicating them in relations of power as voluntary agents.

My study of Tocqueville suggests how the invisibility of power can facilitate the broader dynamic of forgetting that is under consideration in this book. The structure of disavowal hinges on micro-mechanics of self-governing which normalize the functioning of disciplinary power and legitimate the exclusionary techniques mobilized against the nation's internal and external others. Entrusting power to individuals, while indispensable in the construction of a democratic imaginary, may render invisible the mechanisms that subjugate individuals, and obscure structures that maintain white hegemony over racialized groups and immigrant communities. More specifically, in the context of my argument, micro-mechanisms of self-governance have been essential in developing disciplinary apparatuses that regulate the everyday practices of aliens as a response to immigration. As I will elaborate in chapter 5, the enactment of a broad array of disciplinary practices that are less visible at the nation's borders in the national imaginary facilitates a normalized articulation of cultural identity. Diffuse and seemingly minor strategies of discipline easily elude critical scrutiny, and in this way become vital in enabling a normalized notion of civic identity and encouraging an exclusionary form of citizenship in the United States.

3

Immigrant America

Liberal Discourse of Immigration and

the Ritual of Self-Renewal

It is striking, if not ironic, that the liberal discourse of immigration, which so celebrates the nation's plural cultural identity,
is often produced during times of xenophobia and national prejudice.
Walt Whitman's *Leaves of Grass*, for example, celebrated the idea of
the United States as "a nation of many nations" during the rise of
the Know-Nothings and the divisive debate over slavery in the mid-
nineteenth century. Similarly, Oscar Handlin's *The Uprooted* and John
F. Kennedy's *A Nation of Immigrants* further claimed the United States
as an immigrant nation precisely at a time when the strict quota laws of
1921 and 1924 had codified the nation's exclusionary attitudes toward
immigrants. And in more recent history, the dominant discourse of
multiculturalism in the American academy and educational system was
produced in an era of new nativism, exemplified during the 1980s by
the passage of Proposition 187 in California and a militarism intended
to exclude migrant workers at the border with Mexico (I will discuss
the significance of the border to national imagining more specifically
in chapter 5). The co-presence of such liberal discourses concerning
immigrants and the nation's exclusionary practices of nativism speaks
to the ambivalent form of national identity in the United States, an
identity that entails a perpetual vacillation between xenophobia and
xenophilia, hospitality and hostility. I will discuss the role of nativism
in fashioning an exclusive form of nationalism in chapter 4, but here
I wish to consider in particular how the nation's liberal discourse of
cultural identity—the myth of asylum, the nation of many nations,
a nation of immigrants—itself proves on examination to be an am-

nesiac form of nationalism, at once neglectful of its own exclusionary tendencies and inattentive to the nativism with which it coexists.
Like every national myth, the myth of immigrant America blots out
the historical conditions of its formation and masks the politics of
exceptionalism that motivate its celebratory discourse. The nation's
humanitarian acceptance of immigrants, I argue, should therefore not
be treated as an oppositional force in the formation of American national consciousness. It too carries the binary logic of "us" and "them"
in a *symbolically* violent discourse that either reproduces the stereotype
of the immigrant as the "wretched refuse" in need of help from benevolent Americans or else tokenizes the "model minority" to bolster
patriotism and national pride. A celebrated example of this patriotic
benevolence is Emma Lazarus's poem written to boost the fundraising
campaign for the Statue of Liberty:

Give me your tired, your poor,
Your Huddled masses yearning to breathe free,
The Wretched refuse of your teeming shores,
Send these, the homeless, tempest-tost to me,
I lift my lamp beside the golden door![1]

Written at a time when the United States systematically subjected new
arrivals to a draconian form of discipline at Ellis Island and other
ports of entry, the poem represents the nation as a fount of benignity
and altruism. In this kind of liberal narrative of national identity—the
idea of America as a benevolent asylum of oppressed humanity—the
stereotype of the immigrant is not so much that of a menace as that
of a poor but motivated figure needing assistance from a benevolent
America to achieve the democratic ideals of liberty and prosperity. But
it is still a stereotype, and stereotyping, as Homi Bhabha has claimed
in another context, is an "ambivalent mode of knowledge," one that
ensures its repetition across historical periods and masks its excess
through a strategy of individuation.[2] The benevolent discourse of immigration in the United States is a stereotypical discourse that reproduces the cliché of newcomers as huddled masses only to shore up
such exclusionary sentiments as national pride and patriotism, while
reaffirming America's exceptionalism. Xenophilia is thus entailed in
xenophobia, just as hospitality toward immigrants involves a certain
degree of hostility toward them.

Reading the mid-nineteenth-century discourse of pluralism in the

United States against the mid-twentieth-century discourse of multicultural America, my aim in this chapter is twofold. I want to discuss the stereotype of immigrants as either victimized huddled masses or model citizens. I will do so by considering the discursive shift that occurs in the nation's liberal narrative about its immigrant roots and its benevolent relation toward newcomers, a shift that enables its repetition and guarantees its durability. But I wish also to provide a genealogy of the contemporary discourse of multiculturalism in the United States by examining its problematic history and ideological ambivalence, with a view to delineating the circular relation between xenophilia and xenophobia. America's love-hate relationship with its immigrants, paradoxical though it may be, is productive of national identity.

The Nation's Bard:
Walt Whitman and the Epic of Multicultural America

In the second volume of *Democracy in America*, Tocqueville addresses the predicament of literary and intellectual culture in the United States. "The inhabitants of the United States," he observes, "at present, properly speaking, have no literature," a fact that he attributes to "their strictly Puritanical origin" and "their exclusively commercial habits," which draw "the native of the United States earthward" (571, 549). In America, he argues, "The spirit of gain is always on the stretch, and the human mind, constantly diverted from the pleasures of imagination and the labors of the intellect, is there swayed by no impulse but the pursuit of wealth" (548). Though Tocqueville may have been right in describing Americans as practical beings in pursuit of wealth, he ultimately proved wrong in claiming the absence of literary and intellectual culture in the United States. Great poets such as Emerson and Whitman and important writers such as Melville and Poe emerged shortly after Tocqueville made the above observations in 1840, producing a rich body of literary works that have been widely read and celebrated to this day as the nation's canonical literature.

Nevertheless, I begin my discussion of Whitman with Tocqueville because his observations about the practical or earthward aspect of the democratic nation provide interesting insights into how a new literary tradition emerged in the United States in the mid-nineteenth century as a way of articulating the nation's distinctly American cultural identity. Focusing on the preface to the 1855 edition of Whitman's *Leaves of Grass*, I want to discuss how the emergent liberal tradition of multiculturalism in the mid-nineteenth century borrowed from Tocqueville's discussion of democracy, equality, and individual liberty in the United States to produce a uniquely American expression of its cultural identity, one marked by pluralism and exceptionalism. Such an aesthetic expression, I demonstrate, resolves the Tocquevillian contradiction of the practical and the imaginative in a democratic society, as it renders poetic and patriotic the ordinary practices of Americans' everyday lives. Poetry becomes praxis and the practices of everyday life become patriotic poetry.

Fifteen years after the appearance of the second volume of Tocqueville's *Democracy in America*, Whitman published the first edition of his *Leaves of Grass*, inventing a distinctly "American" poetic style that artistically fashioned a unique form of cultural identity at a time when the nation was divided over the issues of slavery, territorial expansion, and immigration. The book, rewritten and expanded six times throughout Whitman's life, offered to America an epic expression of its multicultural identity by celebrating its plurality and its democratic acceptance of cultural differences. Roland Takaki's claim that in *Leaves of Grass* "the poet sings of an America where people of all colors come together, mixing indiscriminately in a great democracy yet respecting each other's rich cultural heritage and diversity" reflects how this "epic project" has remained a powerful ur-text for the discourse of multiculturalism in the United States.[3] As the Whitman scholar and biographer David Reynolds points out, *Leaves of Grass* gave America "a profoundly democratic vision in which all barriers —sectional, racial, religious, spatial, and sexual—were challenged in unprecedented ways."[4] The appearance of over twenty books about Whitman and his poetry just around the centennial year of his death (1992)—a year that interestingly coincided with the nation's celebration of the quincentennial of the "discovery" of America by Christopher Columbus—offers further historical proof of the cultural influence that his text has enjoyed throughout 150 years of American history, shaping the perception of multicultural America as it has been read and interpreted by different generations of Americans.[5]

Some recent critics have questioned the liberal tradition's assumptions that Whitman's "racial politics" were an exemplary and seminal form of multiculturalism. Dana Phillips, for example, has argued that

"Whitman's racial politics are more complicated, more conflicted, and considerably less admirable than his reputation for a broad and easy tolerance of others suggests."[6] "Whitman's belief in the idea of America as a redeemer nation," another reader has more pointedly suggested, "can be made out to be consonant with American imperialism, with its implicit dependence on ideas of American expansionism and exceptionalism."[7] To cite an example, a few years before the publication of *Leaves of Grass*, Whitman published several editorial pieces in the *Brooklyn Daily Eagle* in which he urged the federal government, in an imperialist and jingoistic discourse, to annex Texas and California, arguing that the nation must continue to pursue its "great mission of peopling the New World with a noble race."[8]

In spite of such critical moves to question the "idolatry" of Whitman by contemporary scholars, *Leaves of Grass* has continued to be treated as a "manifesto" for multicultural America, "a case study in multiculturalism at its best."[9] What interests me, therefore, is not the debate over Whitman's own racial politics—whether he was a "true" multiculturalist—as much as the politics of his representation of America as a democratic nation of many nations—what made him and his text representatives of multicultural America. What exactly, we may ask, has enabled this text, like Tocqueville's *Democracy in America*, to enjoy the status of an "epic" work about multicultural America? What are the particularities of its discursive practice that give it currency to this day? And finally, what are the aesthetic and cultural contexts that gave rise to the dominant discourse of multicultural America in the mid-nineteenth century?

Whitman's preface to the 1855 edition offers important clues in answering these questions.[10] Whitman begins his manifesto with what amounts to an acknowledgment (through denial) of the nation's anamnestic attitude toward its history: "America does not repel the past or what it has produced under its forms or amid other politics or the idea of castes or the old religions . . . accepts the lesson with calmness . . . is not so impatient as has been supposed that the slough still sticks to opinions and manners and literature while the life which served its requirements has passed into the new life of the new forms."[11] The preface thus begins with a typical Whitmanesque contradiction, or what I will describe as discursive ambivalence or equivocation: claiming continuity between past and present history while remaining forgetful of the past and maintaining a pseudo-historical consciousness toward the

present. What is striking in this beginning is how the poet problematically represents America's relation to its past as ideologically settled
and self-consciously informed, asserting, ironically, that the nation has
accepted what it has historically done and produced at a time when
the country was politically fractured over the issues of slavery, annexation, and immigration. Whitman recapitulates the nation's ritual of
self-renewal by arguing that the past propels the nation forward, constantly producing new forms and new life. Writing at a time of political uncertainty caused by the nation's conflictual views toward slavery,
its geographic expansion, the Mexican War, and the "open-door" immigration policy, Whitman reconciles the nation's contradictory perceptions of its history by positing, in patriotic fashion, a harmonious
relation between past and present that enables renewal and regeneration. The past is invoked only to be stripped of its relevance to current political events. "The 1855 preface," as Jerome Loving remarks,
"signals Whitman's intention to celebrate America poetically rather
than criticize it politically." [12] The nation accepts the lessons of its past
with calm, which is possible only by forgetting the trauma that constituted the violent beginning of the nation. Like Tocqueville, Whitman pushes the genocide of the native population and the horrors of
slavery to the margins of his text, for he too wants to put the nation's
historical traumas to rest in order to be able to sing a patriotic song
that celebrates the nation's ability to reinvent itself as a plural society.[13]
Though such radical imaginings as Whitman's can be great rejoinders
to a flawed history, they risk monumentalizing the past through denial and disavowal, instead of seriously and critically engaging it. In
Whitman's case, the nation's violent history and its current political
breakdown and imperialistic policies are overlooked instead of being
thoroughly worked through, in order to fictitiously claim a harmonious multicultural community.

The issue of the nation's self-conscious awareness of its history appears throughout the preface, as Whitman tries to delineate the task
of the democratic poet: "Past and present and future are not disjoined
but joined. The greatest poet forms the consistence of what is to be
from what has been and is. He drags the dead out of their coffins and
stands them again on their feet . . . he says to the past, Rise and walk
before me that I may realize you. He learns the lesson . . . he places
himself where the future becomes present" (13). As in the first passage,
Whitman's view of history is marked here by an uncritical move that

is linear and pointed toward the future. In spite of the poet's emphasis on the need for historical consciousness, his vision is anything but historical, as he constantly looks into a future that is the culmination of a forgotten past and a neglected present.

Before I pursue further my discussion of Whitman, a theoretical caveat is in order. To claim that his text is forgetful—"ahistorical"—is not to deny that it is historical in the sense of addressing events such as the siege at the Alamo and issues such as slavery. Indeed, Whitman criticizes the nation for its enslavement of Africans in his anti-slavery poems such as "Black Lucifer" and "I Sing the Body Electric," and in other political poems such as "The Eighteenth Presidency!" Nonetheless, I suggest that Whitman's representation of the United States in the preface conforms to what Nietzsche deemed monumental historiography, an approach in which "much of the past [has] to be overlooked if it [is] to produce that mighty effect" to which such ambitious works aspire.[14] Unlike a more finely grained and critically engaged historiography, Whitman's portrait of the United States and its history mythologizes the past not only through patriotic cant but also by diminishing the cultural and political differences that divide the nation. I describe Whitman's preface as historically amnesiac because it does not engage with historical and current events to bring about a more emancipatory politics of memory.[15] As a result, the preface can continuously perform the ritual of self-renewal by neutralizing historical tensions and political conflicts. "The past," as Whitman states pointedly earlier, "is the past," a tautological statement that undermines his own comments about America's anamnesis while also overlooking the political implications of the historical tensions and conflicts that would soon culminate in the Civil War (10). The task of the national bard is to find consistencies and links between past, present, and future, perpetuating, like the myth of "manifest destiny," the nation's ritual of self-renewal that enables its forward move toward the future, a future that yields only new life and new forms to an ever-expanding nation. The past, like the symbolic dead in their coffins, only comes to life to be learned from, but the lesson that it offers is an idealist and monumentalizing vision that involves historical blindness, if not erasure. It is striking that immediately after the poet "learns the lesson," he is able to place "himself where the future becomes present." History, in other words, is significant only to the extent that it enables self-renewal and patriotism. In such a monumentalizing mode of historiography, the violence of the past is to be forgotten through the nonviolent act of forgiveness: "The power to destroy or re-mould is freely used by him but never the power of attack" (10).

Conjuring an ideal society as Whitman does is not inherently problematic, but it becomes so when it encourages mythologizing the present through disavowal. Whitman's attitude speaks on the one hand to an Emersonian form of transcendentalism that mystifies the present, and on the other to a monumental mode of historiography that mythologizes the past. The messianic task of the nation's bard, Whitman points out, is to be "the equalizer of his age and land," "the arbiter of the diverse," a task that entails squaring historical inconsistencies and contradictions while looking for continuities and similarities: "and if to him is not opened the eternity which gives similitude to all periods and locations and processes and animate and inanimate forms, and which is the bond of time, and rises up from its inconceivable vagueness and infiniteness in the swimming shape of today, and is held by the ductile anchors of life, and makes the present spot the passage from what was and what shall be, and commits itself to the representation of this wave of an hour and this one of the sixty beautiful children of the wave—let him merge in the general run and wait his development" (24). The transcendental notion of an eternity in which all historical periods, geographical locations, and social processes are bonded together into a massive unity through similitude is fundamental to understanding Whitman's notion of historiography. The poet, according to him, must look for similarities in differences, and thus find commonalities in disparities. Consequently, the celebration of difference in Whitman is constantly undermined by his valorization of similarity. Cultural and racial difference here does not imply indeterminacy or undecidability but is rather always subject to the neutralization of disrupting divisions and the flattening of productive tensions. For Whitman, the ideal poem that captures the essence of the nation must therefore transcend its time, become monumental by being timeless, or trans-historical: "A great poem is for ages and ages in common and for all degrees and complexions and all departments and sects and for a woman as much as a man and a man as much as a woman" (24). What is emphasized in this homogenizing formulation is a denial of difference and a valorization of commonality. The timelessness of the nation betrays a profound sense of idealism, typical of the liberal discourse that underwrites much of Whitman's discussion of individual liberty and democratic equality, both of which give the nation its poetic harmony. In the nation's trans-historical poem, contemporary predicaments of democracy are brushed aside, with the present represented as a transitional point between a providential past and a utopian future. The political divisions, imperial pursuits, and economic disparities of the nation during the 1850s, for example, are never contextualized in relation to its previous history, which begins with the divided discourse of the founding fathers about the issues of slavery and immigration. What is at stake is a manifest destiny that compels the nation to move forward, forgiving the violent acts that mark its past and forgetting the divisions that mark its present.

The forgetful, monumentalizing attitude of Whitman toward history provides an important point of departure from which to consider the ambivalences of his representation of the United States, ambivalences that constitute an important beginning for the solidification of the nation's liberal discourse in the 1850s. The monumental and nondifferential articulation of national identity in Whitman, I argue, enables both a virulently populist mode of liberalism and a violently expansionist form of patriotism. Whitman's representation of the United States as "a teeming nation of nations" acknowledges America's plurality in a neutralizing way, thus pushing aside the historical conditions that enabled its production and smoothing out the divisions and inequalities that mark the nation's racial landscape. At the same time, the forgetful forgiving of the past reflects and allows an expansionist view of the nation, "moving in vast masses," that has no limit to its power of future inclusions, not to say invasions, perpetuating in this way what will become the myth of the frontier (5). Let us consider the preface more closely to evaluate the implications of these claims.

Above all, Whitman privileges the diversity of the American population by way of positing a specifically American identity as "the race of races" (7):

> To him the hereditary countenance descends from both mother's and father's. To him enter the essences of the real things and past and present events—of the enormous diversity of temperature and agriculture and mines—the tribes of red aborigines—the weatherbeaten vessels entering new ports or making landings on rocky coasts—the first settlements north or south—the rapid stature and muscle—the haughty defiance of '76, and the war and peace and formation of the constitution . . .

the union always surrounded by blatherers and always calm and im-
pregnable—the perpetual coming of immigrants . . . the noble character of the young mechanics and for all free American workmen and
workwomen . . . the general ardor and friendliness and enterprise—the
perfect equality of female with the male . . . the large amativeness—
the fluid movement of the population—the factories and mercantile life
and laborsaving machinery—the Yankee swap—the New-York firemen
and the target excursion—the southern plantation life—the character
of the northeast and of the northwest and southwest—slavery and the
tremulous spreading of hands to protect it, and the stern opposition to
it which shall never cease till it ceases or the speaking of tongues and
the moving of lips cease. (8)

On the surface, this passage is a typical Whitmanesque catalogue,
offering a long list of historical events, people, and their occupations,
defining in this way the nation as a plural and populist community.
No hierarchies are posited here, and no single race occupies a privileged social position in the list. But read more closely, and there also
emerges a mythological—amnesiac—story of how the nation was born
and populated. As in Tocqueville, the nation begins with "the weather-
beaten vessels entering new ports or making landings on rocky coasts"
where white European pilgrims founded "the first settlements north
or south." Symbolically, the use of "or" instead of "and" smooths the
differences between the northern colonies of white Puritans and the
plantation colonies in the South, thus making the initial white European settlements appear as a homogeneous community. The reference
to the "rapid stature and muscle" of European settlers, followed by
"the haughty defiance of '76, and the war and peace and formation of
the constitution" represents the building of the nation as the work of a
superior race realizing the fundamental human ideals of equality and
liberty. The "perpetual coming of immigrants" has further expanded
the nation by moving to its "unsurveyed interior." In *this* (hi)story,
white European pilgrims constitute the core of the nation's population and its life, even though neither the issue of whiteness nor race is
mentioned. As monumental historiography, Whitman's account thus
"deal[s] in approximations and generalities, in making what is dissimilar look similar" and "diminish[es] the differences of motives and instigations so as to exhibit the *effectus* monumentally, that is as something
exemplary and worthy of imitation, at the expense of the *causae*," to
use Nietzsche's words (70).

But such a monumental historiography does not simply "write off" the other two major races in the United States out of existence, as some critical readers of Whitman have suggested.[16] Indeed Whitman's poetry, especially in the 1855 edition, portrays slave characters, such as a black man at a slave auction and a fugitive slave hounded by white people. Rather, I want to argue, the tale is spun from a form of populist acknowledgment that nonetheless remains historically amnesiac. As an example of discursive negation, the above passage embodies a strange nexus of acknowledgment and denial. In Whitman's populist (hi)story of America the other two races are acknowledged, but in a historically forgetful way that both neutralizes racial difference and rewrites the history that has rendered them so unequal ever since the nation was founded. The reference in the beginning of the passage to "the tribes of aborigines" and the final acknowledgment of slavery and how it has divided the nation—"slavery and the tremulous spreading of hands to protect it, and the stern opposition to it which shall never cease till it ceases"—point to a desire in liberal discourse such as Whitman's to acknowledge the presence of other major races in the polity without mentioning either their cultural and economic contributions or the inhumane conditions under which they have been forced to live. The first reference uses an ethnological vocabulary to acknowledge the indigenous population of North America in a "politically correct" way as *aboriginal* (instead of *Indian*). This short passing reference does not forget the native population, but it overlooks the political, historical, and economic implications of its gradual disappearance through genocide, annexation, and war. The ethnographic term "tribes of red aborigines" is an empty signifier, since it is used without any reference to the history that has divested the indigenous people of the Americas of their land and the rights of citizenship. The notion of "aborigine," contrary to its acknowledgment of an "original" people, is a timeless term, one that like Tocqueville's representation of "Indian tribes" accepts the historical fact of their disappearance by denying the genocidal acts of territorial expansion that still continued throughout Whitman's life in the mid-nineteenth century. The violent encounter between the races perpetuated by the nation's westward expansion is thus left out of the national song, now a harmonious narrative that invokes the indigenous population of the Americas only to forget their history in the land, not to mention ignoring their contemporary situation. What replaces this history is a more detailed and monumentalizing account of the pilgrims and their "haughty" act of defiant nation building.

As in Tocqueville, the nation's black population is also represented in a way that disavows the politics of race in the United States. Blacks appear in the nation's song only in relation to the political debate over slavery that threatened to divide the nation during the time Whitman wrote *Leaves of Grass*. The representation of blacks as slaves betrays the ideological ambivalences of a mid-nineteenth-century liberal discourse that condemned the horrors of slavery but failed to acknowledge, and even often opposed, equal rights for blacks. Such a history disregards the racial politics that underwrite the institution of slavery, as well as the economic factors that introduced and enabled the slave trade in southern plantation societies in the first place. Here the black person does not appear as a full citizen, or even as a racialized human category, but as a subject of political debate. In her illuminating reading of the third (1860) edition of *Leaves of Grass*, Rosemary Graham uses the theoretical insights of Louis Marin about utopian literature to argue that the aim of Whitman's poetics is "to dissimulate contradiction and conflict to project 'onto a screen,' as Marin says, a 'structure of harmonious and immobile equilibrium.' "[17] *Leaves of Grass* obscures the volatile issue of slavery that was being fiercely debated, especially after the nation's acquisition of California and Texas, so as to fashion a utopian vision of America defined by racial harmony and social equality.

My point about the representation of blacks as slaves is in keeping with Marin's and Graham's observation, but my aim is to historicize the discursive production through negation of an ideological equilibrium in the mid-nineteenth century. Whitman's representation of racial politics, I suggest, is able to dissimulate conflicts and create a utopian vision of America through negation, or an amnesiac mode of historiography keen on monumentalizing the past instead of critically working through it. The word "slavery" in the above passage is followed by a long reference to the debate over slavery in antebellum America, a move that erases both the role of the southern plantation economy in introducing slavery in North America and the predicament of the free black population in the abolitionist North, where blacks were second-class citizens with no territorial point of origin that divested them of citizenship rights. To focus on the sociopolitical issue of slavery is a historically amnesiac way of reflecting on the position of the black population in America, for it obscures both the role of slavery in national founding and racial politics that have perpetuated the inequality between blacks and whites. Whitman can thus declare, "I am the poet of slaves and of the masters of slaves," because he omits the economic and historical roots of a racial politics in America that had dichotomized the nation's people into masters and slaves since its inception. Salutary though Whitman's condemnation of slavery was at a time when the nation debated its legality as an institution, it nonetheless fell short of addressing the incommensurable cultural differences and wide economic inequalities between whites and blacks in America. It also failed to engage with the issue of race in a critical fashion and thus to enable an emancipatory politics that would ultimately grant equal rights to African Americans.

For a poet who himself admitted his contradictions in the much quoted lines of "Song of Myself"—"Do I contradict myself? / Very well then . . . I contradict myself; / I am large . . . I contain multitudes"—it should come as no surprise that Whitman's readers would view his representations of race in diametrically opposed ways, as both inclusive and exclusive. While his liberal readers have championed him as the bard of multiculturalism, others have read him more critically as a poet who espoused the racist views of his time. The historical point I am making about his problematic representation of the nation's two "other" major races is not to engage in this debate about Whitman's own racial views but to contextualize the absence of the historical implications of race from the liberal discourse of the mid-nineteenth century, an absence that enabled that discourse to "balance" its own ideological contradictions—the contradictions that have divided modern readers. Whitman's representation of the nation's racial landscape is situated in the interstices of a nondifferential and populist form of pluralism—America as the nation of many nations—and the conformist rhetoric of "out of many one," or what one reader calls his "curious national arithmetic of *e pluribus unum*."[18] Whitman's *Leaves of Grass* is at once a poetic attempt to make the nation whole again through a discourse of plurality and an intensely individualist poem celebrating the assimilationist tendency that eclipses cultural differences and economic inequalities.

The forgetting of history, above all, enables Whitman to tell a mythological narrative of American people who transcend their differences and sing in one voice in spite of their differences. Whitman's representation of the "common people" who constitute "the genius of the United States" provides an example of the will to homogenize the people into a unique mass, or a "race of races": "Their manners speech dress friendships—the freshness and candor of their physiognomy—the picturesque looseness of their carriage . . . their deathless attachments to freedom—their aversion to anything indecorous or soft or mean—the practical fierceness of their roused resentment—their curiosity and welcome of novelty—their self-esteem and wonderful sympathy" (6). Ethnic and economic differences, even within the white community, are flattened in this romanticized representation of Americans. The common people share a similar physiognomy and picturesque life-style, and thus constitute an imagined community of equals whose inherent love of freedom makes them sympathetically acknowledge each other as equal citizens. What is emphasized here is a conformist concept of community that makes one out of many, ignoring the historical fact that the "common people" were quite divided about what constituted the Union even during the time Whitman wrote these very lines, and ignoring as well the class divisions that disunited them as a community. The notion of citizenship suggests a civic sense of duty to the nation and its masses, a notion symbolized in the act of "the President's taking off his hat to them, not they to him" (6). Like the president, the symbol of national authority, the poet "sees health for himself in being one of the mass"; he too is "commensurate with a people" (7). From the prostitute to the president, every individual is blended into one people, one race, and one nation. Difference, in short, is made to make no difference, as plurality is displaced by conformity. Moreover, as Reynolds points out, such a "deep faith in common people and in the power of populist poetry" ironically corresponds to the political vision of "anarchism, Know-Nothingism, and the emergent Republican Party," which advocated an exclusive form of national identity, and also to the populist claims of working-class reformers such as George Lippard and George Thompson (86) (in the following chapter, I will discuss more specifically the significance of the xenophobic politics of Know-Nothings to national imagining). Like these political movements, the homogenizing narrative of Whitman constructs an ideologically monolithic notion of the American people that forgets its historical divisions and cultural differences. Like the Know-Nothings, Whitman advocates a patriotic notion of cultural identity marked by ribald pride and coarse intolerance.

Whitman's seemingly inclusive form of national identity thus re-
sembles less a radical form of egalitarianism than a populist mode of
utopian individualism. Throughout the preface to the 1855 edition,
Whitman returns to the general theme of individual liberty and the
sovereign autonomy of the citizen. Behind the communal spirit of
Americans is the individual quest by the poet and the reader for individuation, for a defiant "soul" to "re-examine all you have been told at
school or church or in any book" (11). As for the nation's bard, Whitman emphasizes his uniqueness: "He [i.e., the poet] is a seer . . . he is
individual . . . he is complete in himself . . . the others are as good as he,
only he sees it and they do not. He is not one of the chorus . . . he does
not stop for any regulations . . . he is the president of regulation" (10).
This valorization of the poet as a unique, self-contained visionary, in
contrast to Whitman's view of the poet as a figure commensurable with
the people, suggests an individualist notion of national identity that is
both populist and élitist. Whitman espouses a populist discourse by
claiming, "There will soon be no more priests," because "every man
shall be his own priest" (25). But he also speaks of a "superior breed,"
"the gangs of kosmos and prophets"—the national poets—who will
take the place of priests. Such an élitist notion of artistic praxis assumes an unequal relation of power between the masses, who cannot
see and speak for themselves, and the nation's bard, who must represent and guide them.

In a prescriptive moment in the preface, Whitman even directly
guides the reader about how to become an exemplary citizen. Let
us consider this passage as an example of how the mid-nineteenth-
century liberal discourse is split between élitism and populism, and
between secularism and religion:

> This is what you shall do: Love the earth and the sun and the animals,
> despise riches, give alms to every one that asks, stand up for the stupid
> and crazy, devote your income and labor to others, hate tyrants, argue
> not concerning God, have patience and indulgence toward the people,
> take off your hat to nothing known or unknown or to any man or num-
> ber of men, go freely with powerful uneducated persons and with the
> young and with the mothers of families, read these leaves in the open
> air every season of every year of your life, re-examine all you have been
> told at school or church or in any book. (11)

Believing, as Emerson did, that the nation's progress toward the future
had to start with the individual, Whitman offers to the reader a code of

behavior for becoming an ideal citizen. In the first part of the passage, citizenship is represented in populist and religious terms as a loving relation between the individual and nature and a benevolent attitude toward the needy. The responsible citizen is altruistic and unmaterialistic, despises wealth, and is unequivocally committed to philanthropy. In the last part of the passage, however, a more secular and individualist notion of citizenship is advocated, in which the individual is an autonomous and free subject who questions the norm and defies any authority. As the defiant tone of this passage indicates, the common spirit of Americans can only be performed as an individual quest, a quest that pedagogically and prescriptively conduces to the nation's imagined community. Here the nation's bard does not "absorb" the diversity and plurality of the national community but instead prescribes an individual code of populist behavior for imagining an ideal society. Whitman's command to "read these leaves in the open air every season of every year of your life" self-reflexively acknowledges that national identity is something to learn and perform: the reader must perform the national song, reading it defiantly against what he or she has been told in school or church. In contrast to the first part of the passage, in which Whitman posits a religious notion of the national self as benevolent and dutiful, here he advocates a secular and modern notion of citizenship as autonomous, consensual, and free. Here the doctrine of individual sovereignty characterizes both the pedagogic role of the poet and the performative act of the reader, displacing the notion of "the people" as the originary principle of national culture. Both the poet who composes the national song and the reader who performs it act as autonomous subjects, voluntarily participating in the project of nation building as unique and free individuals.

The productive tension that characterizes Whitman's ambivalent articulation of national identity—between a populist notion of community and an individualist quest for an autonomous self—provides the ideological underpinnings that inform his description of the country's geographic boundaries. Like its individual citizens, the nation's states are represented both as a united nation and as autonomous units, a contradictory representation, I argue, that enables an expansionist, if not imperialist, ideology in the name of "largeness" and "hospitality" (5). The question of geography and territorial boundaries is a central theme in Whitman's poetry, as he idealizes the American landscape and romanticizes its natural beauty. It is not fortuitous that he begins his preface with the remark that "the United States themselves are essentially the greatest poem," a patriotic statement that celebrates the unique geography of the vast nation as the ultimate poetic expression (5). Indeed, the notion of the United States as a "teeming nation of nations" can be understood as a reference not to the ethnic plurality of the country but to the diversity of America's landscape. Disregarding the territorial divisions that marked the nation during the 1850s and the violent wars that enabled its expansion, Whitman transforms the divided states into a single poem, "the United States."

That *Leaves of Grass* is a populist quest intended to unite the states into a singular imagined community has been widely acknowledged by Whitman scholars. But what have been rarely broached are the discursive and ideological ambivalences of such a poetic representation; these ambivalences bring into focus Whitman's disavowing attitude toward the multiple histories of conquest and expansion, conflict and resistance that foreground that unified nation. Whitman's inclusive representation of America's natural landscape provides an exemplary context in which to further elaborate these issues:

[The poet's] spirit responds to his country's spirit . . . he incarnates its geography and natural life and rivers and lakes. Mississippi with annual freshets and changing chutes, Missouri and Columbia and Ohio and Saint Lawrence with falls and beautiful masculine Hudson, do not embouchure where they spend themselves more than they embouchure into him. The blue breadth over the island sea of Virginia and Maryland and the sea off Massachusetts and Maine and over Manhattan Bay and over Champlain and Erie and over Ontario and Huron and Michigan and Superior, and over the Texan and Mexican and Floridian and Cuban seas and over the seas off California and Oregon, is not tallied by the blue breadth of the waters below more than the breadth of above and below is tallied by him. When the long Atlantic coast stretches longer and the Pacific coast stretches longer he easily stretches with them north and south. He spans between them also from east to west and reflects what is between them. (7)

In the above Whitmanesque catalogue, aesthetics and geography displace politics and history. Whitman's aestheticized representation of the nation's diverse geography, like that of its people, is marked by inclusion and homogenization. Not only is the poet commensurable with the people of the nation, but he also embodies its diverse landscape. Undifferentiated and egalitarian, the passage above posits a nonrational and apolitical relationship between the individual and the natural world. The inclusive poet embodies the nation's geography, natural life, rivers, and lakes, just as he incarnates its heterogeneous inhabitants. Whitman's obsessively inclusive representation of America's landscape connects the nation's cultural identity to geography, and the boundaries between culture and nature are dissolved: the country's rivers open into the poet, as the national self becomes at once an extension and the embodiment of the nation's geography.

Benevolent though such a representation of America's diverse landscape may appear on the surface, upon closer examination it reveals an expansionist ideology that depoliticizes, and therefore obscures, the violent history underlying the nation's movement westward, along with its very recent annexation of California and Texas. The romantic celebration of the nation's geography, coupled with the poet's liberal individualism, constitutes a form of historical disavowal, for it enables the poet and the democratic citizen to evade the economic and political implications of territorial expansionism, as well as the complicated histories of conquest and resistance that characterize it. The reference to the newly acquired territories of Texas, California, and Oregon, for example, forgetfully validates the idea of American settlement by connecting them with the original colonies of Massachusetts, Maine, and New York. Flattening out the regional and cultural differences between the Atlantic and Pacific coasts, the North and the South, the individual poet "spans" between them and stretches with the nation's expansion. In such an aestheticized representation of new territories, expansion, imperialism, and settlement are viewed as "the poetic outcomes both of natural processes and the progressive consequences of willful human activity," as Robert Olsen points out.[19] The poetic language that connects new and old territories of the nation obscures both the historical violence that enabled the nation's expansion and the social forces that facilitated the European settlement of new states. There is no critical reference to the recent Mexican War through which the nation acquired its southwestern states, nor any mention of how the "tribes of red aborigines" were divested of their lands in northwestern states to create space for new white immigrants. Instead the poet sings about "the spirit of peace, large, rich, [and] thrifty" of American geography that makes way for "building vast and populous cities, [while] encouraging agriculture and the arts and commerce" (9). The undifferentiated and homogenizing representation of territories, like his vision of the American people, thus reaffirms the nation's myth of manifest destiny, with expansionism transformed into the liberal notion of progress through poetic fiat.

In a curiously self-reflexive moment in the preface, Whitman insightfully remarks, "As soon as histories are properly told there is no more need of romances" (20). And yet what he poetically represents throughout the preface is precisely a national romance that forgetfully tells the story of nation building in America. Whitman's aestheticization of national ideologies of expansion and commercialism, and his disavowal of racial and geographical divisions, unveil how mid-nineteenth-century liberal discourse re-presented the (hi)story of the nation in monumentalizing terms, in such a way as to posit a unified and inclusive imagined community. In its romantically utopian tale, abstract concepts such as "the soul of the nation," not the concrete national policy of expansion, account for the nation's greatness. "Blind to particulars and details," the preface aestheticizes the nation's landscape and people, creating a harmonious vision of national identity that transcends racial and geographic boundaries and neutralizes the political tensions that divide it (5). Whitman was right to claim that his "great poem is for ages and ages in common and for all degrees and complexions and all departments and sects and for a woman as much as a man," because its monumental and utopian vision of America had little to do with the history and politics that constituted it as a nation. Indeed, his poetic project aestheticizes the nation's geography by way of disavowing its expansionist history. Whitman was thus able to transform the divided states into the "greatest poem" by "repelling" the nation's violent past and slighting its divided present.

From a Nation of Nations to a Nation of Immigrants

Even a cursory glance at the liberal discourse of the mid-twentieth century would reveal its genealogical continuity with that of the mid-nineteenth century. John F. Kennedy's posthumously published *A Nation of Immigrants*, for example, begins with a chapter entitled "A Nation of Nations," borrowing extensively from both Whitman and Tocqueville to make its argument for an immigration policy that is "generous" and "fair" (82). Kennedy describes the nation as a land of equal exiles, "a society of immigrants, each of whom had begun life anew, on an equal footing" (2). Equally invested in the ritual of self-renewal, the celebratory discourse of mid-twentieth-century liberalism, like its forerunner in the mid-nineteenth century, represents Americans in a monumentalizing fashion as a heroic people who "dared to explore new frontiers," and whose love of freedom and independence made them build a great and new democratic nation. "The interaction of disparate cultures, the vehemence of the ideals that led the immigrants here, the opportunity offered by a new life," he states in celebratory style, "all gave America a flavor and a character that make it as unmistakable and as remarkable to people today as it was to Alexis de Tocqueville in the early part of the nineteenth century" (3). America's unique cultural identity is once again articulated in terms of its ability to renew itself through immigration. A hundred years later, the liberal discourse of immigration now includes the excluded of the late nineteenth century—the Jews and Italians, the Poles and the Syrians—in its claim about the plurality of the nation and its tolerance of difference. The new immigrants allow the nation to re-invent itself anew, becoming even more plural as a polity.

To explore the political and cultural implications of this genealogical link, in the remainder of this chapter I want to read Oscar Handlin's (hi)story *The Uprooted* and Kennedy's *A Nation of Immigrants* against their mid-nineteenth-century intertexts, Whitman's *Leaves of Grass* and Tocqueville's *Democracy in America*. The aim of my reading is not merely to demonstrate the discursive regularities of the nation's monumentalizing historiography, but rather to show the subtle way in which the nation's liberal discourse of immigration undergoes a crucial discursive shift in the mid-twentieth century from a romantic to a "realist" representation of America's past and racial landscape, becoming in this way less forgetful of the nation's past and more attentive to the actual condition of immigrants in America. The liberal discourse of the mid-twentieth century, in contrast to its mid-nineteenth-century counterpart, sheds its happy national narrative and acknowledges the pain of immigration, as it recounts in detail the economic and social hardships that newcomers faced in nineteenth-century America. Though the discourse still idealizes the nation as a plural society of equals and as an asylum for oppressed humanity, thus masking the cold war politics that foreground it, the representation is more truthful about the history of immigration in the United States and attempts to write the "bleaker pages of our history," to use

Handlin's words.[20] The new discourse of liberalism, therefore, does not completely romanticize the experience of immigration but instead offers a more historically informed account of the economic and social factors that enabled the mass immigration to America. In this sense, it is a less forgetful mode of representation than its mid-nineteenth-century forebear; and in a liberal way it even offers a sort of apologia for the nation's forgetting and mistreatment of immigrants. Such an acknowledgment of forgetting, I argue however, does not make the new liberal discourse completely anamnestic, for it too disavows and obscures many important issues to write "the epic story of the great migrations that made the American people," to borrow the subtitle of Handlin's *The Uprooted*. I will return to the political and cultural implications of these discursive negations later, but first let us consider how the liberal discourse of immigration in the mid-twentieth century differs from that of the mid-nineteenth century.

The shift from romance to realism in liberal discourse is enabled by a new vision of the nation's historical origins. Whereas nineteenth-century liberal discourse begins the (hi)story of America with the New England Puritans, valorizing their love of liberty and equality as the origin of American democracy, in the mid-twentieth-century discourse of immigration the "great migrations" of the nineteenth century and the early twentieth are privileged as the source of America's greatness. The new liberal discourse of immigration in the twentieth century problematizes the earlier association of the word "native" with white European Protestants in the Northeast by positing a more plural view of national identity that considers everyone a "stranger in the land." Handlin, for example, begins *The Uprooted* with the radical acknowledgment that the history of America *is* the history of immigration: "Once I thought to write a history of the immigrants in America. Then I discovered that the immigrants *were* American history" (3). The new discourse of immigration reflects a more sincere understanding of America's national identity, in which displacement is viewed as the source of what constitutes the nation and as the force that compels it forward. Kennedy in the first pages of *A Nation of Immigrants* also writes, "Another way of indicating the importance of immigration to America is to point out that every American who ever lived, with the exception of one group, was either an immigrant himself or a descendant of immigration" (2). Kennedy cites Will Rogers's claim that "his ancestors were at the dock to meet the *Mayflower*" but uses the authority of "some anthropologists" who "believe that the Indians themselves were immigrants from another continent who displaced the original Americans—the aborigines" to suggest that even the Native Americans were not the original people of North America (2–3). Like its nineteenth-century intertexts, *A Nation of Immigrants* softens the historical fact of genocide by using scientific claims about how the native population itself displaced another people, and it forgetfully represents the involuntary displacement of Africans by casting them as immigrants from Africa, yet its claim about the ubiquity of immigration in the United States testifies to a demystification of any originary claim about national identity. No one can claim to be "native," the "original" American, because everyone is an immigrant, a stranger from another land. In the liberal discourse of the mid-twentieth century, the shadow of exile and displacement falls on notions of citizenship and nationality. America begins with immigration, a potentially radical idea because it fundamentally questions the notion of an "original" or "superior" race or ethnicity in defining national identity.[21]

An important way in which the liberal discourse of the mid-twentieth century problematizes the notion of an "original" race is by insisting on the plurality of the original inhabitants of the United States. Kennedy begins his chapter on the pre-revolutionary waves of immigration with a bluntly anamnesiac statement that demystifies the problematic view of the original colonies as ethnically homogeneous: "The name 'America' was given to this continent by a German mapmaker, Martin Waldseemuller, to honor an Italian explorer, Amerigo Vespucci. The three ships which discovered America sailed under a Spanish flag, were commanded by an Italian sea captain, and included in their crews an Englishman, an Irishman, a Jew and a Negro" (10). At the origin of American national identity is ethnic and cultural diversity. The liberal discourse of the mid-twentieth century promotes a multicultural view of the American polity by dispelling the myth of a monolithic and original English "stock," reminding the nation of the diverse group of people who first populated it. Although it does acknowledge that the first wave of settlements in Jamestown (in 1607) and Plymouth (in 1620) were "predominantly English in origin," it goes on to add, "America was settled by immigrants from many countries, with diverse national, ethnic and social backgrounds" (10–11). Throughout his text, Kennedy reminds Americans that the so-called

British colonies were ethnically plural: Dutch settlements on the Hudson River; Swedes in Delaware; Polish, German, and Italian craftsmen in Jamestown; German and Swiss farmers in Pennsylvania, Virginia, New York, and the Carolinas; French Huguenots who settled from New England in Georgia; Scots and Irish who "advanced the frontier beyond the Alleghenies"; and two thousand Jews who came to pre-revolutionary America from Spain and Portugal all made the original colonies ethnically and culturally heterogeneous. "When Britain conquered Nieuw Amsterdam in 1664," he reminds his readers, "it offered citizenship to immigrants of eighteen different nationalities" (11).

In addition to debunking the myth of an original British stock by showing how the nation was ethnically diverse even before the Declaration of Independence, Kennedy undermines the claim that what impelled Europeans to immigrate to America was a desire for religious freedom, by reminding his readers of the diverse social backgrounds of early immigrants: "They were both indentured servants and profit-seeking aristocrats from England. There were farmers, both propertied and bankrupt, from Ireland. There were discharged soldiers, soldiers of fortune, scholars and intellectuals from Germany" (11). Kennedy further elaborates the new context and role of immigration in the post-revolutionary era, during which "the spreading westward of the new nation" and "economic diversification and industrialization" made the nation even more ethnically diverse. Citing Handlin's *The Uprooted*, Kennedy argues that the post-revolutionary waves of immigrants radically changed the nation, as each new group "helped meet the needs of American development and made its distinctive contribution to the American character" (17). Although Kennedy still offers an ideological narrative in which religious and political freedom is privileged above all as the cause of European immigration to the United States—a move that reflects the political exigencies of the cold war during which he was articulating his pro-immigrant position—his account nonetheless offers a more complex view of immigration that acknowledges the plurality of immigrant communities and their particular contributions to the nation. There is, in other words, a subtle shift from a purely monolithic and homogeneous perception of the nation's cultural identity to a more multicultural and heterogeneous one.

To explore the ideological underpinnings and political implications of Kennedy's multicultural view of the American polity as an exemplar of the mid-twentieth-century liberal position, we may consider Handlin's *The Uprooted*, the Pulitzer Prize winner in history in 1951, which profoundly influenced liberal politicians' views of immigration. This best-selling book made Handlin, a professor of history at Harvard, a significant public intellectual whose views, adopted by politicians like Kennedy and Lyndon Johnson, radically shaped the nation's immigration policy for many years, an issue to which I will return by way of conclusion. As the subtitle of the book indicates, Handlin tells the epic (hi)story of the great migrations of the nineteenth century that fundamentally altered America, a (hi)story that begins with the socioeconomic "push" factors in early-nineteenth-century Europe and ends with the restrictive laws governing the nation's immigration policy during the mid-nineteenth century.

Handlin links America's immigrant identity to the rise of industrialism that uprooted traditional peasant communities in Europe. In contrast to the mid-nineteenth-century liberal discourse of immigration that emphasized the "pull" of immigration, Handlin argues that the "immigrant movement" "started in the peasant heart of Europe," a heart that was shattered as industrialization displaced peasants, transforming them into the proletariat of urban cities. This sociohistorical transformation, which forced the already uprooted peasants to come to the United States, was central to the nation's population growth and economic development (7). Already by the late eighteenth century, Handlin points out, the consolidation of land and the creation of large agricultural units by European feudal lords had put peasants at a competitive disadvantage, forcing some to migrate to urban industrial cities to seek work in factories and mills while impoverishing others who remained behind. Compounded by a precipitous and unprecedented rise in the population of Europe between 1750 and 1850, the socioeconomic changes made immigration the only means of survival: "Year by year, there were fewer alternatives until the critical day when only a single choice remained to be made—to emigrate or die. Those who had the will to make that final decision departed" (37). Though Handlin's use of the word "will" introduces a certain level of agency, he represents European immigrants as economic refugees who migrated out of material necessity rather than political choice. Neither politics nor ideology played any role in the "cataclysmic transfer of population" that enabled the expansion of the nation westward (32). Throughout his text, Handlin thus undermines the nation's ideological myth of asylum by positing "the disintegration of the old village ways" as the major cause of the great migrations of the nineteenth century.

In addition to the "push" created by industrialism and the disintegration of the old agricultural system in Europe, Handlin discusses the technological changes that facilitated immigrating to America for the uprooted. He draws attention, for example, to the "changes in the techniques of ocean travel": the "introduction of steam in the transatlantic services in the 1840's" made the journey faster, reducing it to less than ten days, and also cheaper, because of the large steerage space available on steamships (53). Moreover, various European nations granted "heavy subsidies to the operators of the lines bearing their flags" in the mid-nineteenth century, and these made the journey still less expensive for immigrants. Later, large shipping transportation companies emerged on both sides of the Atlantic to transport uprooted Europeans to the United States. Handlin's discussion of these and other technological developments, such as the expansion of railroad lines in Europe and the United States, historicizes the material conditions that enabled the transatlantic migrations of the nineteenth century, thus making immigration less an ideological choice and more a socioeconomic necessity.

Just as Handlin qualifies the political myth of asylum by elaborating the economic and technical causes of transatlantic migration, he qualifies the benevolent aims attributed to the nation's open-door policy in the nineteenth century by elaborating the disenfranchised conditions of some immigrants in the "promised land." Far from the "land of opportunity and equality" that they were promised in the popular genre of "Letters from America," the country upon which these immigrants landed proved to be anything but socially equal or economically advantageous. Although politically speaking the European immigrants did hold equal legal status with the older residents, the harsh and hostile circumstances of work made them both socially alienated and economically disenfranchised. Handlin contextualizes the disempowered position of immigrants in nineteenth-century America in terms of the nation's brutal capitalist economy. Though recounted in a humanist language that focuses on the misery of immigrant life, his text nonetheless draws attention to several reasons why America was hostile and alienating to newcomers. First of all was the "practice of peonage" that existed in many states until 1907, when the federal government intervened to stop it (67). Many poor immigrants who could not afford to pay for their transatlantic fare came to this country as indentured laborers, a condition that virtually enslaved them in a patronage system. The law was on the side of unscrupulous contractors, condemning the unwitting immigrants to a life of servitude that lasted until they could pay the debt. With no prospect of security, the indentured laborers worked for subsistence wages, unable to reach "a point that permitted a man to accumulate the stakes of a fresh start," remaining thus forever second-class citizens, unequal and disenfranchised (68). Handlin goes on to remind his readers that it was the exploited labor of these indentured workers that enabled the growth of the nation from 1830 to 1930. "Intricate systems of aqueducts, of gas pipes, of electric wires, of trolley tracks [that] supplied water and light and transportation for the new city millions," he states, "depended for [their] execution upon an ample fund of unskilled labor" (68).

The situation of those who could pay their fare to America was not radically different. Their inability to get to the West, where inexpensive land was still available for cultivation, forced them to take up menial jobs in industrial cities. Because "in the 1820's and 1830's, factory employment was the province of groups relatively high in social status," these newcomers could not find work in industry and had to accept low-paying jobs as janitors and sweepers in eastern metropolises (71). The disenfranchised status of these newcomers did not change much during mid-century, when rapid economic expansion produced new jobs in the industrial sector. Though a few immigrants had the necessary skills to find work as operators and mechanics, the majority had to toil in coal mines, construction, and maintenance services, jobs that kept them at the bottom of the economic ladder. With the second industrial revolution in the 1870s, some immigrants were able to penetrate into the older textile and shoe industries. But here too the conditions were oppressively harsh, reflecting "an inhuman lack of concern with human needs that was characteristic of the entire system" (73). Handlin cites long working days, a "high rate of industrial accidents and a stubborn unwillingness to make the most elementary provisions for the comfort of the employees" as evidence of the "penetrating callousness" of industrial capitalism in nineteenth-century America (73). The capitalist exploitation of immigrant labor—compounded by "the trap of an expensive credit system" to which immigrants turned in "the bitter intervals between earnings" and the oppressive living conditions of overcrowded tenements created by greedy landlords—"made the peasant less a man" in the new world (78, 79). Handlin thus offers a more realistic, perhaps even anamnesiac, representation of the socioeconomics of immigration by bringing into focus the inhumane and oppressive conditions of newcomers in America: "no hands extended to assist them" and no way to make "their voices heard," as callous forces of industrial capitalism reduced the helpless immigrant to "the driven cog in a great machine" (81, 108).

The alienated and disenfranchised condition of Europe's uprooted in capitalist America, Handlin goes on to argue, accounts for the social ills associated with new immigrants in the nineteenth century. Writing against the nativist arguments of the late nineteenth century and the early twentieth, he discusses the predicaments of pauperism, alcoholism, disease, and crime as the natural consequences of the socioeconomic conditions of immigrants, not as evidence of the inherent characteristics of "inferior races." If the immigrant had to surrender to pauperism, he points out, "No blame could attach here to him who could not always earn a livelihood, who came to depend for his sustenance on the gifts of charity" (157). Poverty, not a "lack of foresight," a "hopeless future," not a "dissolute character," economic disparity, and not "spendthrift habits," were the reasons for the high rate of pauperism among immigrant communities. Moreover, Handlin devotes a whole chapter to "The Ghettos," in which he blames the crowded and unsanitary spaces of tenements and the filthy streets of eastern cities' poorest quarters for the spread of disease among the nation's newcomers. In the ghettos of New York City, for example, the lack of adequate water closets in apartments or hallways, a primitive and ineffectual sewerage system, and poor sanitation services transformed immigrant quarters into insalubrious and disease-infested spaces (152). The oppressive and confining conditions of living were also what channeled many immigrants into alcoholism and gambling. "After a day's effort to hammer happiness out of the unyielding American environment," he remarks half ironically, "it was good, now and then, to go not to the narrow realities of home but to the convivial places where the glass played the main part" (159). Alcohol was a "means of release," allowing the immigrant to "dissolve in alcohol the least soluble of problems" (159). Gambling was "another way of entering immediately into a realm of hope that shone in bright contrast to the visible dreariness about them" (160). Trapped in the poor ghettos of American cities where a "hopeless future" awaited them, immigrants found in gambling "the comfort of hope," as the possibility of winning "conjured up the most heartwarming dreams" (160–61).

The aim of Handlin's elaboration of the social ills associated with Europe's uprooted is not merely to provide a liberal apologia for immigrant delinquency. It is also to demonstrate how an ahistorical understanding of the predicaments of immigration provided the necessary ideological ammunition for the new nativism of the late nineteenth century and the early twentieth in its push for the racially exclusionary quota acts of 1921 and 1924, both of which severely curtailed the arrival of newcomers. "The stranger," according to Handlin, has historically been "the butt of attack" by nativists in America, at least since the Know-Nothing movement blamed immigrants for the nation's economic and political problems in the mid-nineteenth century. But in the late nineteenth century, the socioeconomic problems of the immigrant ghettos were authoritatively and ideologically interpreted by American social scientists so as to advance their racist theories about new immigrants, theories that were eventually adopted by the politicians who passed the quota laws. (I will discuss the new nativism of this era and its political consequences in chapter 4.) Discussing the birth of sociology as a "discipline of independent stature" in the late nineteenth century, Handlin writes, "The American social scientists approached their subject through the analysis of specific disorders: criminality, intemperance, poverty, and disease. Everywhere they looked they found immigrants somehow involved in these problems. In explaining such faults in the social order, the scholar had a choice of alternatives: these were the pathological manifestations of some blemish, either in the nature of the newcomers or in the nature of the whole society. It was tempting to accept the explanation that put the blame on the outsiders" (278). Borrowing the biological dictum of European race theorists of the late nineteenth century, such as Gobineau, Drumont, and Chamberlain, that "social characteristics depended upon racial differences," these scholars argued that "flaws in the biological constitution of various groups of immigrants were responsible for every evil that besets the country—for pauperism, for the low birth rate of natives, for economic depressions, for class divisions, for prostitution and homosexuality, and for the appearance of city slums" (278). Convinced that "their conclusions must be capable of practical application," these social scientists were not only scholars but also activists who became involved in reform movements that advocated a eugenic approach to the problem of immigration: "the control of the composition of the population through selection of proper stock based on proper heredity" (179). This idea, Handlin argues explicitly, provided the "scientific" rationale behind both the literacy test in 1917 and the quota laws of 1921 and 1924. In these exclusionary acts, the racist theories of social scientists "acquired the force of law," making race a crucial component of the nation's immigration policy (286). The literacy test, for example, was racially motivated because it worked as "a means of barring southern and eastern Europeans without excluding those from the northern and western parts of the continent where the facilities for elementary education had become common by 1917" (290). The restrictive laws of immigration in the early twentieth century, he thus concludes, at once perpetuated and reaffirmed a monolithic notion of national identity by giving "official sanction to the assertions that the immigrants were separate from and inferior to the native-born" (294).

Handlin, like other liberal thinkers of the mid-twentieth century, worked against mythologized representations of America's Puritan origins by reminding Americans that their nation began with an immigration that was heterogeneous, a welcome move that called into question the monolithic constructions of national identity in the United States. The liberal discourse of the mid-twentieth century, unlike its precursor, remembered the trauma of displacement in order to critique the binary distinction between native and alien through which narrow nationalists justified their struggle against "lax" immigration laws and their discriminatory attitude toward "lower elements in the population" (284). Forgetting one's own trauma of immigration, Handlin correctly observed, is what fueled the "agitation against the Orientals, the Negroes, and the newest immigrants": such fixed and homogeneous claims about nationalist identity "implied a rejection of their parents who had themselves once been green off the boat and could boast of no New World antecedents" (284-85). The nation's disavowing attitude toward its immigrant foundation made America move toward a restrictive and homogeneous view of society and a fixed and conformist view of American culture.

Learning from the activist role played by social scientists of the late nineteenth century and early twentieth in changing the nation's immigration policy, liberal intellectuals of the mid-twentieth century did not allow their discourse to be limited to academic analysis or historical study. They became actively involved in dismantling the racist quota laws of the 1920s. As I have already suggested, Handlin's history of the nation's immigration in *The Uprooted* was itself an important intertext for Kennedy's liberal thinking, shaping in distinctive ways his legislative proposals to eliminate the national origins quota system. But Handlin also wrote political essays to convince the general public of the need for changes in the nation's immigration policy. Two years after the publication of his book, Handlin voiced his strong opposition to the quota laws in an article titled "We Need More Immigrants" published in the *Atlantic*. Here he directly addressed the racist assumptions of the immigration laws, founded on the "pseudoscientific pseudo facts" of social scientists (28). Responding to the passage of the McCarran-Walter Immigration and Nationality Act of 1952—which did not eliminate the national origins quota system, though it made all races eligible for naturalization and eliminated race as a bar to immigration—Handlin used the authority of new race theories to push for the more far-reaching revision of eliminating altogether the "racial features" of the nation's immigration policy. Writing at a time when "No respectable scientist now accepts the racist dogma of inherent biological differences among men," Handlin demystified the idea that "American civilization was the work of the Anglo-Saxon branch of the great Nordic, or Aryan, family" (27–28). He acknowledged both the economic and cultural contributions of immigrants throughout American history, arguing that "people from every cultural background are capable of leading creative lives within the free institutions of the United States" (29). Race, therefore, should not be a criterion in admitting new immigrants: the nation's immigration laws, he concluded, should "rest upon a calculation of American interests and not upon racial prejudice" (31).

Through such convincing arguments, liberal intellectuals like Handlin played an important role in shifting the nation's immigration policy in the mid-twentieth century. It is not an accident that the proposals President Kennedy offered to the 88th Congress in 1963 to eliminate the national origins quota system of the 1920s—proposals that were eventually written into law through the passage of the Immigration and Nationality Act of 1965 after his death—closely resembled those formulated by Handlin in his articles: abolition of racially discriminatory provisions in the immigration laws; dismantling of the national origins quota system; preference given to unifying the families of American citizens; and the inclusion of political refugees from communist countries as one of the preferred categories of admission.

The similarities between Handlin's recommendations and Kennedy's policy proposals demonstrate that mid-twentieth-century liberal discourse directly influenced the shift in the nation's immigration policy toward a multicultural perception of national identity in the United States. In reminding the nation of its uprooted "origins," liberal thinkers made the idea of "national origin" obsolete in defining cultural identity. In his reflective concluding chapter of *The Uprooted*, Handlin appeals to memory to urge the removal of racially discriminatory quota laws. Critiquing such exclusionary views of national identity in the United States, he ends his (hi)story of the uprooted by reminding Americans one more time that they were once immigrants themselves: "we cannot push away the heritage of having been once all strangers in the land; we cannot forget the experience of having been all rootless, adrift" (306). This shift from romance to "realism" in the liberal discourse of immigration provided a powerful critique of exclusionary notions of national identity in the United States, and this critique mediated the transformation of the nation's immigration policy and the enactment of the Immigration and Nationality Act of 1965, in which the racial and ethnic biases of quota laws were eliminated.

The Limits of Liberal Pluralism

To the extent that mid-twentieth-century works such as Handlin's *The Uprooted* and other liberal defenses of immigrants[22] helped to eliminate the racially discriminatory national origins quota system, the shift from romance to realism in the liberal discourse of immigration must be viewed as salutary. And yet to acknowledge as much is not to deny that the liberal discourse of immigration, like nineteenth-century discourse, reenacted the ritual of self-renewal and perpetuated the ideology of American exceptionalism; it did so by simultaneously dissimulating the conflictive politics of race in the United States through deployment of the ethnicity paradigm and masking the economically and politically expedient nature of immigration reform that motivated the reforms of 1965. Above all, in the act of celebrating the nation's multiculturalism, the liberal discourse of immigration remained peculiarly Eurocentric. Handlin's *The Uprooted*, for example, focused narrowly on the experience of central and southern European peasants, using their story to construct a master narrative of national identity that overlooks the economic contribution and social condition of other immigrants, not to mention African Americans. While Handlin's approach allowed him to diversify and denationalize mythic images of a white, Protestant United States, the resulting ethnically diverse picture went only so far, failing to address the qualitatively different historical experiences of various ethnicities. Written at a time when most African Americans and Chinese immigrants were still denied full citizenship, *The Uprooted* avoids any discussion of the nation's racialized landscape and writes a triumphant, if not monumentalizing, history of immigrant America that begins with the arrival of disenfranchised European peasants and ends with their successful incorporation into the industrial society. To produce such an immigrant narrative of progress, however, one must either overlook certain historical facts or omit them altogether. Left out of this narrative, for example, are the blacks in the South who had toiled as slaves in the cotton plantations that produced raw material for the textile factories in the North, where the newly arrived European peasants found work. Similarly absent from the picture were immigrants from Mexico and Latin America, who as *braceros* enabled the massive development of agribusiness throughout the Southwest. In addition, Handlin's triumphant narrative of immigrant America ignores the work of indentured Chinese coolies, who in spite of providing the necessary cheap labor to build railroads throughout the West became subjected to violent discrimination, including exclusionary laws, in the late nineteenth century. That an Irish immigrant like Denis Kearney led the anti-Chinese movement in California in the early 1870s disproves Handlin's claim of civic unity achieved through the common experience of having "all been strangers in the land and . . . passed through the trials of the uprooted" (275). Far from being a harmonious mosaic, immigrant America was (and remains) a divided community, splintered by racial divisions and economic inequalities. In reducing "the issue of race to an element of ethnicity," as Omi and Winant point out, the liberal discourse of the mid-twentieth century ignored "ongoing processes of discrimination, shifts in the prevailing economic climate, the development of sophisticated racial ideology of 'conservative egalitarianism' . . . in other words, all the concrete sociopolitical dynamics within which racial phenomena operate in the U.S." (20–21). The kind of multiculturalism that mid-twentieth-century liberals fashioned was a new form of universalism designed, as Lowe insightfully argues, "to accommodate the irreducible diversity of American society" by " 'forgetting' the material histories of racialization, segregation, and economic violence" (30). For Handlin this universalism takes a more ambivalent form, since it makes a gesture of inclusion that is in fact partial, thereby recognizing some while doubling the exclusion of others from the national narrative—I say "doubling" because their absence staged the inclusions that Handlin sought.

In the liberal narrative of immigrant progress, moreover, the European peasant proves useful to the nation as an agent of renewal whose material success perpetuates the common belief in class mobility while his or her cultural assimilation reaffirms the myth of an immigrant America receptive to every stranger willing to embrace the nation's democratic ideals. The transformation of European peasants from serfdom to citizenship privileges a linear narrative of assimilation in which the model immigrant shores up the popular belief that America is the land of equal opportunity, accessible to anyone willing to abandon his or her "old" identity and embrace the new form of modern citizenship. The twentieth-century literature of immigration is replete with sociological and historical studies of individual white ethnic communities, acknowledging and celebrating their contributions to American society while forgetting the material histories of race in America.[23] While these works aim to refute the nativist claim that immigrants threaten the nation's unity, they offer distinct accounts of America's exceptionalism, with each immigrant community represented as embodying the ideals of democracy, for example "family values," dedication to hard work, and the possibility of upward mobility. The liberal literature of immigration in this way perpetuates the myth of immigrant America, because it represents "the foreigner as a supplement to the nation, an agent of national reenchantment that might rescue the regime from corruption and return it to its principles," as Honig remarks (74). These liberal accounts therefore do not constitute an oppositional moment in the discourse of immigration: they are ideologically affirmative, shoring up patriotism and national pride by corroborating the idea of American exceptionalism. This literature inadvertently recuperates the figure of the immigrant for national reinvigoration; it also indirectly functions as a disciplinary force for the poor and the less successful ethnic communities, since its endorsement of a meritocratic perception of class mobility that assumes economic success or failure to be purely a function of the individual immigrant's drive devalues the qualitative historical differences demarcating racial meanings and dynamics in the United States. By claiming that newcomers begin life on an "equal footing" in a society that does not "restrict their freedom of choice and action," the liberal discourse of immigration denies the material history of race and dissimulates the social and political inequalities that undermine the American dream, holding unsuccessful immigrants fully responsible for their disenfranchisement (Kennedy, *A Nation of Immigrants*, 2).

Ideologically affirmative as the liberal discourse of immigration was, the policy changes that it mediated were predictably geared to favor the "model" immigrant and the traditional family structure, while ironically barring from entry the economically uprooted whom Handlin celebrated in his work. Although the Immigration and Nationality Act of 1965 abolished the racially discriminatory National Origins Act of 1924, it instituted a new restrictive legislation that privileged a professional class of immigrants and the idea of the nuclear family. The 1965 act established a preference order in which highly skilled and professional immigrants whose services were in demand could claim up to half of the residency visas assigned to each country, thus excluding from the American polity the needy and those belonging to lower social classes. Class and symbolic capital, rather than race and nationality, thus became the determining categories for citizenship, as the legislators unabashedly embraced the economic expediency that has historically motivated the nation's immigration policy. The law identifies citizenship with class and profession, pointedly privileging the needs of a capitalist economy over political and humanitarian ideals.

Moreover, the 1965 act promulgated the traditional model of the nuclear family by making family reunification the cornerstone of the nation's immigration policy. The new immigration act exempted from preference requirements and numerical national quotas unmarried adults whose parents were U.S. citizens, and the spouses and offspring of permanant residents. By instituting family reunification as a rationing criterion of immigration policy, the law implicitly defined citizenship in heterosexual and patriarchal terms. The law helped reenchant the institution of marriage at a time when the women's liberation movement threatened to undermine the patriarchal order.

Passed in the middle of the civil rights movement, the Immigration and Nationality Act of 1965—enabled by the liberal discourse of immigration in the mid-twentieth century—has been credited with helping to abolish racial discrimination and bring about an "authentic" form of multiculturalism in the United States.[24] This view of immigrant America, I have been suggesting, overlooks how the nation's liberal discourse and the passage of a race-free policy of immigration also made possible a normative form of citizenship characterized by capitalist and familial principles that were codified through the preference requirements of the new immigration law. The two major considerations that President Kennedy recommended for inclusion in his proposal in 1963 to liberalize immigration statutes were "the skills of the immigrant and their relationship to our need" and "the family relationship between immigrants and persons already here, so that the reuniting of families is encouraged" (103). The cornerstone of the Immigration and Nationality Act of 1965, these proposals bring into focus how the nation's liberal immigration policy and discourse were embedded in what the president's brother, Robert Kennedy, in his introduction to *A Nation of Immigrants* called "our faith in the American ideal" (x). Salutary as it was in replacing the nation's Anglo-conformity with multicultural pluralism, the shift in the liberal discourse and policy of immigration deliberately repositioned the immigrant as the agent of national renewal by making him or her once again "reflect [citizens'] faith in the American ideal," again in the words of Robert Kennedy (x). So while the immigration act of 1965, for example, finally ended discrimination against Asians by nullifying the Chinese Exclusion Act of 1882, it recuperated them as model immigrants by allowing only those who were either professional or skilled workers to immigrate. In modeling immigration policy in terms of class instead of race, the liberal immigration law transformed the immigrant from a threat to the nation (such as the "yellow threat" represented by Asians) to a figuration of its ideals, such as those enshrined in the ideas of "family values" and a meritocratic economy.[25] Now the incarnation of American values, the new immigrant was thus figured as the agent of the nation's ritual of self-renewal, reinforcing national pride while perpetuating a normalized notion of citizenship.

4

Discourses of Exclusion

Nativism and the Imagining of a "White Nation"

In one of his campaign commercials during the gubernatorial race in California in 1994, Pete Wilson used footage of undocumented border crossers at the San Diego–Tijuana checkpoint. The advertisement opened with a black-and-white video of a dozen presumably Mexican immigrants scurrying across the border, dodging cars and running from the checkpoint, as the announcer intoned, "They keep coming! Two million illegal immigrants in California. The federal government won't stop them at the border, yet requires *us* to pay billions to take care of *them*" (my emphasis). Although the alarmist commercial sparked charges of immigrant bashing by many Democrats and activists—who compared it to George H. W. Bush's commercial using the convicted murderer Willie Horton's story to campaign against Michael Dukakis for the presidency in 1988—Wilson's campaign continued to run the commercial for about two weeks, claiming that it was "a real commercial about real issues."[1] Ironically, less than a decade earlier Wilson had successfully lobbied as a "pro-immigration" leader in the U.S. Senate by supporting the continued admission of farm labor from Mexico, a position also expediently adopted to appease western growers, who were concerned that the employer sanctions imposed by the Immigration Reform and Control Act of 1986 would raise labor costs and damage their earnings. In contrast to his earlier position, in 1994 Wilson claimed to be a crusader against lax immigration policies, fighting to stop (illegal) immigrants from stealing Californians' jobs, services, and tax dollars.

Wilson's campaign ad offers a striking example of how the nation's anti-immigrant discourses rely on a form of disavowal marked by retreat from truth to omnipotence. Like earlier manifestations of nativism, the anti-immigrant campaigns in California during the 1990s—such as Wilson's and that in favor of Proposition 187—systematically distorted and misrepresented the socioeconomic problems of California so as to blame immigrants for them. Denying the fact that "undocumented workers pay far more in taxes than they receive in services," these campaigns, as Lipsitz points out, worked to "insulate white voters and property owners from the ill effects of neoconservative economic policies" by "[b]laming the state's fiscal woes on immigrants rather than taking responsibility for the ruinous effects of a decade and a half of irresponsible tax cuts for the wealthy coupled with disinvestment in education and infrastructure" (51, 48). This form of denial, as Wilson's commercial further demonstrates, is articulated through the binary logic of "us" and "them," with specific referents mutating into general ones—"they" originally meant Mexican and other Latin American immigrants and eventually meant (illegal) immigrants in general. As Darry Sragow, the campaign director for the Democrat John Garamendi, correctly pointed out, "The word *they* is obviously a veiled reference to a specific group of people who tend to be perceived as having certain attributes in common. One of those attributes, of course, is that if they are illegal, they don't belong in this country. But in the perception of most voters, these people also are not white and don't speak English as a first language."[2] Predictably, Wilson's campaign pointedly denied that the pronoun "they" implied immigrants from Mexico and Latin America, claiming that the phrase "they keep coming" was a reference to illegal immigrants in general. Like earlier forms of nativism, this new anti-immigrant expression embodied a *differential* mode of national identification—differential because it relied on a binary form of cultural and political classification in which national identity was articulated through and depended upon an alien other: this other, by threatening to invade, helped to define the citizen as a white, English-speaking person who, as the commercial went on to point out, "work[s] hard, pay[s] taxes and obey[s] the laws."

The sentiment that Wilson's commercial expressed so bluntly was not merely that of an opportunist politician exploiting cultural anxiety about immigration to get reelected, as most immigrant-rights activists claimed. It was (and is) also that of a broader nativist population, ranging from second- and third-generation immigrants and members of labor unions to older citizens and people who classify themselves politically as "moderate" to "conservative." According to most surveys—including those of the American Institute of Public Opinion, Associated Press–NBC, the *New York Times*, Gallup, Roper, and Harris—an overwhelming proportion of Americans (close to 80 percent) wishes to limit legal immigration and stop "illegal" immigration to the United States, even though most Americans rely on some form of cheap immigrant labor to fulfill their everyday needs.[3] Curiously and disturbingly, according to a nationwide survey in 1992 even 75 percent of Mexican-Americans believe that too many immigrants are arriving.[4] Whence comes such a broad-based anti-immigrant consensus? How can a "nation of many nations," a "nation of immigrants," be so adamantly anti-immigrant?

Many sociologists and most immigrant-rights advocates consider the nation's anti-immigrant views as arising from economic conditions.[5] Echoing the economism of the restrictionists, they argue that hostility toward "aliens" is an ephemeral and cyclical reaction to the nation's swelled unemployment and economic slump. These observers cite the historical tendency of periods of receptivity to alternate with periods of exclusion—the "open door" era of 1776–1881 preceded the era of regulation of 1882–1924, the admission of political refugees during and after the Second World War preceded "Operation Wetback" of 1954, which sanctioned the mass deportation of Mexican farm workers—to demonstrate the "bipolar" pattern of welcoming immigrants when they are needed and turning against them when times are hard. The conventional liberal wisdom about the public reaction to immigration is this: "When things are going well and there's a shortage of labor, people either look the other way or are actively supportive of bringing cheaper labor into the United States. But when jobs are tight, and the cost of supporting people goes up, then we suddenly redo the calculus."[6]

Empirically convincing though such an economic view of anti-immigration consensus may seem, it fails to address immigration as both a necessary mechanism of social control in forming the state apparatus and an essential component of national identification. What the view of cyclical anti-immigration misses is that immigration as a practice, and as a discourse, of exclusion has *always* been a part of the American polity (though it may occasionally be exacerbated by a poor economy). Contrary to Wilson's claim that he introduced the agenda of immigration control, the practice and discourse of excluding aliens are hardly new. Even during the so-called era of the open door, anti-immigrant sentiment ran high against newcomers: against Germans for their "clannishness," against Jews for their "parvenu spirit" or radicalism, against the Irish for their "low and squalid" way of life, against Italians and Poles for their Catholicism, and against the Chinese for their "criminality" and inability to assimilate.[7] The cultural and ethnic differences of these immigrants helped to bolster a differential mode of national identification, while their social disparities gave the state a political rationale for regulating their practices of everyday life. The discourse and practice of exclusion, as I discussed in chapter 1, had its beginnings in the writings of the founding fathers, whose fear of seditious foreigners led at least some of them to pass the early Alien and Sedition Acts of 1798, which invested the president with the power to exclude undesirable aliens and delineated the requirements for U.S. citizenship. These requirements, embodying the regulatory exercise of state power, were already symptomatic of the nation's differential form of cultural identity.

To acknowledge the prevalence of an anti-immigrant consensus since the very beginning of American national consciousness is not to suggest, however, an unchanging attitude toward immigration throughout American history. Indeed, fundamental shifts such as the Chinese Exclusion Act of 1882, the quota laws of the 1920s, and the McCarran-Walter Act of 1952 have gradually transformed the ways the United States has treated its immigrants, from more lenient and receptive to more restrictive and regulatory. These critical moments constitute ruptures in the nation's discourses and policies of immigration, and as such they demystify linear histories of immigrant America. Neither successive nor continuous, the nation's response to its immigrant formation and its immigrants has always entailed complex, and often contradictory, shifts in relations. I will return to these shifts in policy and public perception later, but for the moment I wish to make a broader, more theoretical point about how immigration has functioned throughout American history as a nodal point for the exercise of state power and as a differential mode of national identification. My contention is that the United States, as a modern nation-state, has always relied upon the phenomenon of immigration to construe and delineate its national, geographical, and political boundaries. The figure of the immigrant confirms the nation's myth of asylum for the oppressed, as I have proposed in previous chapters, and also constitutes a signifier of otherness that differentially makes possible a normalized notion of national identity.

The myth of immigrant America perpetuated by the nation's liberal discourse obscures the history of immigration in the United States as a disciplinary and differential relation between the nation-state and its "alien" subjects. The national discourse of hospitality constitutes a form of historical negation, which disavows the nation's hostility toward newcomers. In what follows, I hope to demonstrate that immigration in America offers a differential discourse of cultural identity through which the nation imagines itself as a homogeneous community and a field of sociopolitical practices whereby the state exercises its disciplinary power. As I have shown in chapter 3, the United States of America has always characterized itself as an *immigrant* nation, celebrating its diverse ethnic composition and taking pride in its hospitality toward newcomers. And yet, by engaging in historical scrutiny one notices powerful strands of anti-immigrant sentiments that have played an equally fundamental role in how a nation-state is imagined in the United States.

In this chapter, I want to consider two particular historical moments in the public debate about the nation's immigration policy by way of demonstrating the complex ways in which nativist representations of immigrants have informed constructions of national identity to this day, as well as shaped the nation's immigration policies. These historical moments are the mid-nineteenth century, when the Know-Nothings launched a powerful anti-immigrant movement to exclude newcomers, and the early twentieth century, during which doctors of the U.S. Public Health Service, in alliance with eugenicists, mounted a scientific form of opposition to new immigration. Read contrapuntally, these historical moments above all shed light on how nativist representations of new immigrants have historically enabled, through disavowal, a normalized notion of national and cultural identity in the United States, one that belies the nation's equally constant celebration of its ethnic diversity and its claim to total hospitality. Nativism, I suggest, is not contradictory to the nation's benign image of itself as a haven for the oppressed and persecuted masses of humanity; it is rather a disavowed, but necessary, component of its formation. Moreover, my contrapuntal reading of these two historical moments suggests that nativism is itself not a monolithic phenomenon that remains the same throughout history. I study the pivotal shift that occurs in its articulation over the course of the nineteenth century and the early twentieth. Focusing on this historical shift in the discourse of nativism—a shift from ideology to science—I will also argue that in this period nativism, by articulating its anti-immigrant stance on "scientific" or "objective" grounds, helped to inaugurate a disciplinary mode of exclusion that was institutionalized and has been exercised by the state ever since.

Forgetting Nativism

Most Americans know virtually nothing about the Know-Nothings, the powerful secret movement of the mid-nineteenth century that made hating the "alien" and the immigrant an integral component of American identity.[8] The movement that vowed to reclaim American asylum for Anglo-Saxon "natives" disappeared from the national memory just as quickly as it disappeared from the political scene in 1860, when the Native American Party to which it had given rise dissolved. The myth of asylum, in which immigration is defined as a matter of national hospitality, has always obscured the role of xenophobia in the construction of national identity. Although an anti-foreign tendency has been culturally and politically prevalent in the United States since Hamilton, who compared immigrants to a "Grecian horse"[9] destroying the nation from inside, the Jeffersonian myth of asylum and hospitality has actually dominated the discourse of national identity. As I demonstrated in chapter 3, the latter idea, of America as an immigrant-loving nation, permeates every expression of American nationality, from the speeches of presidents and politicians to the poetry of Emerson and Whitman to the historical interpretations of American nationalism by liberal intellectuals like Oscar Handlin and Louis Adamic. Crèvecoeur's description of America as the asylum for the needy humanity of the globe has always been the quintessential description of American national identity.

What the myth of the nation as a refuge for the oppressed of all nations disregards is the ideological underpinnings of the myth's own production, as well as the importance of nativism in imagining a national consciousness in America. Latent in the nation's benevolence toward immigrants are both the political desire to appropriate new territories and the economic need for labor, which are denied in rep-

resentations of America as an asylum of freedom. But more importantly, the myth of immigrant America obscures the nation's xenophobic attitude toward newcomers, as expressed both in the nativist
movement and in the nation's expectation from immigrants that they
shed their cultural diversity and political difference to be accepted
as citizens. The obscuring of xenophobia by the myth of immigrant
America raises questions as to both the nature and the function of
national amnesia. What is it about nativism and xenophobia that liberal America wishes to forget? What role does the forgetting of nativism play in the construction of national consciousness in the United
States? And what can we learn about the dynamic relationship between
xenophobia and xenophilia, as alternative and cooperative modes of
defining national identity?

A starting point to address these questions is the organization of
xenophobia as a viable mode of national identification by the mid-
nineteenth-century nativists. My intention in beginning here is not
to treat this particular historical moment as a point of origin, for as I
have stressed and as students of nativism have demonstrated, the roots
of xenophobia in America go back to the nation's colonial heritage.
For example, the great historian of nativism John Higham has traced
the nation's xenophobia to the early English colonizers' anti-Catholic
and anti-radical tendencies, as well as their belief in the racial superiority of Anglo-Americans.[10] Rather, my aim here is to show the seminal role that mid-nineteenth-century nativism played in legitimating
xenophobia as a form of national belonging and community building.
Since the short-lived Alien and Sedition Acts of 1798 that authorized
the president to expel political dissidents, a paranoid fear of "foreign
influences" has always existed in the United States. But it was not until
the mid-nineteenth century that xenophobia became an organized political movement, legitimizing its claim to an exclusive form of national identity. The rise of anti-foreign parties in New York and other
cities in the eastern United States during the late 1830s, which eventually grew into the powerful Know-Nothing movement of the 1850s,
helped transform xenophobia into an acceptable and powerful form
of patriotism, which has survived to this day. But before discussing the
broader cultural and political implications of this ideological transformation by reading an exemplary piece of Know-Nothing literature,
let us briefly consider how historians of nativism have contextualized
this era.

Historians of nativism have attributed the rise of organized xenophobia in the mid-nineteenth century to both economic and political factors. Some have argued that the sudden surge in the number of unskilled immigrants from 1845 to 1854 fueled the anti-foreign sentiment of the mid-nineteenth century. Almost three million people immigrated to the United States during this period, most of whom were unskilled Irish and German laborers. Concerned about the nation's demographic homogeneity and anxious about the social effects of pauperism and crime associated with new immigration, many Americans espoused the nativists' anti-foreign stance to protect their nation from cultural and political "contamination." Americans, the historian Ray Allen Billington argues, "believed that the influx of aliens threatened their established social structure, endangered the nation's economic welfare, and spelled doom for the existing governmental system."[11] Nativism, according to the historians of this camp, was a defensive form of nationalism that viewed America as a "threatened paradise" in need of a patriotic movement to save it from the "alien invasion."

Other historians have cited the political turmoil of antebellum America over slavery as the source of nativism's popularity in the mid-nineteenth century. The sectional tension between the South, which favored slavery, and the North, which was against it, threatened the Union with disintegration, fueling a great deal of political anxiety about American nationality. The Fugitive Slave Act of 1850, which as a compromise bill was meant to ease this tension by obliging free northern states to return runaway slaves to their southern owners, only weakened the two-party system, as it made the Whigs and the Democrats internally divided. Moreover, the passage of the Kansas-Nebraska Act of 1854, which made slavery possible in both states by repealing the Missouri Compromise of 1820 (which had set the geographical limits of slavery between the North and the South), practically dissolved the Whigs' unity, making the nation even more politically divided. Many historians have claimed that the sectional conflict over slavery was the political origin of nativist parties in the mid-nineteenth century. The historian Tyler Anbinder, for example, argues that "slavery played the key role in transforming the Know Nothings from a small nativist organization into a national political power."[12] Throughout the eastern cities, the Know-Nothings exploited anti-party sentiment, which was caused by the conflict over slavery, to gain the support of various constituencies. Nativism, according to this view, was an opportunist movement that capitalized on the nation's fear of sectional conflict to fashion an exclusive form of national identity.

Though the economic and political histories of mid-nineteenth-century nativism have greatly contributed to the understanding of antebellum xenophobia, they have often overlooked the intellectual contribution of nativist movements. By concentrating on the political *activities* of Know-Nothings and other xenophobic movements, instead of their *theoretical* contributions, these histories have tended to treat mid-nineteenth-century nativism as "an aberration in the nation's liberal tradition," an exception to the general tendency of the nation to welcome and help its immigrants.[13] Even the liberal historian Handlin, who eloquently recounted the marginalized position of newcomers during the nineteenth century, claimed that the Know-Nothings, like the American Protective Association of the 1890s and the anti-German movement of the First World War, were merely "brief lapses" in the nation's history that "had no enduring effects upon legislation or upon the attitudes of the mass of the native-born" (*The Uprooted*, 269). The study of the theoretical literature of the Know-Nothings, however, is crucial to understanding the broader cultural and political implications of mid-nineteenth-century nativism, demonstrating that anti-immigrant sentiment in the United States has been a lot more enduring and significant than liberal historians have liked to believe. What makes this literature important is the light that it sheds on the philosophical and ideological underpinnings of nativism, which assured its longevity as a political ideology in spite of its disappearance as a social movement. That a best-selling book like Peter Brimelow's *Alien Nation* can make its immigration policy argument in the late twentieth century around notions of racial and ethnic exclusivity, claiming that the American nation must protect its white ethnic core and prevent social decline by barring nonwhites from immigrating, attests to the durability of nativism as a political ideology in defining national identity in the United States. The philosophical writings of Know-Nothing intellectuals, marginalized though they may be in multicultural America, continue to inform new forms of nativism today. Calls for race-based immigration laws by best-selling authors such as Brimelow demonstrate that nativism was not merely an aberration in the nation's liberal tradition but an important component of its very formation.

I treat one of the most important works of the Know-Nothings,

Thomas Whitney's *A Defence of the American Policy* (1856), as a syn-
ecdoche for Know-Nothing literature, a useful lens through which to
see the ideological significance of nativist political theory in the construction of an American national identity. Whitney was an important
political activist: he co-founded the United Sons of America, a fra-
ternal nativist organization, in the 1840s and was elected to Congress
as a Know-Nothing in 1854. In the *Defence* he took a more scholarly
turn, providing a compelling theoretical justification of nativism as a
political ideology in keeping with the principles of American Republicanism. What sets his work apart from other intellectual works by
nativists, such as Samuel Busey's *Immigration: Its Evil and Consequences*
(1856) and Samuel Morse's *The Foreign Conspiracy against the Liberties
of the United States* (1835), is the power of its rhetoric, together with
its rigorous theoretical approach. This voluminous book offers critical
analyses of a broad range of topics, from the general notion of American republicanism as "Human Equality, and the innate right to Life,
Liberty, and the Pursuit of Happiness," to specific issues of citizenship, naturalization, and immigration.[14]

*Discursive Formation of
Mid-Nineteenth-Century Nativism*

The full title of the book, *A Defence of the American Policy, as Opposed
to the Encroachments of Foreign Influence, and Especially to the Interference of the Papacy in the Political Interests and Affairs of the United States*,
sounds typically jingoistic and xenophobic. Yet the actual content of
the text offers a powerful and subtle polemic against the myth of immigrant America. As the word "defence" in the title indicates, the book
attempts to make a historically legitimate argument in support of the
policy of excluding foreigners in general and Catholics in particular from the national polity. Whitney defends this exclusive form of
nationalism on three grounds. On a historical level, he sees the conditions that gave birth to American republicanism as making foreigners
unfit for American citizenship. Immigrants' ties to despotic powers
and oppressive regimes make them by nature anti-republican. On a
political level, Whitney claims that the Declaration of Independence
entitles everyone to certain inalienable rights, but that not everyone
is fit to enjoy them fully. The hierarchical structure of political rights

demands an unequal relation of power between the "native" and the "alien." Finally, on an economic level, he argues that "superabundant immigration from Europe" cheapens the value of labor, creating a disequilibrium between capital and labor that destroys the principles of American republicanism (308). Let us consider these arguments more closely with a view to disentangling the cultural and political contributions of nativism to the construction of national identity.

To defend his nativist demand that the nation be rid of "foreign influence," Whitney first reflects on the historical conditions that gave birth to the nation. He attributes the success of American republicanism, in contrast to the Robespierrian Republic and the Cromwellian Commonwealth, to five historical factors, all of which he borrows, interestingly, from Tocqueville's *Democracy in America*:

> Their remoteness from the parent government, whose authority was exercised more by tacit consent than by absolute dictation, so far at least as its effects were felt by the hardy populace; their exemption from the constraint of aristocratic intercourse; the local dangers by which they were surrounded and exposed, forcing upon them a community and equality of interest for mutual protection; their wild and romantic habits of life, tempered with an uniform reliance on Divine Providence; together with the innate spirit of resistance to despotic authority, inherited from their Puritan ancestors; all contributed to qualify the people of the United Colonies for a system of self-government, at the very moment which saw their national independence consummated. (17)

That is, what enabled early settlers to found an independent, democratic nation was a unique combination of historical factors. This idea of historical uniqueness embedded in the narrative of American exceptionalism, I will argue, is central to Whitney's construction of Anglo-Saxon "natives" as true, patriotic Americans and other immigrants as political dissidents. Colonial Americans' geopolitical distance from England, their lack of a hierarchical class structure, their perilous frontier life, their "romantic habits of life" as "pioneers," and their Puritanical tradition of anti-despotism made them uniquely situated as a chosen people destined to form a true democracy. As in Tocqueville, what these historical factors have in common is a general notion of community that is ambivalently articulated through both equivocation and disavowal. Whitney's history of nation building, like Tocqueville's, forgetfully vacillates between the personal and the political, the natural and the cultural. "Anglo-Saxon pioneers" were personally liberated as romantic adventurers as much as they were politically emancipated because of their distance from England; the natural environment contributed as much to their building of an independent nation as did their cultural heritage as Puritans. Also, echoing Crèvecoeur's bivalent description of colonial America as a romantic but enlightened community, Whitney represents European settlers as both romantic pioneers driven by a personal desire for autonomy and enlightened Puritans propelled by a political desire for freedom.

Whitney's historical overview of America's bivalent beginning is important to his nativist argument in two important ways. First, on a theoretical level it justifies the exclusion from the national polity of immigrants and Catholics. The historical view of America as quintessentially anti-authoritarian, borrowed from the liberal literature, supports the nativist view that Catholics and new immigrants, because of their ties to despotic powers and lack of democratic education, are not only unfit to become Americans but dangerous to democracy. As the reference to Anglo-Americans' "innate spirit of resistance to despotic authority, inherited from their Puritan ancestors," suggests, Whitney's claim is that there is something fundamentally antiauthoritarian and anti-despotic about America. Hence his policy recommendation to stop Catholics and most immigrants from coming to America: their attachments to despotic power and authoritarian regimes in their countries of origin mark them as "un-American." Later in his text, Whitney recommends that only "men of business, capital and respectability, who take little or no interest in politics" be allowed to become naturalized Americans (167).

What motivated the Know-Nothings like Whitney and Busey against Catholics was not their religion, for the American Party, following the Constitution, advocated the protection of religious opinion and worship. Rather, it was Catholics' presumed affiliation with an autocratic, hierarchical, and centralized institution that made them an anathema to American democracy and its valorization of individual rights. Whitney's anti-Catholicism is a form of republicanism grounded in non-authoritarian, popular government, an idea he shared with his liberal contemporaries like Whitman and Emerson. But Whitney uses the idea of republicanism to articulate an exclusive mode of nationalism in which immigrants play a differential role as others, inassimilable and dissident. In this sense Whitney is not ideologically different from the founding fathers who claimed that to "possess the genuine character of true Americans," one must "have no attachments or exclusive friendship for any foreign nation," though of course the historical circumstances in which he makes his argument differ from those in which the founders made theirs.[15]

Second, on a political level Whitney's overview of early Americans' historical uniqueness legitimates the view of Anglo-Saxon people as the only patriotic native Americans. His overview of the nation's beginning forgets (intentionally disavows) that the land was indeed populated with "native Americans" before the arrival of European colonizers, not to mention that colonial America was more ethnically heterogeneous than Whitney claims. This disavowal allows him to identify the political community of the nation with the Anglo-Saxon race. Although race is not explicitly mentioned in the factors that he enumerates, it is clearly central to his historical understanding of American national identity. What enabled colonial Americans to form an independent nation, according to Whitney, was their unique situation as a homogeneous community of equals whose anti-authoritative spirit "qualified" them "for the grand experiment of a popular government" (17). Like Tocqueville, he maintains that there was something personally and culturally "exceptional" about Anglo-Saxon Americans that made them the founders and true patriotic subjects of the American nation. Their anti-authoritarian personality, their romantic adventurism, and the anti-despotism of their Puritan culture made them a superior race, ready to enjoy a life of liberty and equality. The category of the "native" is obviously a racial term, in the sense that it identifies Americans differentially and exclusively with the Anglo-Saxon ethnicity. But the biological notion of the Anglo-Saxon race is culturally constructed in Whitney's text. Anglo-Saxon Americans constitute a superior race because their Puritan heritage made them defy despotic powers and their "romantic habits of life" made them rebel against a hierarchical and oppressive England.

To elaborate his hierarchical and differential distinction between the patriotic native and the dissident alien, and to further substantiate his policy of denying naturalization to foreigners, Whitney next returns to the foundational text of American republicanism, the Declaration of Independence. In chapter 4, he interprets the most important statements of this document, namely "That all men are created equal; That they are endowed by their Creator with certain inalienable rights, among which are Life, Liberty, and the pursuit of happiness." Whitney begins by claiming that we must go beyond "the simple letter of the text" and try to understand what the framers of the Declaration truly meant by the general principle of equality and the inalienable rights of the individual (43). He argues that equality and the inalienable rights of life, liberty, and the pursuit of happiness are general principles that must be qualified according to individuals' "moral, political, and social capacities" (42). That "men are *created* on a moral, political, and social equality," in other words, does not mean that everyone will have equal opportunity in life, because the inequality of people's "intellectual faculties" and cultural heritage positions them unequally in society (42). "Men," Whitney argues, "are created equal in all natural, social and political rights, and those rights are to be enjoyed and exercised in proportion to the natural social and political faculties of the individual" (49). The principle of equality, in short, is unevenly accessible because of individuals' unequal faculties.

Similarly, Whitney qualifies the fundamental principle of liberty. Liberty, by which he means "the liberty of conscience, the liberty of opinion on all subjects" and "the unabridged right to speak, proclaim, write, and publish whatever sentiments the individual may entertain, whether in politics, religion, or ethics," is an inalienable political right (45–46). This inalienable right, he argues however, was not meant by the framers of the Constitution "to promulgate the idea that all men possess the irrefragable right to do as they please at all times, and under all circumstances" (46). Liberty, like equality, is hierarchically afforded according to the intellectual and social faculties of the individual. Although everyone is entitled to this inalienable right, not everyone is fit to enjoy it fully. One is afforded by the Declaration "the enjoyment of intellectual freedom, and political and social equality to the extent of [one's] capacity and adaptedness or fitness" as an individual (47).

The notions of "capacity" and "fitness," tacitly cast in racialized terms, are paramount to an understanding of Whitney's political theory, since they determine the individual's access to citizenship and political representation. What makes non-Nordic immigrants unfit to become naturalized citizens of the United States, which would endow them with the inalienable rights of life, liberty, and the pursuit of happiness, is their cultural unadaptability on the one hand and their political inferiority on the other. Since they are "taught by sad experience to regard the rulers of their native land as tyrants, they do not realize the possibility of a government of equal and liberal laws," Whitney argues (179). But the permissive immigration and naturalization laws of the United States furnish immigrants with "more liberty than they are capable of 'enjoying and employing rationally' " (179). The immigrants' inability to adapt to the political principles of American republicanism creates social disorder. Because the differences in people's intellectual capacities create a hierarchical social structure in which political power is unevenly distributed, the large presence of "unprepared aliens" disrupts the nation's unity and corrupts its political principles.

It is the immigrants' lack of intellectual, cultural, and political qualifications that tilts Whitney against lax immigration and naturalization laws. "To believe," he points out, "that a mass so crude and incongruous, so remote from the spirit, the ideas, and the customs of America, can be made to harmonize readily with the new element into which it is cast, is, to say the least, *unnatural*" (165; emphasis in original). Whitney therefore considers it "an important duty on the part of the statesman, to encourage all that pertains to unity of character and custom, and to discountenance every influence that tends to produce the opposite results" (69). That in the United States "the conflict of individual character and custom is kept so constantly active by an unceasing and multifarious emigration" makes this duty particularly imperative (69).

Immigrants disturb not only the nation's cultural and political homogeneity but also its economic equilibrium. Claiming that "no feature of political economy [is] more deserving [of] the careful consideration of the statesman than that of immigration," Whitney devotes a large part of his text to the economic consequences of lenient immigration and naturalization laws (164). To justify the exclusion of foreigners on economic grounds, he first historicizes the rationale behind the nation's liberal immigration policy:

The United States, in the early history of their government and nationality, adopted a more liberal policy, a policy corresponding with the necessities of an infant nation. The territory of the new government was vast and fertile, and its population comparatively trifling, and utterly inadequate to the natural resources of its domain, and the requirements of a young, but vigorous independency. Under such circumstances, it was a wise stroke of policy to encourage a healthy immigration. . . . The

primary effect of this law was rapid immigration from the most valuable classes of Europeans; men, who brought with them respectability,
intellect, industry, and capital, and whose presence was an immediate
and valuable acquisition to the *morale* and the *material* of the country.
(145; emphasis in original)

In this passage Whitney, like the liberal Jefferson, acknowledges the
immigrant character of the nation and remembers that the natives
were once immigrants themselves. But this acknowledgment does not
lead to mythologizing the nation as a free asylum open to the oppressed humanity of the globe, as it does in liberal thinkers and politicians like Jefferson, Whitman, Handlin, and Kennedy. Unlike the liberal discourses of immigration, Whitney's text does not discount the
real reasons behind the nation's encouragement of immigration, which
are the economic need for labor and the political desire to appropriate new territories. What he does mythologize, however, is the social
class of early immigrants as well as their democratic roots. In addition to denying that early European immigration to the United States
was mostly motivated by economic necessity, as Handlin convincingly
demonstrated in *The Uprooted*, he fails to remember the "despotic"
structure of power in Britain, from which the Anglo-Saxons migrated.
Forgetting that a large number of early European immigrants were
indentured workers, brought to the country as cheap labor, Whitney
mystifies the earlier economic refugees as valuable immigrants whose
"respectability, intellect, industry, and capital" helped "the morale
and the material of the country." In this way he too engages in a monumentalizing form of historiography that blurs the differences of motives and instigations among founders and overlooks much of the nation's past.

Whitney's mystification or disavowal of early European immigrants'
social class enables him in turn to make a distinction between "old"
and "new" immigrants, a differential mode of national identification
that continues to this day, I would argue, to dominate the discourse
of immigration in the United States (see chapter 5). In Whitney's binary logic the "old" immigrants are represented as intelligent, indus-
trious, and wealthy, while the "new" immigrants are crude, unskilled,
and poor. The distinction between "old" and "new" immigrants provides Whitney with the economic rationale to claim that the liberal
policy of immigration is "suicidal in the present attitude and condition

of the United States" (148–49). By "present attitude and condition of the United States," he is referring to two pressing issues. First is the political problem of national homogeneity. The "unfitness" of immigrants for the political culture of the United States, combined with their power as a large mass, makes them "dangerous to the national identity" (150). "The intellectual character of the great mass of immigrants who have, for several years past, come to the United States from foreign lands," Whitney claims, "is not adapted to the political duties of the citizen, and liable, if vested with full political rights, to subvert rather than strengthen our institutions of civil and religious liberty" (149). Naturalization, he argues, cannot provide the immigrant with the cultural capital and political intelligence necessary to becoming a citizen with political privileges and duties. This is why Whitney calls naturalization the most "unnatural" practice. But because of permissive immigration and naturalization laws, foreigners are given rights and privileges that they are not ready to enjoy. The large number of "unqualified" citizens, according to him, has disrupted the nation's social equilibrium, thus depriving the average Anglo-Saxon citizen of his or her inalienable rights.

Second is the economic factor of supply and demand. Whitney argues, not entirely unjustifiably, that "the necessity for a rapid increase of population has passed away," yet the number of immigrants has greatly increased in recent years (149). The large supply of immigrants and the low demand for them in the United States create an economic imbalance that can only be remedied by a more restrictive immigration policy. Whitney elaborates this point in chapter 14, in which he discusses "the effects of the competition of immigrant labor on the industrial interests of the United States" (306). Unlike his European counterpart, the average American worker, he maintains, has traditionally been able to occupy an important position in society, since the "dignity of labor" is recognized in the United States and the nation's social structure is meritocratic—Whitney can of course make this statement only by ignoring slave and indentured labor. But, he further argues, the competition of immigrant labor has pushed the American laborer from "his rights and high social position" by cheapening the value of labor (307). The effect of this devaluation has been to benefit what Whitney calls "the aristocracy of wealth" in America, a social class "which is the worst of all aristocracies" (311). By "aristocracy of wealth" he means the great capitalists and industrialists who benefited from the exploitation of cheap immigrant labor. "The effect of excessive cheap labor," Whitney correctly observes, "is to aggrandize capital" (311). The excess of cheap immigrant labor in the 1840s forced the average worker out of his job, making him "seek subsistence on the broad prairies of the far West—to build his house in the wilderness, and endure the hardships of a pioneer life" (310).

Whitney may seem dramatic in his representation of the white American worker's fate, but the point he makes about the effects of excessive cheap labor is potentially a radical critique of industrial capitalism in the mid-nineteenth century. Radical, I mean, because unlike the liberal discourse of immigration in America, his discourse exposes the self-interested intention of those who advocated lax immigration and naturalization laws. In the liberal discourse of immigration, the capitalist need for cheap labor is often deceptively couched as benevolence toward the oppressed, in disregard of the economics of immigration that belie the myth of hospitality. Since the nation's social "equilibrium is destroyed" by the antagonism between capital and labor resulting from cheap immigrant labor, the problem ultimately destroys the political foundations of American republicanism, according to Whitney. The effect of "excessive immigration of the poor of Europe," he observes, "is to promote *caste*, and stimulate a puerile aristocratic taste among the rich," a taste that runs contrary to republican "sentiment" (311; emphasis in original). Whitney's argument brings into the open the duplicity of the liberal discourse of immigration by demonstrating how the myth of immigrant America serves, in reality, the interests of the capitalist class. It increases their wealth, while creating social divisions that deny to the average American his inalienable rights.

Whitney concludes his conservative argument against the nation's open immigration policy with a curiously liberal remark: that the question raised by his "native American" policy is "a question of *humanity* in the true sense of that word," since Whitney's Native American Party sought not only "the physical emancipation of a few blacks, but the political and moral freedom of the whole human race" (326). This remark may seem contradictory, if not duplicitous, given the exclusionary and differential form of national identity that Whitney posits throughout his text. But the remark appears more consistent with his political ideology when read in the context of his historical, political, and economic discussions of American republicanism. Whitney's concluding remark suggests that nativism as a political ideology does not contradict the liberal myth of immigrant America but is rather a repressed component of its formation. True, American historians have often described mid-nineteenth-century nativism as the ideological opposite of liberal America, an exception in the history of an immigrant-loving nation. But Whitney's historical, political, and economic arguments against the nation's lax immigration policy demonstrate the productive function of nativism in the liberal discourse of immigration. I say productive because, as I have noted, the nativist movement introduced a politically volatile distinction between old and new immigrants which legitimated the unequal and differential relation between the "native" and the "alien," between citizen and immigrant. This nativist distinction has been the covert theoretical underpinning of the liberal discourse of immigration. It has supplied liberal America with the political rationale to justify assimilation, or to deny cultural heterogeneity, in spite of claiming a pluralistic view of national identity. The binary logic of native and alien settles the contradiction in the liberal discourse of immigrant America between its claim of a pluralistic view of American nationality and its expectation that new immigrants must shed their cultural and ideological differences to become Americans. The liberal and nativist discourses of immigration, in sum, are cut from similar cloth, for they both stem from the desire to create a homogeneous America and rely on a differential mode of cultural identification.

The (Pseudo-)Science of Nativism

In an article published in 1902 entitled "Immigration's Menace to the National Health," the commissioner general of immigration, Terence Powderly, warned the nation about dangerous diseases brought into the country by "new" immigrants: "If we remain indifferent simply because these diseases do not prove fatal to life, we evade our duty; for the health of the nation is imperilled while one man is diseased. The old cry, 'America is the asylum of the oppressed of the world,' is too threadbare to withstand the assault of disease. There is a danger that the oppressed may, through the burdens they fasten on others, become oppressors. At any rate, there exists no reason why the United States should become the hospital of the nations of earth, even though it does afford an asylum for those who come here to escape oppression."[16]

This alarmist statement brings into relief a new form of nativism concerned about the health, not the ideology, of newcomers, a concern that foregrounds the shift from focusing on immigrants' minds to focusing on their bodies. The problem with new immigration, according to Powderly, was not political dissidence but physical contamination. The nation's powerful myth of asylum, he remarked, had unwittingly transformed the hospitable United States into the world's hospital, a place where every nation sent its feeble and diseased citizens. Like most nativists of the late nineteenth century and the early twentieth, Powderly relied on a form of disavowal marked by retreat from truth to omnipotence, blaming the new immigrants, "the tide of immigration . . . from the countries of southern Europe and the Orient" for the spread of "loathsome" and contagious diseases, among which he specifically named favus, a dermatological disease of the scalp, and trachoma, a chronic eye infection caused by chlamydia. The new immigrant was once again differentially marked as the "other" of the "native," but this time it was the newcomer's body, not his or her political ideology, that became the sign of alterity. The foreign threat was to the nation's health, not its political system. Unlike the supposedly healthy immigrants of the early and middle decades of the nineteenth century—"the sturdy Englishman, Irishman, Scotchman, Welshman, German and north countryman who came strong in limb and pure in blood"—Powderly claimed that the newcomers were both physically and mentally unfit to become American citizens (53). Ignoring that the "old" immigrants he idealized were once the unwanted "new" immigrants, he went on to predict that unless the government curbed the arrival of new immigrants, future generations of Americans would be made "hairless and sightless" by the spread of favus and trachoma (60).

The commissioner's foreboding remarks, I argue, mark a decisive shift in the discourse of nativism from politics to medicine, from ideology to health.[17] As I suggested above, until the late nineteenth century opposition toward immigrants was mostly articulated in political and economic terms. While some claimed that the affiliation of "aliens" with despotic European powers threatened national security and undermined the foundations of American republicanism, others emphasized that immigrants increased the nation's burdens of pauperism and crime. Even when the immigrants' ill health was mentioned, say in the case of the Irish in Massachusetts, it was seen not as an inherent characteristic of the immigrants but as the effect of "the very wretched, dirty, and unhealthy condition of a great number of the dwelling houses" that they occupied.[18] The issue of health, therefore, was never a reason for excluding new immigrants. But in the late nineteenth century there emerged a pseudo-scientific approach to excluding the new immigrant that led to the labeling of the newcomer as a figure of physical contamination. Whereas in the discourse of mid-nineteenth-century nativism the immigrant was a political dissident threatening the ideological foundations of the republic, in the late nineteenth century he or she became the polluter, endangering the physical health of the nation by bringing into the country dangerous germs and bad genes.[19] As Powderly claimed, the immigrant's "menace to the national health," not his or her subversive political ideology, would "oppress" America and its children.

This shift in the discourse of nativism from ideology to health was enabled by the changes in the field of medicine. The ascendancy and influence of medical discourse in the late nineteenth century, as historians of medicine have demonstrated, was largely due to the consolidation of the medical profession and the radical changes that had occurred in the science of medicine itself.[20] Until then there had been various and competing schools of medicine, and no group of doctors could claim a "clear therapeutic superiority" over others, as Elizabeth Yew has remarked.[21] But with the development of germ theory and the discovery of bacteria as the cause of infectious diseases (by Louis Pasteur in France and Robert Koch in Germany during the second half of the nineteenth century), the discourse and profession of medicine gained tremendous authority in the United States and became a significant factor in the nation's immigration policy. The advance of germ theory and the bacteriological revolution ended the reign of competing schools of medicine and the notion of "medical freedom." People could no longer choose the course of their medical treatments, as health became a public issue to be controlled and regulated by medical experts.[22] The medical breakthroughs of the late nineteenth century helped the new physicians to claim exclusive therapeutic power, as a unitary theory of disease authorized them to become the legitimate and monopolistic protectors of national health. Doctors, as one public health official remarked, represented the "essence of the newer patriotism" because they defended the nation against such mortal enemies as typhoid and tuberculosis, cholera and leprosy, diphtheria and malaria.[23]

The physicians of the U.S. Public Health Service (USPHS),[24] trained

in German and Viennese hospitals, were the first and most significant segment of the American medical establishment to embrace germ
theory and bacteriology enthusiastically.[25] Buoyed by the Progressive
movement, which advocated a more interventionist and bureaucratic
government, and discursively enabled by new scientific discoveries that
authorized them as medical experts, this small group of physicians was
in a unique position to advocate measures that would conserve human
life and natural resources. Under the new leadership of Dr. Walter
Wyman, a highly dedicated and efficient surgeon general who took
command in 1891, the doctors of USPHS were not just healers who
cured illnesses but hygienists who reformed the administrative system
of health and maintained the physical well-being of the social body.
They were medical authorities who studied and cured diseases, and
also political experts who proselytized and wrote on the broader social implications of public health and hygiene. It was the "scientific"
writings of these experts, I suggest, that eventually led to the exclusionary quota laws of 1921 and 1924, as a result of which the flow of
immigration from eastern and southern Europe to the United States
nearly ceased.

Given the scientific power of these doctors, it is not surprising that
the issue of immigration should have become the central locus of
the nation's war against harmful germs, dangerous bacteria, and bad
genes.[26] As the fear of contagious diseases and a concern about "national eugenics"[27] entered the public debate, the question of whom to
admit became a volatile political issue, forcing the federal government
to regulate and control immigration. In 1891 Congress for the first
time passed an immigration law that excluded any immigrant "suffering from a loathsome or a dangerous contagious disease," a law signaling the new nativists' assumption that dangerous germs and bacteria were brought from abroad by new immigrants. The category of
"loathsome" is suggestive, because it is an unscientific term that can
be applied to just about any pathology. Among the other categories of
exclusion were the "feeble-minded," "idiots," and the "insane," categories, as I will show later, that reflect a concern about the negative
effect of new immigration on national eugenics.

The law charged the physicians of the USPHS with the responsibility
of inspecting the physical and mental health of new immigrants so as
to determine their eligibility for landing, a responsibility that transformed the public health official into the nation's gatekeeper. A certifi-

cate of health became the primary requirement for landing. At every port of entry, doctors first observed immigrants for any sign of physical or mental deformity and disease, and decided whether they were physically healthy and mentally fit enough to not become a "public charge" upon landing. Then the doctors subjected every immigrant of the steerage class[28] to a painful eye examination by rolling back his or her eyelids with a metal buttonhook to check for trachoma. More specialized doctors further investigated those suspected of an illness or disability in private examination rooms. In Ellis Island the "line" doctors would chalk the back of the suspected immigrant's clothing with letters, each indicating an abnormality worthy of further investigation. Writing in this way on the body (or clothes) "thingified" the subject, reducing him or her to a commodity devoid of human agency. In a disquieting way, the examination of new arrivals also resembled the selection of enslaved people by plantation owners who looked for strong and healthy slaves to maximize their profit, a resemblance that is obviously repressed in the new discourse of health.

Having empowered themselves as patriotic protectors of national health, the physicians used immigration stations like Ellis Island and Angel Island as laboratories where they tested new drugs and medications, experimented with new diagnostic and therapeutic techniques, and developed more efficient and effective medical inspection procedures, all in the name of safeguarding the nation against contagious diseases from abroad. In the Ellis Island station, for example, a large hospital and a quarantine facility employed doctors of the USPHS as physicians and researchers: there they could develop and refine their diagnosis and treatment of various bacteriological diseases. These doctors also tried to develop and refine the best methods of examining new immigrants. At Ellis Island, the nation's public health officials "put to the test" new methods of medical and mental examination and "modified [them] in the light of experience" to be used at other ports of entry, as one doctor wrote (Reed, "Immigration and the Public Health," 328–29). These doctors assumed "the first line of defence" against infectious diseases, and also used their medical expertise to proselytize about the nation's immigration policy (336). The medical and popular journals of the early twentieth century are filled with articles by USPHS physicians who criticized the nation's open-door policy of immigration for medical reasons.

One of the most prolific and opinionated of these writers was Alfred C. Reed, who worked at the Ellis Island station during the peak immigration years of the early twentieth century. His articles, mostly published in the *Popular Science Monthly*, offer valuable insight into the central role that medicine played in ending the open-door era. Reed, who viewed Ellis Island as "an experimental station in the mental and physical examination of immigrants," used his knowledge as a doctor and experience as a medical inspector to convince the public and the federal government of the danger of a lenient immigration policy, while at the same time, of course, using his warning to authorize himself as a doctor (329). In every article he warned the nation about the danger of contagious diseases and inferior genes pouring into the country from abroad. Like Powderly, he claimed that unless better and more thorough methods of medical inspection were instituted at various ports of entry, the physical, mental, and social health of the nation would be fundamentally jeopardized.

For Reed medicine was not just a profession but the essence of a new form of patriotism. In an article entitled "Immigration and Public Health," he described the medical work of the nation's public health officials as heroic, demanding that the average citizen become a supporter and a participant in the patriotic task of creating a "cleaner and better America." Let me quote his remarks at length to demonstrate the significant role that physicians like him played in defining a new form of nativism based on pseudo-scientific claims:

> Truly it is sweet to die for one's country. But even in the battles of peace the need of this sacrifice is rare. Greater is the need and grander the opportunity to live for one's country, and wage war against the powers of ignorance, indifference, disease and degeneracy. And this is the essence of the newer patriotism, which in no way removes or lessens the ancient duty of defending the land and honor of one's country, but at once idealizes and transcends that duty. If this be true, it follows that the man who is awake to his civic responsibility and who appreciates the honor of his American heritage will be in hearty sympathy with all agencies engaged in this distinctly modern line of endeavor. He will take part in, and aid to his utmost ability, those influences making for a cleaner and better America, because he realizes that this is not only his opportunity but his patriotic duty. (314)

This passage points to a historical shift in the meaning of patriotism: from lives sacrificed to lives saved. Patriotism is no longer "measured in terms of human life sacrificed" or "weighed in the balance of territorial or financial advantage." Rather, in the modern world the true patriotic citizens are those who "fight the more terrible foes of ignorance, disease and public wrong." The new form of patriotism transcends the old one because in an age of newly discovered bacteria, it is disease and not political ideology that threatens the health of the nation. Medicine and hygiene constitute the essence of this newer form of patriotism, the differential markers that separate the citizen from the "alien," the native self from the immigrant other. The binary opposition between citizen and alien takes an *embodied*, as opposed to ideological, form. Given this historical shift, the truly patriotic citizen must participate and aid agencies such as the USPHS in their effort to make, in Reed's words, a cleaner and better America. Helping public officials in their fight against disease is every American's civic responsibility and patriotic duty. Reed's remarks echo Powderly's admonition that "every citizen should do his part, use his influence, to safeguard the homes of the poor of the United States against disease from abroad" (60). The discourse of health, as I will argue later, conduces to an exclusive form of national identity marked by vigilantism, for it mobilizes every citizen in the battle against disease and degeneracy and does so by scientifically legitimating the binary of us and them. In depicting immigrants as infected and impaired, the new discourse of nativism at once shores up vigilantism and normalizes—indeed boosts—the state's disciplinary practices as patriotism.

Reed's observations, moreover, underscore how the medical profession provided nativism with the "objective" or "scientific" criteria needed to fight the nation's loose immigration laws. At least on the surface, what made new nativists like Reed and Powderly critical of the new wave of immigration was public health, not xenophobia. In another article, "The Medical Side of Immigration," Reed even embraced the myth of immigrant America, acknowledging in a celebratory fashion that "the history of the United States is the history of alien immigration," and that "the earliest pioneers were themselves alien immigrants" (383). Unlike the mid-nineteenth-century nativist, the medical reformist of the late nineteenth century was not against immigration *tout court*. But he used his experience as a physician at Ellis Island to argue against the "tide" of *new* immigration, claiming that his anti-alien sentiment was not directed against immigrants but sprang from a rational concern about the health of the nation. The issue of public health helped new nativists like him to posit and defend an exclusive and differential form of national identity on "objective" grounds. More importantly, concern over public health compelled the average citizen to become a health vigilante, participating in the medical battle against the foreign threats of disease and degeneracy, as both Reed and Powderly suggested in their writings. "Immigration's menace to the national health," in other words, was productive of a disciplinary power exercised over both the citizen and the immigrant. While the body of the immigrant was examined, labeled, marked, and disciplined, the citizen was forced to interiorize the disciplinary system and participate in it as a vigilante.[29]

Reed's notion of patriotism was not limited to barricading against the physical ill health of new immigrants. Even more important, he went on to elaborate, was the battle against the mental disorders of new immigrants. The threat of new immigrants' mental illnesses was particularly urgent, because whereas "acute diseases" could be "easily recognized," "the detection and diagnosis of mental conditions in immigrants [was] a matter of exceeding difficulty" (318, 329). In a typically disavowing discourse that blamed the immigrant for the nation's ills, Reed claimed that there was an "intimate relation . . . between immigration and the prevalence and increase of insanity and mental defectiveness in the United States" (326). He cited the works of other physicians, H. M. Friedman, H. H. Goddard, and T. W. Salmon, to prove his claim that "the alien population of the United States [was] furnishing considerably more than its proportionate number of feebleminded and insane persons" (325). Noting that "more than four fifths of the immigrants entering the United States come from southern and southeastern Europe," he argued that new immigrants had a "racial tendency toward . . . mental instability and predisposition to a neurotic and psychopathic constitution" (321, 325). The fight against "mental impairment," according to Reed, was "absolutely essential in order to conserve our national mental health and to ensure a normal mentality to coming generations" (327). Just as favus and trachoma would make the future generation of Americans hairless and sightless, the "inferior" mental condition of new immigrants would "result in the transmission of hereditary taint or predisposition or actual disease to posterity" (319). What was at stake for Reed was the negative "eugenic aspect" of new immigration (317). Racially "inferior" immigrants from eastern and southern Europe transmitted "a tainted heredity or actual mental disease to [their] descendants," eventually rendering the native population less intelligent and more prone to mental retardation (325).

To drive home his point about the long-term effects of new immigrants' mental disorders, Reed gave the alarming example of one "Englishman of good ancestry who contracted an illegitimate union with a feeble-minded girl" (325). From this union descended 480 persons of whom "36 were illegitimate, 24 were chronic alcoholics, 3 were epileptics, 33 were immoral, 8 kept houses of ill-fame and 3 were criminals; [and] 143 were feeble-minded" (325). Reed used this pseudo-empirical example to argue that new immigrants' "bad" genes profoundly affected the "social health" of the nation, because "the mentally diseased and defective" were "predisposed to crime" and tended to reproduce a "large class of morally defective children and border-line types" (325). Bad genes associated with certain racial categories therefore had negative social and ethical consequences. But equally important was the economic burden of unhealthy immigrants. Mental and physical ill health in the new immigrant, Reed argued, "decreased his productivity and power of self-support, consequently laying an additional and undeserved burden on the rest of the community" (319).

My aim in critically reading Reed's discussion about "the medical side of immigration" has not been to claim that the United States should have allowed every diseased person into the country. Reed was right to make the policy recommendation that for the sake of "self-preservation," it was "absolutely essential to exclude unsound immigrants" (338). Nor is my goal to repudiate entirely his claim that many new immigrants at the turn of the century were indeed unhealthy, laying an "undeserved" economic burden on the nation as a whole. As the historian of medicine Alan Kraut also acknowledges, "immigrants can be and, from time to time, have been the bearers of diseases harmful or even fatal to the native-born population" (9). Rather my point is to draw attention to how medicine proved central in perpetuating an exclusive form of national identity that was at once *forgetful* and *disciplinary*.[30] Let me elaborate these terms by way of concluding my remarks about early-twentieth-century nativism.

As in the writing of mid-nineteenth-century nativists like Whitney, Reed's progressive discourse of medicine adopted a form of historical denial marked by retreat from truth to omnipotence and assumed a binary distinction between the "native," or "old" immigrant, and the "alien," or new immigrant, a distinction that is possible only through an act of forgetting. The new nativist discourse of health disavows historical facts: that the white man's contagious diseases such as smallpox, syphilis, typhus, and yellow fever killed half the indigenous population of the New World,[31] and that the more recent epidemics of cholera were brought into the East Coast ports in the 1830s by the "old" immigrants whom Reed and Powderly valorized as healthy and able.[32] Reed completely represses the ample evidence that epidemic diseases brought by earlier European immigrants had caused similar alarmist responses in the late eighteenth century and the early nineteenth. The forgetting of the history of disease in America helped the new nativism to blame immigrants for the nation's ills by construing the body of the new immigrant once again as "other," the differential marker of all that stands in opposition to being American.

The cultural construction of the new immigrant as diseased was politically productive in that it necessitated a disciplinary approach to immigration. The war against disease now helped to create a powerful apparatus of medicalized control at the nation's ports of entry, where every underclass immigrant was subjected to examination and discipline. The medicalization of immigration control made the nation's "gateway" into a cross between a hospital and a prison, institutions that create and perpetuate the disciplinary system of power, as Michel Foucault has demonstrated. In his article "Going through Ellis Island," Reed referred to Ellis Island as "the immigration plant," where "there is system, silent, watchful, swift, efficient," words that closely echo the description of the panoptic prison system's disciplinary apparatus.[33] The diseased immigrant constituted an object for medical knowledge and as such was transformed into a "hold" for the exercise of disciplinary power—that some immigrants are physically unhealthy or mentally feeble does not necessitate the casting of "the immigrant" as diseased and inferior. The perception of the immigrant as diseased legitimated the federal government's disciplinary practices at the nation's ports of entry. The management of the so-called crisis of health made the state's disciplining of aliens, the multiplication of its regulatory strategies and techniques of coercion, a necessary and legitimate assertion of political sovereignty—having been refined and perfected since then, these strategies and techniques are utilized at every port of entry to this day (see chapter 5).

At the same time, the figure of the diseased immigrant is also useful in manufacturing a permanent "state of emergency" that perpetuates an exclusive and differential form of national identity. In the discourse of new nativists like Reed and Powderly, the embodied binary relation between the healthy "native" and the diseased "alien" is construed in terms of a national crisis—thus enabling at once their self-authorization and their nativist agenda. Both officials warned the nation about the immediate and permanent effects of illness on the nation and its social body, claiming that "every advance of loathsome, dangerous or contagious disease should be challenged at sea coast and border line" to prevent the republic from becoming another "dead empire" (Powderly, "Immigration's Menace to the National Health," 60). The fight against disease, commonsensical though it was, played a vital role in normalizing the exercise of disciplinary power over the alien by construing its exercise as a national duty. The medicalized discourse of immigration control in the early twentieth century points to the usefulness of reifying "immigration's menace to the national health," because doing so facilitates the production of a national consensus about political power and citizenship. Seeing the immigrant as posing a threat to the nation's health helped to create a simulated civil war in which the citizen and the imagined community of the nation willingly participated in the state's politics of exclusion. As such, it transformed every citizen into a vigilante and participant in the exercise of disciplinary power. Health, in short, became a national duty, defining the border between the "native" and the "alien," the citizen and the immigrant.

Uses of Aliens: Nativism and the Ritual of Self-Purification

Scholars of contemporary nativism have located the roots of today's anti-immigrant sentiment in the United States at the beginning of the nineteenth century. Joe Feagin, for example, has argued that "contemporary attacks on immigrants do not represent a new social phenomenon with no connection to past events. Anti-immigrant nativism in North America is at least two centuries old."[34] The critics of new nativism cite four common themes running throughout the discourse of nativism to prove that new nativism is "old poison in new bottles," to borrow the title of Feagin's essay: the new immigrants are racially and culturally inferior; they are not willing or able to assimilate to the dominant culture; they are taking jobs from the "natives"; and they create political crises that the government must deal with. Although these scholars are right in arguing that "certain essential components of nativism remain more or less constant," their "monolithic" and unchanging view of nativism misses the important role played by historical shifts that enable the renewal and perpetuation of the structure of denial and the binary logic upon which American cultural identity is founded. As I have suggested in my contrapuntal reading of the mid-nineteenth century and the early twentieth, important historical shifts in the discourse of nativism transform how the anti-immigrant sentiment is articulated to fashion a homogeneous imagined community. While the general binary of native and immigrant remains constant throughout the discourse of nativism, what guarantees the longevity of this exclusionary mode of national identification are the new ways in which distinctions are made between "us" and "them," as well as between new and old immigrants. The shift from an ideological and political form of nativism in the mid-nineteenth century to a medical and embodied mode of nativism in the late nineteenth century and the early twentieth, for example, inaugurated a new phase in the nation's discourse of exclusion that gave scientific authority to racist views of new immigrants. Whereas in the political discourse of Know-Nothings the figure of the immigrant is represented as a social deviant who disrupts the nation's polity by cheapening the worth of labor and weakening the country's democratic institutions, the turn-of-the-century nativists manufactured a pseudo-scientific discourse of otherness that made the newcomer a medical and genetic threat to society.

In addition, the works of medical doctors and public health officials at the nation's gateways such as Ellis Island and Angel Island introduced a eugenic perspective into the discourse of exclusion, one that made race an essential component of the national identity. A racialized framework borrowed from European colonialism has existed in the United States since its very inception, as historians of nativism have already demonstrated, but what distinguishes turn-of-the-century nativism is the scientific authority that made the exclusion of certain races appear to be a rational project. The shift toward a pseudo-scientific form of racism enabled both a normalized form of cultural identity and a restrictive approach to immigration by the state. On the one hand the sciences of biology, medicine, anthropology, and eugenics gave ample ammunition to racial ideologues of the early twentieth century, such as Madison Grant and Kenneth Roberts, to justify their claims about the superiority of the "Nordic" race and the danger of mongrelization that the new immigrant posed. In the popular discourse of these nativists, racial biology displaced racist ideology, thus perpetuating the binary opposition of native and immigrant by normalizing it as an "objective" fact.

On the other hand, the scientific nativism of the turn of the century played a crucial role in inaugurating new immigration policies through which restrictive laws to curtail immigration were racially articulated. Until 1899 the Bureau of Immigration had no racial system of categorization to classify newcomers; it divided and recorded immigrants only by country of birth. But as the debate over the racial inferiority of new immigrants from southern and eastern European countries generated scientific "facts," the government started categorizing new arrivals according to race and ethnicity. By 1911 the Committee on Immigration, led by Senator William Dillingham, produced the *Dictionary of Races or Peoples*,[35] to give immigration officers a reliable source of information for help in uniformly classifying new immigrants and also to provide the government with what it called a "better understanding of the many different racial elements that were being added to the population of the United States through immigration" (2). The introduction of "race" into the nation's discourses and policies of immigration provided the political impetus for the state to adopt a racial policy of immigration in the early twentieth century. From 1907 to 1910 Dillingham led the U.S. Immigration Commission, which recommended a new restrictive technique to reduce the number of "unwanted" immigrants: using quota laws to limit the number of immigrants from each ethnic category based on the number of its natives already resident in the United States before 1890—that is, before the arrival of southern and eastern Europeans. These recommendations were written into law in 1921 and 1924 with the passage of the quota acts,[36] which gave official sanction to the claim that new immigrants were racially inferior people who posed a genetic and medical threat to the nation, and remained in effect until 1965.

Nativism and the discourses that its advocates have produced are often viewed as aberrations in the history of an immigrant-loving America. This view obscures the formative role that xenophobia plays in defining citizenship and cultural identity in the United States. American nationalism has always embodied a nativist or anti-foreign component in its manufacturing of an imagined sense of community. Nativism provides the modern nation with a "ritual of purification," through which cultural, social, or political crises are contained and resolved.[37] The binary logic explicit in every nativist claim is always constructed in terms of a national crisis. The immigrant other always threatens the foundation of the American polity, creating a state of national emergency that can only be overcome through more rigid regulation and control of the nation's border. Xenophobia is therefore productive in manufacturing a national consensus against free and nondiscriminatory immigration. The redundancy of nativist claims about the menace of new immigrants demands a conception of immigration history in keeping with Walter Benjamin's insight that "the 'state of emergency' in which we live is not the exception but the rule."[38] The so-called crisis of immigration is neither a historical exception nor a series of cyclical eruptions of a unique disorder. Rather, the state of siege is the rule of the narrative of American nationalism: it is what legitimates national pride and state power. The repeated scapegoating of immigrants in the United States as a discourse of denial marked by a retreat from truth to omnipotence, though perpetuated in each instance by different historical conditions, and articulated at every point in new terms, underscores the productivity of immigration crises in imagining a nation-state. The perpetual threat of new immigrants reinscribes a notion of difference on the national community, a difference that must be constantly maintained to propagate a space of contestation where concepts of nationality as citizenship and state as sovereignty can be rearticulated and reaffirmed. The crisis of immigration manufactured by discourses and practices of nativism, in sum, awakens the community to self-consciousness as a nation, while legitimating the disciplinary power of the state apparatus.

5

Practices of Exclusion

National Borders and the Disciplining of Aliens

One cold Sunday afternoon during the Gulf War, long before the terrorist attacks of 9/11 normalized the state's disciplinary practices throughout the nation's airports and other ports of entry, I was returning from Montreal to Rochester, New York, a trip that would take me across the border with Canada outside Watertown, New York. Still savoring the pleasant weekend I had spent with an exile friend—himself on intimate terms with the ins and outs of immigration control—I did not think ahead to the violent experience of the border, the place where I had always felt the power of immigration laws over my body and mind. It was therefore with a sense of cool forgetfulness, gingerly holding my newly acquired Resident Alien Card in my hand, that I encountered the primary inspector, who upon briefly examining my papers sent me in for secondary inspection.[1] Once inside the institutional space, which was covered with disciplinary warnings and posters that made me even more vigilant and apprehensive about the dangers of transgressing the immigration law, I could not but remember all my traumatic experiences at the border—the first time I arrived in New York City, alone, as a boy of seventeen, unable to communicate much with the inspector; or the time I had been kept in a claustrophobic room and strip-searched in the Detroit airport; or the time when I had to discuss my love life with an agent at the Niagara borderline because he could not understand how I could be traveling with a female friend while carrying a probationary "green card" that meant I was married.

That Sunday, the secondary inspection for me, a Middle Eastern "subject," consisted of being asked to stay inside the station and hand over the keys to my car to the inspector so that it could be inspected. For what? I wondered. Guns, bombs? What else could they expect to find in the car of a Middle Eastern man? While waiting, I distracted myself by watching the inspections of others, perhaps to comfort myself that I was not alone and that others had it even harder. Two blond agents were body-searching a group of African American youths (for drugs?); soon after, another Middle Eastern–looking man was subjected to the same inspection as I; and finally, toward the end of my wait, another male inspector began a "flirtatious" inspection of two white women who had been stopped, perhaps for no other reason than to entertain the predominantly male staff. As I was waiting, I wondered why we were being inspected so differently at the border that Sunday afternoon. Was it our race, nationality, and gender that made us symbolize different kinds of threats to American security? Could the law be so nakedly blunt about its modes of regulation? If it wasn't the law, could it be particular procedures of the law that allowed inspectors to categorize us differently along such crudely stereotypical lines as the terrorist, the drug dealer, and the babe?

I begin this final chapter by remembering and recounting the above encounter, partly because the questions I asked myself that day were what initially ignited my interest in the (micro-) politics of immigration in the United States, an interest closely intertwined with my own biography as a naturalized citizen. My exposure to the disciplinary laws of immigration and my desire to ward off the fear that I always experience at the border as an immigrant and naturalized citizen from an "undesirable" nation have informed my critical study of the myth of immigrant America. On a theoretical level, my border experience in Watertown and various other encounters with the INS have made me think critically about the cheerful theories of border and immigration that forgetfully view the border experience as allowing the "subversion of all binarism, the projection of a 'multicultural public sphere.'"[2] Since 9/11 the idea of "border culture as a utopian model for dialogue is [at least temporarily] bankrupt."[3] The border, as I argue in this chapter, is not a metaphor of subversive transgression and radical hybridity, as some cultural critics have suggested, but rather a site of policing and discipline, control and violence.

I cite the above incident at the border at this juncture in my discussion also because it provides an anecdotal example of what I explore more specifically in this chapter: how borders as sites of disciplinary

practices by the state are expedient and indispensable to constructions of otherness and illegality, and therefore important in defining
the boundaries of citizenship and nationality. The border provides a
privileged locus where the state's disciplinary practices can be articulated and exercised, practices that are minor, modest, and detailed but
whose overall effects are significant in normalizing an exclusive and exclusionary form of national identity. Drawing my examples from both
narrative (anecdotal) accounts of border control and official immigration enforcement documents, I ask two interrelated questions: how
does the application of immigration laws by border agents systematically contribute to the construction and normalization of the state's
policing power? And how does the anxiety over undocumented ("illegal") aliens and the formation of a national consensus about regulating illegality transform the border into a useful, though violent, site
of national identification?

More generally, my aim in this chapter is to extend my cultural
analysis of forgetting in the constitution of the nation-state, which
I have elaborated up to this point, by turning to a more experiential
and material account of how immigration laws, which reflect the national ideology of immigration, impinge on the bodies and minds of
immigrants. My focus on disciplinary practices at national borders
may seem narrow on the surface, but my goal is to make a broader
argument about the nation's "laws of hospitality" by demonstrating
that immigration is not just a juridico-political phenomenon, as Derrida suggested, but works on a micro-mechanical level as a set of concrete disciplinary procedures. As a nation committed to forgetting,
the United States enacts its laws and policies of immigration not at the
center but at its border zones, marking the bodies that are less visible
in the national imaginary. These strategies are "minor" and "discretionary" and therefore less visible, which enables a kind of immigration policy that too often eludes critical scrutiny. My argument here is
a continuation into the contemporary era of my analysis in chapter 4
about the proliferation of exclusionary immigration laws since the late
nineteenth century, laws that have made immigration increasingly a
matter of policing and administrative enforcement, not national hospitality. Using the example of the border between the United States
and Mexico, I elaborate the ways that the state's practices of immigration control dovetail with the contradiction between the demands of
capitalism and the theory of human rights. Disciplinary practices of

border control, I argue, produce a docile and cheap labor force, necessary to the development of capital. At the same time, these micromechanical practices, in expanding the state's disciplinary exercise of power over immigrants, play a critical role in normalizing an exclusionary form of citizenship and national identity.

Micro-Mechanics of Immigration Control

Nowhere is the disciplinary nature of immigration law more evident than in the procedures and mechanisms of border inspection, increasingly too familiar to anyone who has traveled outside the country since 9/11. Border inspection, marginal though it may seem, constitutes a field of power relations in which minor and modest procedures of immigration law subject aliens, and increasingly citizens, to a whole set of regulatory techniques, ranging from embarrassing questions about one's personal life to the humiliating, if not violent, experience of a strip-search. An important document to consider in understanding these regulatory practices is one not publicly circulated, the U.S. Department of Justice's "Guide for the Inspection and Processing of Citizens and Aliens by Officers Designated as Immigration Officers."[4]

This corpulent document, a quick procedural reference for INS agents, initially describes the task of the inspector as one of "immeasurable importance in the protection of national interests, fostering of good will in foreign relations, and facilitation of international travel," casting the inspector in the role of metonym for the nation's sovereign right as well as its claim of national hospitality (1). As the representative of his—the document shamelessly assumes that its user is male—national interest, the officer is asked to keep in mind the importance of "courtesy, consideration, tact, and a genuine interest in people" and of projecting a positive "image of the United States to the nationals of other countries who come our way" (1). Disciplinary procedures of immigration are here couched as "laws of hospitality." The "Immigration Detention Officer Handbook," another manual published by the Department of Justice, similarly reminds the INS agent that "the attitude with which [he] should exercise his authority is best defined by the old-fashioned word 'courtesy'" (chapter 2, unpaginated). "In the long run," the handbook goes on to assure him, "courtesy will make the officer's job easier, and everyone, including himself, will feel better about it" (chapter 2). Authority, in other words, is defined here as a "humane and liberal administration of the Immigration and Nationality laws," and the disciplinary practices of admitting or detaining aliens take the respectable names of pleasant service, hospitality, and courtesy toward foreigners (Guide, i). The exercise of policing power, as D. A. Miller has demonstrated in another context, never passes as such, but is "visible only under cover of other, nobler or simply blander intentionalities."[5] Although the nature of immigration and customs inspection is one of policing, these documents construe the agent as a cordial helper, an affable gatekeeper, more interested in assisting the law-abiding citizens and being hospitable toward visitors than in exercising his disciplinary power over "aliens." The handbook even devotes a whole section to "Dignity and Self-Control," engaging in a humanist discourse of hospitality by reminding its users that "it is a small man who builds his own ego by tearing down the dignity of others" (chapter 2). Like the police, the INS officer is at the border to "protect and serve."

Not surprisingly, the discourse of courtesy and hospitality is soon displaced by that of regulation and control, as these documents outline the basic procedures of inspection, thus revealing the disciplinary nature of immigration law at the border. The guide begins its discussion of basic inspection procedures by emphatically stating the policing authority of the agent, pointing out that sections 235 and 287 of the Immigration and Nationality Act grant to the inspector the right to question under oath any person entering U.S. territory, and to search without a warrant that person and his or her effects. At the border the Fourth Amendment does not apply, at least not to foreign nationals. The guide is quite blunt in noting that its disciplinary practices apply to aliens alone. "The immigration laws," it states, "do not apply to United States citizens," and "examination under those laws should cease as soon as it is found that the applicant for entry is a citizen" (1). Legitimated by the state's claim to sovereignty, immigration law is founded on a profound, binary distinction between citizen and alien—a binary, I should add, that has become increasingly blurry since the terrorist attacks of 9/11 justified the extension of disciplinary practices over anyone who can be constructed as a national threat, regardless of citizenship status. I will later address the broader political and cultural implications of this distinction in the context of border control. For the moment, though, suffice it to say that the binary logic of inspection implicitly associates the "alien" with criminality, illegality, and transgression, an association, I further argue, that enables a normalized perception of citizenship and nationality.

These manuals, furthermore, invest the agent with a tremendous discretionary power in executing the law. Immigration enforcement laws and procedures are often too vague in defining the distinct boundaries of legality and illegality. Consequently, "Immigration inspectors possess extensive discretion stemming from broad delegations of legal authority and from the organizational characteristics of enforcement,"[6] as Janet Gilboy has documented in her empirical study of border inspection.[7] In outlining the basic inspection procedures, the guide, for example, often emphasizes the significance of "careful observation, study, and use of ingenuity" in detecting the "law-breaker" (1). In a sense the guide undermines its own role as guiding principle by acknowledging the experiential nature of the inspection job. The agents are expected to use such tools as "behavioral analysis," "cool logic," and observational techniques, developed through "experience," to help them exercise their authority efficiently. Consider the following advice about establishing citizenship by oral statement: "Pay careful attention to what the individual says and the way he says it, as well as his actions and appearance. Experience will quickly sharpen your ability to detect accents in speech and unusual statements which might indicate foreign origin" (Guide, 2). This instruction makes evident the fluidity and flexibility of immigration procedures. The category of "experience" is all-important, because it means that not only inspection, training, and knowledge of immigration law make a good and efficient agent but also "working the line" (Gilboy, "Deciding Who Gets In," 577). Working as an INS agent requires a "feel" for how and where to apply the procedures and laws of immigration. Border inspection is not just about knowledge, but also about experience. This is why job training for inspection work consists of watching experienced inspectors for several days as well as formal instruction and language training.

Discretionary power in immigration control suggests that many of the state's regulatory practices at the border have to do with the interpretations of particular agents. This interpretive authority in most cases means the sanctioning of a whole range of cultural stereotypes in the practice of border inspection. These stereotypes lead agents to impose different kinds of inspection for, say, a Middle Easterner suspected of being a terrorist, a Chicana with an accent suspected of being an illegal immigrant, and a young Ethiopian woman suspected of being a drug carrier. As Gilboy's empirical research confirms, "categorization of an individual as from a 'high-risk' nation routinely results in the [primary] inspector treating the individual as referable with no further inquiry to take place at [secondary inspection] stage," where the traveler is subjected to further questioning, baggage search, and sometimes strip-search (582). One may add to Gilboy's findings that this kind of decision making and the categorization of travelers into types by immigration inspectors, on which the decision making is based, are not simply functions of organizational knowledge and institutional criteria but result also from cultural prejudices and stereotypes concerning immigrants that are embedded in nativist perceptions of cultural identity in the United States—Muslims and Middle Easterners are terrorists, African Americans are drug dealers and criminals, and so on.

Immigration inspectors routinely classify different nationalities into positive and negative types, as well as into different categories of illegality. The following statements by two INS agents vividly illustrate the agency's prejudices, as well as its agents' freedom to exercise their discretionary power:

> Any male [from one specific Asian country] you secondary. You don't waste your breath. They're not going to tell you anything. They're going to give you a sing-song language, or they are going to lie to you anyway.
>
> What you're asking is mainly, "does that person appear to be what he says he is." Quite often the national background makes a difference. Let's say he's from [a specific European country]. Now [they] come, and they say they backpack. . . . In most cases, that is just what they are going to do. (Gilboy, 586)

These comments make clear that border inspection is an explicitly differential mode of policing, as the agents assume the power to assess the traveler's credibility on the basis of the stereotypes of Asians as charlatans, liars, and deceivers and Europeans as guileless and straightforward.[8] While the second agent presupposes the truthfulness of the European traveler, the first automatically subjects the Asian man to secondary and more brutal inspection simply because he happens to be from a country categorized as "high-risk." As a disciplinary practice, border inspection entails a classificatory mechanism through which the agent can sort and differentiate aliens, to expedite passage for the law-abiding and deny admission to the law-breaking. The classificatory mechanism, sanctioned by nebulous immigration laws and procedures, provides the inspector with a general field of comparison and a space of differentiation to gain maximum visibility over border crossers. The exercise of power at the border therefore becomes subjective and normative, as those upon whom it is exercised are stereotypically classified.

The use of discriminatory stereotypes in border inspection does not imply inattention to the characteristics of individual travelers. Quite the contrary: the scale of control in border inspection as a disciplinary practice is minute; it mobilizes mechanisms that can distinguish infinitesimal differences in appearance, clothing, gesture, accent, and attitude. General categories, such as the traveler's national origin, are useful only to the extent that they allow the inspector to quickly single out "suspicious" aliens for secondary inspection. Border inspectors, Gilboy remarks, "take great pride in their knowledge of their setting— for instance, in identifying the nationality of passengers by the height of the men, by the straightness of the inspection queue, or the existence of pushing in it" (583). No detail is unimportant in border inspection, for any detail has the potential to help categorize people into types that enable the agent to determine whom to inspect, what to look for, and how to interpret what is discovered in the inspection. For example, a young backpacker coming from Latin America with sweating hands may be carrying illegal drugs, while a similar condition in a European woman would be interpreted as mere nervousness.[9]

Such attention to minute details is particularly important in situations where the majority of border crossers happen to have similar national or racial backgrounds. Acknowledging the racial homogeneity of travelers at the MacAllen checkpoint in Texas, one agent remarks:

> We look for clothing, mannerisms, for speech. Speech because if you compare, just to give you an example, a Cuban or a Salvadorean or a Nicaraguan, or someone from the south and central region of Mexico, accents are obviously going to be different from the way people speak Spanish here. At one time, . . . when we were dealing with the typical bracero type, field labourers, [stopping people with particularly Indian features] might be true. Then you were more likely to run across a person wearing huaraches, a type of shoe that is not used on the border,

you would look for a person that looked like he'd worked on the land his entire life. So those are some of the keys that we used.[10]

This statement suggests that border inspection is based on more than just racial and ethnic profiling, and entails a more nuanced approach to locating "illegality." It forces upon both the agent and the "alien" a detailed system of identification, description, and categorization. "Discipline," as Foucault points out, "is a political anatomy of detail."[11] To be a good inspector, the agent must go beyond the general law laid down in the book as well as the broad categories of border crosser, and develop from experience specific rules to place each particular case. As the agent's comments demonstrate, what matters in detecting the "illegal alien" is a "retail" approach that can meticulously single out and distinguish between different styles, gestures, accents, and attitudes, even within the same ethnic and racial category, so as to render visible to the eye of the power the individual and his or her motivation to cross the border. "Instead of bending all its subjects into a single uniform mass," Foucault argues, disciplinary power "separates, analyzes, differentiates, carries its procedures of decomposition to the point of necessary and sufficient single units" (*Discipline and Punish*, 170). The exercise of disciplinary power at the border is a function of individualization and detail.

Detail in immigration inspection, I have been suggesting, is a function of interpretation, or more accurately the *authority to interpret*. Attention to particular details is not merely the effect of an organizational perception or characteristic enforced institutionally by a particular INS bureau, as Gilboy has argued. Rather, detail offers to the disciplinary power a site at which to seize, control, and produce subjected and compliant bodies through the authority of deductive interpretation that procedures of the law allow. Here the agent's interpretation, for certain indicia, takes the form of deductive "reading." In immigration inspection disciplinary power is intertwined with the semantic significance of detail in "clues" that hold back the "truth" about the alien. Border inspection, as a disciplinary form of examination, posits each traveler as a potential "case," which according to Foucault "is the individual as he may be described, judged, measured, compared with others" (*Discipline and Punish*, 191). The act of converting an individual into a case "constitutes an object for a branch of knowledge and a hold for a branch of power" (191). In such a fluid system of regulation as immigration control, individual characteristics, interpreted through a complex network of cultural perceptions and stereotypes about "others," constitute a "hold" for disciplinary power as well as a certain form of knowledge that can be accumulated and used in future inspections.

An example of how the methods of disciplinary individuality are played out in the exercise of border control appears in a story titled "The Revenue Nose" in the governmental magazine *Customs Today*.[12] This is how the story begins:

> Little did Customs Inspector Delmar Baker realize, as he began screening passengers at the Houston International Airport on June 26, 1989, that his observations would set in motion a cocaine smuggling investigation that would span four continents and result in the first-ever controlled delivery of cocaine between the United States and the Federal Republic of Germany. As the passengers were leaving an aircraft which had just arrived from Guatemala, Baker noticed that one of the women was in transit to Amsterdam. Normally such transit passengers are considered low risk and pass through Customs with little notice. But there was something about this passenger, traveling on a Guatemalan passport bearing the name "Funez," that just didn't seem quite right. Baker decided to refer the passenger to Customs Inspector Holt, who was working secondary. Through questioning, Holt determined that Funez was a teacher and was going to Amsterdam on vacation. The fact that Funez did not act like a teacher on a sabbatical, was nervous and was carrying only an overnight bag reinforced Holt's decision to refer her for a personal search. As Funez was escorted to the search room by Customs Inspector Dimple McArthur, she began to cry. A personal search revealed 32 packages of cocaine weighing seven kilograms in a smuggler's corset. Funez' Colombian passport in her true name of Blanca Dominguez was also found.

The story goes on to tell how this arrest, followed up thanks to "international cooperation," led to the breaking of a cocaine ring, and it ends with the following remark: "And so it ended. The long arm of the law had reached across continents to dismantle a drug smuggling organization which had started in South America and stretched through to Europe and Asia. And all because Blanca Dominguez didn't seem right to Delmar Baker's revenue nose."

This story is interesting, above all, in demonstrating how immigration and customs regulations involve a micro-practical understanding of laws and procedures that makes it possible to extend the arms of the law across the world by classifying and forming categories and sub-categories. Inspector Baker is successful in detecting a drug carrier because he does not rely on the general category of the transit passenger as low-risk, but instead focuses on particular signs of difference or exception to the rule. The constitution of Blanca Dominguez and her individualized features as a describable, analyzable object become the determining factor in signaling her as a criminal, and thus in providing a hold for the disciplinary power. But the law works here because it doesn't work. She is brought under the gaze of disciplinary power, her body subjected to its examination and control, not by the general regulations relating to transit passengers but through small techniques of observation and a system of comparative individuation that are described here in supernatural terms as a "sixth sense." Through observation of the traveler's general appearance and luggage, behavioral analysis, and the perception of a discrepancy between how the traveler acted and how a "teacher on a sabbatical" would be expected to act, the agent is able to single her out as a "criminal" in the crowd. Here "the examination, surrounded by all its documentary techniques, makes each individual a 'case,' " to use Foucault's words (*Discipline and Punish*, 191). Blanca Dominguez is a case that can be defined, described, judged, and compared with others in her individuality, and the procedures constitute a disciplinary practice that can finally extract her "true" identity. Immigration procedures make individuation, categorization, and observation a means of control and domination. Immigration inspection is the fixing of individual differences as the new modality of power. What matters in the exercise of border control is not the law but the revenue nose of its agents. What defines the parameters of disciplinary power is not a generalized collectivity but the individual as the effect and object of its knowledge.

This sanctioning of stereotypical interpretation and the emphasis on categorical detail have their origin in the disciplinary practices of the Immigration Bureau in Ellis Island, practices that were eventually codified by the exclusion provisions of the Immigration and Nationality Act of 1952—also known as the McCarran-Walter Act—which systematically, and in a detailed fashion, defined the categories of "undesirable aliens" and instituted for the first time an alien registration system. The broader implications of attention to detail are discernible in the particular context of these provisions, which remain on the books. What matters in the individualized exercise of immigration control, I argue, is not ultimately the isolated cases of law breakers but the organization of surveillance and control that can assure a more general and automatic functioning of power as well as a normalized notion of national belonging. Section 212(a) of the Immigration and Nationality Act lists thirty-three classes of excludable aliens, twenty-two dealing with the "personally undesirable" and six with the "physically or mentally deficient." Visitors, prospective resident aliens, and applicants for citizenship are asked in their applications to indicate whether they belong to any of these excludable categories, which range from "mentally retarded" persons to paupers, drug addicts, aliens "afflicted with any dangerous disease" or "physical defect," polygamists, bigamists, prostitutes, spies, rapists, murderers, anarchists, and communists. This list is an interesting example of the detailed political investment of the alien's body and mind, as the law turns everything to account and tries to name every possible category of "undesirability." In listing these categories, most of which are hard if not impossible to determine either upon border examination or through an INS interview, the immigration law is not so much interested in determining a given form of illegality or delinquency that an alien may conceal as in locating and seizing a site for the exercise of its power. The high volume of cases and the limited resources of INS make it impossible to identify and catch more than a very few "law breakers"—only 2 percent of those crossing the borders are so much as sent for secondary inspection, and only a very small number of criminal aliens are spotted and deported each year. The goal of border inspection or of an immigration interview is therefore not to totally exclude the "undesirable" but to establish a pattern of social control that constitutes a generalized mode of surveillance and a normalized notion of citizenship. Immigration control even depends on a certain level of what Foucault describes as "useful" delinquency or controlled illegality. This justifies the continuing exercise of immigration control, as well as its practices of discrimination. The idea is not to identify a prostitute, an insane person, or a drug addict, but to transform all these types into sites where the law can extract the "truth" of prostitution, insanity, and addiction and thus impose on the average immigrant a sense of visibility and vulnerability, while inculcating in him or her a normalized sense of national identity. It is for this reason, as I have pointed out, that those who apply for permanent residency or naturalization are asked to identify whether they belong to any of these "undesirable" categories. The questions are almost always answered negatively, but the process of interrogation makes resident aliens and citizenship applicants sense the eye of power over their bodies and minds, and also develop a normalized sense of what it means to be an American citizen.[13] The scandal in 1995–96 over the Clinton administration's controversial Citizenship USA program, in which at least five thousand immigrants with criminal records were naturalized and sworn in as citizens before the FBI had completed checks of their fingerprints against its database, confirms my thesis that what is at stake in the categories of excludable aliens is not so much keeping out delinquent aliens as establishing a pattern of sociojudicial control over the immigrant population. The constant reminders to the "alien" of the existence of "undesirable" categories, both in application forms and on the ubiquitous warning posters in inspection and immigration offices, are aimed at inducing in the alien a sense of permanent and conscious visibility that ensures a more economic, if not efficient, operation of immigration power.

INS and Outs: Technologies of Discipline at the Border

The disciplining of aliens is not solely the consequence of microprocedures of border inspection or other INS administrative practices: it is also achieved through techniques and technologies of surveillance used by the INS and the Border Patrol. Fueled by anxiety over "illegal" immigration and the threat of terrorism, new technologies of observation have been employed in the past two decades by these government agencies to build, according to one government pamphlet, "a comprehensive southwest border enforcement strategy."[14] Couched as a necessary and noble step to halt terrorism, deter drug trafficking and the smuggling of aliens, and facilitate legal immigration and commerce, the investment in border control, I argue, entails an intricate apparatus of surveillance that imposes upon immigrants as well as average citizens what Foucault calls "a principle of compulsory visibility" (*Discipline and Punish*, 187).

In *Discipline and Punish*, Foucault uses Jeremy Bentham's plan for the Panopticon, the circular prison with a central watchtower, as the architectural model for the disciplinary regime of power that has permeated western societies since the late eighteenth century. As a machinery of surveillance, the Panopticon puts in place a structure of hierarchical observation in which visibility and the monitoring of prisoners render them subjected and docile. "The exercise of discipline," Foucault demonstrates, "presupposes a mechanism that coerces by means of observation; an apparatus in which the techniques that make it possible to see induce effects of power, and in which, conversely, the means of coercion make those on whom they are applied clearly visible" (170–71). Visibility is precisely the mechanism that entraps individuals in the disciplinary web.

I hope to demonstrate that the Border Patrol's employment of such high technology to detect and apprehend terrorists and "illegal crossers," though far more advanced and sophisticated than that of the late-eighteenth-century reformers discussed by Foucault, functions in a similar fashion to discipline immigrants and enable a normalized sense of citizenship.[15] These technologies of surveillance subject border crossers to a field of visibility where they can be constantly seen and immediately recognized, monitor their movements to control them more effectively, and ultimately induce in them a sense of fear, vulnerability, and passivity. Such disciplinary apparatuses also work to turn the average citizen into a vigilante and impose a normalized form of national identity on the general population. Today, however, disciplinary power is not represented by the architectural figure of the Panopticon but by the "little gadgets" that produce the "hold" of power. There has been a shift from an architectural mode of discipline that invests power in the hierarchical arrangement of space to a technological model in which small machineries of perception form the constraints of power. This "state-of-the-art technology" constitutes a comprehensive and advanced apparatus of observation, while also legitimating and encouraging a broader culture of vigilantism. As a result, a heterogeneous and flexible system of surveillance is imposed across a wide-ranging social sphere.

With the proliferation since the 1970s of alarmist and sensationalist representations of the border with Mexico as a locus of illegality, delinquency, and transgression, and with tensions heightened by the so-called War on Terror since 9/11, the issue of border control has occupied a privileged position in American politics, prompting a wide range of measures to stop terrorists from entering the country and to deter undocumented immigrants at the border.[16] Among the three central recommendations of the prestigious U.S. Select Commission on Immigration and Refugee Policy formed by President Jimmy Carter in 1977 was one to increase resources for the Border Patrol, an underfunded agency created by the Immigration Act of 1924 as a federal police force, initially to catch tequila smugglers but later to regulate the flow of undocumented immigrants into the country.[17] Since the publication of the commission's report in 1981, which laid the policy foundation for the Immigration Reform and Control Act (IRCA) of 1986, the Border Patrol and INS have witnessed unprecedented expansion, including the introduction of high-technology hardware for immigration enforcement. Two publications of the INS, *Meeting the Challenge through Innovation* (1996) and *Building a Comprehensive Southwest Border Enforcement Strategy* (1996), provide a glimpse into these new technologies of surveillance.

Not surprisingly, both documents define immigration issues in terms of border control and "national security" and bluntly advocate "get-tough border initiatives involving more Border Patrol agents and high-tech equipment, better intelligence, and stepped-up enforcement to deter illegal immigration, . . . returning order to communities in border areas."[18] Having thus construed the immigration debate around such binaries as legal and illegal, control and transgression, order and chaos, these documents provide an ostentatious list of INS achievements in its effort to restore the nation's "border integrity." These include the use of such "innovative technologies" as night-vision goggles and scopes, seismic and infrared sensors, surveillance helicopters, and computerized identification and tracking systems. The first pamphlet boastfully describes the "new INS" as an "advanced, professional, high-tech agency, . . . working smarter through new technologies that expand its capabilities and enhance border control and customer service" (i). Similarly, the second pamphlet contrasts the days when broken-down vehicles and equipment handicapped the Border Patrol's "ability to patrol the front line" with the present, when "agents . . . have state-of-the-art equipment and vehicles," making them more efficacious in catching "illegal crossers and criminal aliens" (5). What is celebrated in these official discourses is an economic and efficient mode of disciplinary power in which "tighter control" of the border is achieved through the least amount of effort. "Advanced technologies in use at the border," as the first pamphlet adds, "enable the INS to quickly identify criminal aliens and other illegal crossers, and dramatically reduce the time enforcement officers spend on paperwork" (ii). While new instruments of observation, such as scopes and sensors, enable agents to maintain direct supervision of border activities, the accumulation and storage of such data as the fingerprints and photographs of apprehended illegal aliens in the agency's computerized tracking systems, such as IDENT, help to regulate migrant traffic more efficiently. The INS today uses motor vehicle, credit, and social security databases to locate fugitives for deportation. New technologies of surveillance thus make it possible to perfect the exercise of disciplinary power by obtaining maximum control at the lowest possible cost and in the least amount of time.

To create such an effective and efficient system of surveillance, the new technologies of observation rely on two principles: visibility and unverifiability (Foucault, *Discipline and Punish*, 201–2). The Border Patrol makes its presence visible to aliens to dissuade them from crossing. At Imperial Beach near the border between San Diego and Tijuana, for example, "a Border patrol officer often sits on a bluff overlooking the beach in an attempt to discourage illegal crossings."[19] Similarly, one important strategy of Operation Hold the Line in El Paso, Texas, and Operation Safeguard in Arizona during the 1990s involved placement by the INS of "Border Patrol agents directly on the line at regular intervals" (*Building a Comprehensive Southwest Border Enforcement Strategy*, 4). The sight of the Border Patrol agents raises the possibility of being spotted and arrested and thus induces in border crossers a consciousness of permanent vulnerability. The principle of visibility makes the functioning of disciplinary power more efficient in that the mere presence of an individual agent, if not an empty patrol car, often deters a large number of possible border crossers. The redeployment of agents right on "the line," the principal strategy of Operation Hold the Line, for example, reduced the number of aliens apprehended by about 72 percent, according to the INS.[20] The constant presence of agents at popular corridors of "illegal entry" is aimed at subjecting prospective crossers to a field of visibility, forcing them to become the agents of their own regulation through the fear that it instills in them.

At the same time, new technologies of surveillance allow a principle of unverifiability: the prospective border crosser must never know whether he or she is being observed at any particular moment, but must be made aware that the possibility always exists. As a mode of disciplinary power, border surveillance remains for the most part invisible and the role of its agents attenuated, by which means it simultaneously imposes upon those who are subjected to it a mechanism of self-regulation. To organize this principle, a dissymmetry must be established between the agent as the observer and the alien as the observed. What characterizes the new instruments of surveillance is a panoptic gaze that makes aliens and their movements visible in the eyes of immigration power while the power remains mostly invisible to the aliens. In the past decade, the INS with the support of military personnel and the National Guard has installed brightly shining lights in many parts of the border, turning the anti-immigrant activists' slogan "light up the border" into a major strategy to stop the migratory flow. It has also deployed sensors, seismic monitors, low-light-level television surveillance systems, infrared scopes with remote-imaging capacities, and night-vision goggles to detect undocumented crossings during the night in more remote regions. As in the Panopticon, these technologies entail a hierarchical structure of surveillance in which the eye of power can see without being seen. Buried in the ground, seismic monitors and magnetic sensors, for example, not only detect the subtlest movements but are capable of informing the Border Patrol's communication center about the size of immigrant groups crossing the border. They also provide agents with computer printouts of the exact location and number of people traversing the area. Similarly, a sophisticated camera system, designed to operate with minimal light, makes border crossers constantly visible to INS agents, giving them more mobility and flexibility. The constant visibility of undocumented immigrants and the invisibility of the mechanisms of regulation maintain a kind of collective subjection and assure an elaborated yet illusive exercise of disciplinary power.

The Border Patrol's machinery of observation is significant not so much for its capacity to "catch" aliens, given the vast and porous southern border, but for its ability to make them watchful and insecure about the perils of illegal crossing. As a consequence, the principle of unverifiability also makes the exercise of disciplinary power potentially more economical, since it allows a higher ratio of results to expenditure. The quite sparse installation of sensors and other intrusion-detection equipment at the border between San Diego and Tijuana, for example, has slowed traffic and shifted it east, to areas where the Border Patrol has a tactical advantage in catching undocumented border crossers.

Delinquency and the Economy of Border Control

And yet, in spite of these technologies and strategies of regulation, the Border Patrol's enforcement remains for the most part inadequate in preventing the migratory flow and the illegal entry of terrorist suspects. Despite the agency's recent official discourse of success and progress, most agents openly acknowledge their inability to stop "illegal immigration" into the country, citing a broad range of obstacles such as inadequate funding, the disparate topography and sheer length of the border, and the profound economic divide between the United States and Mexico. As one agent pointedly remarks, "Sometimes you feel like a highway patrolman. He gives a few tickets, but he goes home every night knowing how many speeders are out there."[21] Another officer paints an even gloomier picture of border enforcement: "About the only way you can secure the border is to hire enough agents to stand hand in hand along the U.S. side. Even if you do that, they eventually will get across. This is where the jobs are."[22] These acknowledgments are remarkable as testimonies to the failure of border enforcement, and also as indications of the Border Patrol's recognition of "delinquency" as an essential component of social regulation. By delinquency, following Foucault's use of the term in *Discipline and Punish*, I mean a form of "controlled illegality" sanctioned and even produced by the very disciplinary power that claims to regulate and control transgressions of the law (272). Delinquency, as I will argue briefly, is not a contradiction in the exercise of disciplinary power but rather the consequence of a system of regulation that works precisely because it doesn't. In other words, just as imprisonment does not diminish the crime rate and in fact causes recidivism, the strategies of border control produce delinquent immigrants whose quick deportation makes them only more motivated to try another "illegal" crossing. "Punishment," Foucault insightfully remarks, "is not intended to eliminate offenses, but rather to distinguish them, to distribute them, to use them" (272).

Particular to the perpetuation of delinquency at the border is what one may call the principle of inconsequential retribution. One of the strategies that the Congress has adopted in the past decade to counter illegal immigration has been the streamlining of the deportation process. Because power over aliens has been viewed by the juridical system as having a "political character" and is therefore subject only to narrow judicial review,[23] Congress has been able to enact statutes that have empowered INS agents to deport illegal immigrants without a hearing. Although, as Hiroshi Motomura has critically argued,[24] such statutes have isolated immigration law from the mainstream of American public law and from constitutional principles, they have ironically rendered the punishment for illegal immigration for the most part inconsequential: the penalty for illegally crossing the border is a quick trip to the other side. As one border crosser who made it to El Paso after four attempts put it, "Getting stopped is no big deal. You take the bus back, hang around Juarez near the railroad yards, talk to people, find out about a better spot and then you are across" (Chaze, "Invasion from Mexico," 38). The policy of "voluntary return" has effectively turned the southwest border into what anti-immigrant activists have described as a "revolving door." Indeed, as a veteran patrolman resignedly states, "It sometimes seems Washington really doesn't want us to do the job" (38). Though expressed in the context of the agency's insufficient staff and equipment, this remark lucidly captures the state's desire to produce delinquency.[25]

What the patrolman's statement misses, however, is that the failure to stop the flow of immigration is a kind of success in that it authorizes and justifies a perpetual mode of surveillance. *At the border, we have discipline because we don't have punishment.*[26] That the Border Patrol as an integral component of state apparatus tirelessly attempts to "hold the line" while fully aware of its inability to do so should warn us against the official rhetoric of maintaining "border integrity." What is hidden beneath the glaring cynicism of border control is an attempt to "assimilate the transgression of the laws in a general tactics of subjection" (Foucault, *Discipline and Punish*, 272). The failure to control the flow of (illegal) immigration might imply that the agency simply misses its target, but it might also say that the failure is a success in making the violent mechanisms of discipline legitimate and natural. The regulation of the southern border is not simply about stopping the flow of undocumented immigrants, but also about a general economy of discipline that uses delinquency to authorize its perpetual surveillance and control of the immigrant population and to transform the average citizen into a vigilante who internalizes disciplinary power. Far from being a contradiction, the perpetuation of illegality must therefore be viewed as a necessary component of a disciplinary society.

The goals of delinquency as a strategy of discipline may be sum-marized as a double repression, both parts of which are disavowed in the official discourse of immigration control: to produce a submis-sive and cheap labor force, and to perpetuate a monolithic and norma-tive notion of national identity through the othering and criminaliza-tion of immigrants. Delinquency at the border, or what immigration scholars and policy advisors have called the "benign neglect" of ille-gal immigration in the post-bracero era, has been vitally important in maintaining an elastic supply of cheap labor from Mexico. In her path-breaking research on the bracero program, *Inside the State*, Kitty Calavita has documented the duplicitous role played by the Immigra-tion Service in "fashioning policies to maximize the utility of the con-tract labor system to growers" both during and after the dissolution of the program in 1964 (180). Critiquing both the instrumentalists' argument that reduces the INS to a "lackey of growers" and the struc-turalists' one according to which the "objective relation" between the state and capital makes the agency a " 'bearer' of the structure of capi-talism," Calavita demonstrates that "immigration officials and bracero employers worked out a modus vivendi, the nature of which was con-tingent on the mandate of the immigration bureaucracy to control the border" (180–81). Calavita's research depicts the INS as a regulatory agency that often intentionally does not regulate or regulates by im-perfectly regulating—not to mention the inherent organizational con-flicts and contradictions that further undermine its ability to control the border. The INS, she remarks, is "charged with controlling ille-gal immigration but precluded from doing so by the significant eco-nomic utility of a porous border" (159). In the post-bracero era, un-documented immigrants provide a source of cheap labor not only for the agricultural sector of the economy but increasingly for a broad range of urban employers, from restaurants and construction compa-nies to users of such domestic services as gardening and child care. Many immigration scholars have thus claimed that to facilitate the economic advantages of illegal immigration, the INS and the Congress have adopted a policy of "benign neglect" toward the border, toler-ating and occasionally encouraging a constant flow of migrants into the country.[27] Such a strategy, like other anti-immigrant measures, is "designed to insure the unimpeded importation of low-wage labor in order to drive down wages for all workers while blaming the result-ing social and economic catastrophes on the immigrants themselves"

(Lipsitz, *The Possessive Investment in Whiteness*, 52). Ignoring the predicament of the border thus enables both capital and discipline.

The state's tolerance, if not promotion, of an illegal flow of immigrants does not imply an absence of regulation. On the contrary, the production of a compliant, low-wage labor force hinges upon an apparatus of discipline that must constantly regulate it. Such an apparatus was founded by the Immigration Act of 1924, which made entry into the country without inspection a felony, introduced a new administrative procedure called "voluntary departure" to accelerate the deportation of illegal immigrants, and most importantly created the Border Patrol. The new law engendered a critical distinction between legal and illegal immigrants, while establishing an organizational mechanism to administer and regulate the boundary between them. These changes enabled the institutionalization of an underclass of migrant workers who were included through exclusionary practices at the border—included because "the Mexican migrants are providing a fairly adequate supply of [cheap] labor"—but excluded from the polity since "the Mexican, . . . is less desirable as a citizen than as a laborer."[28] The new Immigration Act essentially changed the status of the migrant worker to that of a fugitive, subjecting him or her to a "shadowed life" in which the fear of being caught or turned in imposes both a sense of compulsory vigilance and an obedient disposition.

The birth of the Border Patrol and the criminalization of migratory workers without inspection, as Jorge Bustamante remarks, "not only modified the interaction between the illegal entrant and the employer, but brought a new fact into being, namely the danger of being apprehended and returned to Mexico."[29] The threat of deportation has forced undocumented immigrants into accepting low wages and substandard working conditions. Especially as Mexican migrant workers went underground in the post-bracero era and the convenient local arrangement between growers and the Border Patrol allowed a constant flow across the border, the potent threat of deportation added new ammunition to the employers' arsenal, enabling them to tighten labor discipline, thus ensuring a tractable labor force that willingly and reliably performed menial jobs for lower wages (Portes, "Of Borders and States," 20). "It is simple," as one undocumented Nicaraguan immigrant remarks, "Everybody knows the situation with illegals, and the bosses know it too. The illegals have to work for whatever they're offered" (20). The discovery of seventy-two undocumented Thai garment workers kept in prison-like conditions at a sweatshop in El Monte in August 1995 may have come as a cultural shock to most Americans, but the exploitation of illegal immigrants is more a rule than an exception. In fact, according to the *Los Angeles Times*, "government regulators say employer exploitation of immigrants is widespread in California's apparel manufacturing, agriculture and construction industries."[30] Such findings are further corroborated by empirical studies and reports of human and immigrant rights organizations that have documented the connection between aliens' fears and vulnerability and their exploitation by employers.[31] Tractable and obedient because of their illegal status, undocumented immigrants work "scared and hard," to cite the words of the ex-secretary of labor F. Ray Marshall.[32] Not only are they willing to accept menial and minimum-wage jobs that are unattractive to citizens and permanent residents, but undocumented immigrants also work diligently and submissively at these tasks.

Furthermore, to the extent that the strategy of delinquency changes the status of the migrant worker to that of a fugitive violating the nation's "border integrity," our attention needs to go beyond the economic consequences of discipline to focus on the political utility of "benign neglect." In addition to enabling the production of a tractable labor force, the seeming failure of border enforcement transforms the border into a site of contestation where the nation-state is constantly engaged in a process of self-assertion and self-definition. Border enforcement, or the management of who gets in and who doesn't, is at once an assertion of political sovereignty for the state and a mode of cultural identification for the nation. While it may be an overstatement to claim that modern nation-states are their borders, the role of the border and the management of its perpetual "crisis" are fundamental in how the nation imagines itself and how the state rationalizes the techniques of coercion and discipline that enable a normalized sense of national identity. The so-called flood of illegal aliens and the threat of terrorism are useful in legitimating the state's disciplining of aliens and the multiplication of its new instruments of coercion as necessary and justified assertions of political sovereignty. That the state is consistently delinquent in controlling its borders should not be taken as a sign of its weakness; rather the failure, I have been suggesting, is politically productive in that it legitimates an exclusionary mode of state power and manufactures a more popular basis for it by making it possible to blame immigrants for the nation's social and economic ills. Delinquency and illegality at the border allow a permanent state of crisis that perpetuates a disciplinary context in which a sense of collective sovereignty is articulated.

Yet simultaneously a normalized notion of national identity based on the rights of citizenship is differentially posited at the border against an alien who by definition does not belong and poses a threat. The border is not just a territorial marker of the modern nation-state, defining its geographical boundary, but an ideological apparatus where notions of national identity, citizenship, and belonging are articulated. Since the concept of the modern nation presupposes a legally and geographically distinct state under the effective power of a government, the border is invested with tremendous symbolic power in defining the imagined community: the border delineates the state's claim to sovereignty and the boundaries of national identity differentially and normatively. It posits a binary and exclusionary relation between a self that obeys the law and an alien who transgresses it.

Since the early 1980s, when Ronald Reagan declared that "this country has lost control of its borders. And no country can sustain that kind of position,"[33] the border between the United States and Mexico has been consistently portrayed in popular discourse concerning immigration as under siege. As suggested by the titles of such journalistic reports as "Losing Control of the Borders" and "Invasion from Mexico: It Just Keeps Growing," the border is represented as a battleground where the Border Patrol strives to defend the nation by upholding its "border integrity" against "the swelling tide of illegal Mexican aliens" and "Islamic terrorists." What such a perception points to is the usefulness of the "crisis" of the border in producing a national consensus about political power and citizenship. The border crisis offers more than a momentary and forcible solution to the contradiction between the economic advantages of an undocumented labor supply and its political and fiscal costs, for it allows the production of an ideology of consent as "common sense" or "public opinion."[34] Since the technological objectification of the state's exercise of power in democratic societies such as the United States requires a consensual basis in civil society, the crisis of the border is particularly useful in creating a simulated civil war in which the imagined community of the nation willingly participates in the state's politics of exclusion because it views the fight against terrorism and illegal immigration as being demanded by common sense. The border's state of emergency plays a vital role in normalizing the state's rationale of regulatory power in the region and beyond, as the discourse of national sovereignty is used to justify the disciplining of aliens.

An illustrative example of the productivity of the border crisis in perpetuating the structural relationship between the state's command and the ideology of consent is Peter Brimelow's national best seller, *Alien Nation: Common Sense about America's Immigration Disaster* (1995). This book begins with the premise that "the United States has lost control of its borders," a situation that has consequently "robbed Americans of the power to determine who, and how many, can enter their national family, make claims to it, . . . and exert power over it" (4–5). As a solution, the author suggests that "the border . . . should be sealed (at long last) with a fence, a ditch and whatever other contrivances that old Yankee ingenuity finds appropriate" (259). And to conclude, Brimelow offers the following remark to justify his reactionary response to the nation's predicament: "It is common sense that Americans have a legitimate interest in their country's racial balance. It is common sense that they have a right to insist that their government stop shifting it. Indeed, it seems to me that they have a right to insist that it be shifted back [to that of 1965 when nearly 90 percent of the population was white]" (264). *Alien Nation* provides a symptomatic example of how the nation's "crisis" at the border can be deployed, both to justify the state's new techniques of coercion and to normalize a broader politics of exclusion that extends beyond this particular region. Concern over the nation's porous border allows the conservative author to defend nativism as a legitimate form of nationalism. As Brimelow's polemics suggest, the "crisis" at the border threatens the very foundation of how the nation is imagined, because it deepens the gap between the citizen, who has the birthright to determine the composition of the national family, and the alien, who threatens the polity. The loss of border control instigates a reactionary response that helps push to the limit the state's mechanisms of exclusion, repression, and marginalization, as the national community actively gives its consent.

Most disturbingly, as the conclusion of *Alien Nation* reveals, the predicament of the border is generalized to the point where the state's politics of exclusion becomes a matter of public opinion and racism against nonwhite immigrants becomes a legitimate form of nationalism. That a national bestseller can so shamelessly advocate a racially homogeneous country is testimony to the prevalence of nativism today, and to the success of the state in marshaling a mobile and productive relationship between command and consensus by simulating a state of siege at the border. This "state of emergency" provides a consensual basis for articulating a discourse of sovereignty that legitimates and rationalizes the state's disciplinary practices. These practices extend beyond the repressive measures of the INS and help to sanction a broader national politics of exclusion.

America's "Open Wound"

Gloria Anzaldúa's poetic description of the border as an "open wound" powerfully captures the violence of this contradictory and volatile space: "The U.S.-Mexico border *es una herida abierta* where the Third World grates against the first and bleeds. And before a scab forms it hemorrhages again, the lifeblood of two worlds merging to form a third country—a border culture. Borders are set up to define the places that are safe and unsafe, to distinguish us from them. A border is a dividing line, a narrow strip along a steep edge. A borderland is a vague and undetermined place created by the emotional residue of an unnatural boundary. It is in a constant state of transition. The prohibited and forbidden are its inhabitants" (3). I have chosen to conclude my discussion of disciplinary power at the border with Anzaldúa's poetic remarks because they help us to reflect on the broader effects and implications of the state's mechanisms of territorial regulation. Above all, the disciplining of aliens must be understood in the context of the uneven encounter between the First World and the Third World. The massive socioeconomic inequalities between the United States and Mexico, the consequence of both capitalist expansion and globalization, have been decisive in encouraging a migratory flow from South to North, though such geopolitical inequalities have been mostly disavowed in the official discourse of immigration. At least since 1911, when the Dillingham Commission on Immigration noted the advantages of a cheap, docile, flexible, and unlimited supply of labor from Mexico, immigration policymakers in Washington have facilitated its exploitation by growers and the service sector of the economy, creating loopholes for continued clandestine immigration while passing restrictionist measures to regulate it and render it tractable.[35] Here the policing and regulatory practices of border control displace the nation's liberal democratic principles, unfolding the contradiction between the demands of global capitalism and the political discourse of human rights. The violence of the border is at once the effect and the expression of this contradictory structure, a structure that in immigration debates has been consistently ignored and denied as a factor.

Moreover, the political economy of the border is indispensable in constructing a differential mode of national identification in which the figure of the alien is necessary for imagining a normative notion of national identity. The border between the United States and Mexico is not just the scene of actual violence, the place where many trigger-happy patrol agents brutalize and violate the rights of defenseless undocumented immigrants,[36] but more importantly the site of a symbolic form of violence. The border is the boundary that relentlessly separates the inside from the outside, the lawful from the prohibited, and the citizen from the alien. It is the limit that must be constantly transgressed so that violence is rationalized and regulation is made the norm. National borders constitute a violent third space where identities are monolithically and normatively inscribed while cultural differences are marginalized. Disciplinary power hinges on this "unnatural boundary" to simulate a state of siege that normalizes its functioning and legitimates its exclusionary techniques. The creation of the border as a "deviant" space, in sum, is in accordance with the fact of its suppression through a national politics of exclusion.

Conclusion

Remembering 9/11

For several months after the terrorist attacks of 9/11, a huge banner hung over ground zero declaring, "We Will Never Forget," a sentiment shared by a nation "unpracticed in the art of remembering," as one insightful reporter pointed out during the first anniversary of the tragic event.[1] That day, as the nation commemorated what many have proclaimed to be its most traumatic day in history, every official echoed the familiar refrain that we must never forget the lessons of September 11, 2001. For a moment it seemed that the nation was finally committing itself to overcoming the tendency to forget by reflecting on its cultural and political values and countering the forces that appeared to threaten them. Throughout the country, government officials remembered the dead in their patriotic speeches, peppered with claims about the nation's resilience and its unwavering commitment to democracy and freedom in the face of terror, while ordinary citizens honored the victims by lighting candles, planting trees, displaying memorial quilts, and waving American flags. Despite the official rhetoric of remembrance and the nation's televisual pageantry of patriotism, however, the immediate memorialization ironically did as much to obscure as to preserve the political and cultural values that it appeared to defend. Indeed, less than two months after the tragic events of 9/11 a nervous Congress had hastily passed the USA Patriot Act, which dramatically extended the surveillance and investigative power of federal security agencies such as the FBI, the CIA, the Border Patrol, and the INS, agencies whose power had already been augmented by the Anti-Terrorism Act of 2001. In an atmosphere of edgy alarm, Congress had spent very little time debating the bill, as it rushed to pro-

vide the federal government with sweeping powers to monitor, wire-
tap, investigate, and incarcerate citizens, immigrants, and foreigners
to prevent another terrorist attack. And so while the nation officially
recommitted itself to democracy and freedom in response to terrorist
attacks, the USA Patriot Act radically infringed Americans' privacy,
civil liberties, and constitutional rights. On a micro-mechanical level,
the bill introduced provisions that took away fundamental constitutional protections of citizens' rights by radically enhancing the federal
government's authority to carry out surveillance of e-mails, telephone
conversations, and credit card transactions. In a manner recalling the
disciplinary practices at the nation's borders, the law created broad and
discretionary powers to implement a detailed system of surveillance,
enabling the meticulous monitoring of the everyday practices of citizens and aliens alike. In short, in the name of preserving our freedom
and defending our democracy, the new legislation sacrificed the values
that it meant to defend.

I begin this concluding chapter by reflecting on the nation's trib-
ute to the victims of 9/11 and the subsequent passage of the USA
Patriot Act to create a context for considering the implications of
my earlier discussion, in which I showed that nation and immigration have had an entangled history marked by disavowal. What was
remarkable about the hurried passage of broad legislation to curtail
the constitutional rights of citizens was how powerfully the figure of
the immigrant-foreigner once again provided the differential other
through whose threatening presence a state of emergency was declared, enabling thus the entrenchment of disciplinary apparatuses
and surveillance procedures to protect the democratic polity from the
other's terror. Notably, a substantial part of the bill was devoted to
enhancing immigration procedures by denying to foreigners, immigrants, and permanent residents the rights of habeas corpus and due
process and permitting the indefinite detention of those who had violated any immigration codes, including those guilty of such minor offenses as overstaying a visa. The act also implicitly depicted the brown-
skinned immigrant—Middle Eastern, Southeast Asian, or Latino—as
a threat to the democratic nation, so much so that apocalyptic measures on the part of the state were required to eradicate the (terrorist) foreigner. The American Civil Liberties Union and the Lawyers
Committee for Human Rights protested the obvious targeting of immigrants as reflected in section 412 of the Patriot Act, which permits

indefinite incarceration of immigrants and noncitizens, but their salutary intervention, necessary as it was, overlooked the more subtle ways in which the immigrant was vilified.

The rhetoric of the immigrant and the foreigner as a threat to democracy and freedom suspended the myth of America as a nation of immigrants until further notice. Rapidly codified discriminatory laws now denied entry to certain immigrants and foreigners and allowed the interrogation, incarceration, and deportation of others. While President Bush and other government officials warned the nation against the misguided mistreatment of Arab and Muslim immigrants, the legislation subtly repositioned them as a national menace, targeting them for their purportedly terrorist ties while radically curbing their constitutionally sanctioned civil liberties and allowing the massive arrest of immigrants for minor offenses. As in earlier manifestations of the nativist trend that I discussed in chapter 4, the figuration of the Arab and Muslim immigrant as a threat to the democratic nation demarcated the boundaries of national identity differentially and normatively, by positing a binary opposition between the citizen who obeys the law and the alien who transgresses it.

On the other hand, the very category of immigrant was strategically enlarged to include at least some (un)certain citizens, as was made clear by the arrests of Yasser Hamdi, an American citizen held captive at Guantánamo Bay, and Jose Padilla, who in an ironic twist had renamed himself Abdullah al Muhajir (the last name meaning "the immigrant" in Arabic). The arrest of Padilla seemed to acknowledge his inscription as an immigrant other in the American polity because of his race in spite of his being a citizen. Though, as Senator Russell Feingold aptly remarked, "to the extent that the expansive new immigration powers that the bill grants to the Attorney General are subject to abuse," immigrants from Arab, Muslim, and South Asian countries are "most likely to bear the brunt of that abuse," the USA Patriot Act deployed the threat of terrorism to justify and rationalize the extension of a disciplinary form of power over anyone who could potentially be constructed as a foreigner or immigrant, regardless of his or her citizenship status.[2] The bill strategically invoked the figure of the immigrant-foreigner as a threat to justify the need for a total and permanent state of visibility. The surveillance of the terrorist foreigner, in short, has made everyone the potential subject and object of the state's disciplinary gaze, as techniques and instruments of regulation and coercion are legitimized as exigencies of war. The figure of the terrorist, like the "illegal alien," enables the production of patriotic ideology, as the imagined community of the nation willingly participates in the simulated war against terror.

In the context of such broad legislation, which has strategically accentuated the danger that the immigrant once again poses, my discussion of America's ambivalent relationship with its immigrants offers a genealogical study. It makes us understand the productive function of the immigrant, whose perennial figuration as a threatening other in the democratic imaginary has perpetually helped to fashion an exclusionary sense of belonging and also to entrench and rationalize the state's disciplinary power over its citizens. Although when I began this project, I could not have known that the United States would be moving through a period that would foreground precisely the issues grappled with in *this book*, my discussion of the inner mechanisms of amnesia deepens our understanding of the contemporary iterations of forgetfulness in the American national consciousness. The hurried passage of the USA Patriot Act manifests exactly the kind of historical amnesia that I thematize throughout this text, a forgetting akin to the Freudian notion of negation in which disavowal is accompanied by a supplementary act of acknowledgment. One of the most striking features of the national debate about the Patriot Act's impact— specifically, whether it strikes an appropriate balance between liberty and security—was the inattentiveness shown by Congress to the nation's history of curbing civil liberties in the name of national security, commonly mobilized through the figure of the immigrant. As a ritual of self-purification, the nation's response to the tragic events of 9/11 brought into focus the often overlooked productive function of the immigrant as the scapegoat through whose expulsion political, social, and economic crises are contained and resolved. Although a few politicians like Senator Feingold and legal scholars like David Cole spoke of the similarities between the USA Patriot Act and earlier misdeeds, such as the Alien and Sedition Acts of 1798, the interning of Japanese-Americans during the Second World War, and the blacklisting of communists and their sympathizers during the McCarthy era, the public generally disregarded history, allowing "these pieces of our past to become prologue," as Senator Feingold warned the Congress (2). As in the earlier cases of historical amnesia that I have elaborated in this book, forgetting here did not entail mnemonic foreclosure: the nation did acknowledge in passing its violent treatment of immigrants in the past. But it chose not to look at the effects and implications of this treatment, let alone take full responsibility for it, thus unwittingly re-enacting its xenophobia as a means of self-preservation by supporting the new legislation. The nation's historical amnesia, in other words, enabled the return of what it was forgetting, namely the xenophobic and inhospitable treatment of immigrants and foreigners. Denial took the form of normalization, through which inhospitality and violence toward immigrants were either unrecognized (by the state) or pas-sively accepted (by the average citizen). The collective disavowal of past brutalities toward immigrants created a culturally desensitized at-titude toward the present, as the nation was encouraged to believe that contemporary events were utterly different from those in the past and that steps taken in response to them were necessary for national secu-rity. Such forgetfulness at once ensured a sense of cultural and po-litical innocence by repressing memories of historical events, while at the same time renewing a defensive form of patriotism, state violence toward the immigrant other, and discipline. In sum, by refusing to re-member its past mistreatment of immigrants, the nation was acting out its violence toward them again, thus reproducing the past not as memory but in action.[3]

In addition to historical disavowal, the nation's commemoration of 9/11 entailed a contemporary form of denial in which forgetting was effected by way of memory in the form of a pseudo-historical con-sciousness. The nation's discourse and its ritual of remembrance dur-ing the anniversary of 9/11 were peculiarly laced with suggestions that the country was ready to move on, which was implicitly understood to mean forget as opposed to work through. General Richard Myers, the chairman of the Joint Chiefs of Staff, for example, declared that the United States is "a nation that refuses to dwell on our past sor-rows," intimating that the country should leave behind the traumatic memory of the terrorist attacks and that the people should get on with their lives (*New York Times*, 12 September 2002). Indeed, one year later, the nation *was* moving on—ground zero had been cleared and plans for construction of new office buildings were under way; the Pentagon was fully repaired; widows of victims were remarrying; blow-'em-up movies that had been considered culturally inappropriate after the at-tacks were making a comeback; Saddam Hussein had replaced Osama bin Laden as the face of terror; and Iraq had replaced Afghanistan as the new battleground against terrorism. And so, contrary to the official rhetoric of remembrance, the very ritual of commemoration constituted a willful act of disremembering 9/11.

In this way, the trauma of 9/11 made acute a dilemma that threatens the national imaginary, a dilemma arising from a dynamic of forgetting that entails both acknowledgment and disavowal. That the nation's memorializing is accompanied by a willful desire to forget speaks to an ambivalent form of national identification, symptomatically manifested, as I have shown in this book, in how the nation views its immigrants. The split positioning of the immigrant in the democratic imaginary of the United States, constructed both as a critical supplement and as a profound threat, demonstrates a schizophrenic form of historical consciousness that perpetually vacillates between a cultural desire to acknowledge the past and a political need to disavow it. While the popular script of immigrant America is constantly invoked to shore up America's exceptionalism, a forgetfully xenophobic invocation of immigrant threat is mobilized politically to resolve the nation's ideological paradoxes and social dilemmas.

Although this book is primarily descriptive rather than prescriptive in dealing with the nation's ambivalent historical consciousness and its predicament of immigration, my argument nonetheless suggests an alternative approach to the production and reproduction of national memory, as well as pointing to what a more hospitable American politics might look like. My critique of the nation's amnesia in the previous chapters does not imply that forgetting is counter-productive *tout court*. On the contrary, as Nietzsche reminds us, "Forgetting is essential to action of any kind, just as not only light but darkness too is essential for the life of everything organic" and "*there is a degree of sleeplessness, of rumination, of historical sense, which is harmful and ultimately fatal to the living thing, whether this living thing be a man or a people or a culture*" (*Untimely Meditations*, 62; emphasis in original). The capacity to forget may be what enables us as human subjects to transcend historical traumas and avoid being psychologically paralyzed. And yet, as necessary and comforting as it is to forget, we can only leave behind what first we have faced and worked through. As Slavoj Žižek insightfully remarks, "in order really to forget an event, we must first summon up the strength to remember it properly."[4] Past traumas that are not worked through, as Freud has already taught us, either engender a neurotic fixation to a particular portion of the past, which alienates us from the present and prevents us from moving forward in our lives, or create the conditions of resistance in the form of repetition and acting out. What the commemorating events during the first anniversary of 9/11 symptomatically demonstrated was the nation's resistance to fully remembering the historical trauma. Therefore, rather than engage such cogent issues as how the U.S. government had aided the rise of the Taliban and bin Laden as part of its anti-Soviet crusade in Afghanistan, or how its Middle East policies of supporting authoritarian regimes had produced profound resentment in the Muslim world—especially in countries that were considered allies of the United States—the nation quickly became engaged in an ideological battle of good versus evil, sanctimoniously disavowing any responsibility for its actions while reproducing the familiar pattern of international engagement that arguably caused the problem in the first place. And so, rather than reflect on the painful question of why they hate us, the country was quickly gearing up to wage an unpopular war in Iraq that would ultimately make them hate us more.

In this manner, the commemorating events of the first anniversary of 9/11 brought into focus the nation's investment in a monumental form of historiography in which, as Nietzsche observed, "much of the past would have to be overlooked if it was to produce that mighty effect" (69). Monumental history, as he elaborates, has "no use for that absolute veracity: it will always have to deal in approximations and generalities, in making what is dissimilar look similar; it will always have to diminish the differences of motives and instigations so as to exhibit the *effectus* monumentally, that is to say as something exemplary and worthy of imitation, at the expense of the *causae*" (70). The nation's monumentalizing engagement with history during the first anniversary thus mythologized the past by ignoring the overdetermined causes of the traumatic event and by dwelling on such political generalities as Americans' love of freedom and their unwavering commitment to democracy.

Although it is impossible to draw a clear line between a mythologized and a real past, my suggestion here is that a critically engaged historiography can bring about a more emancipatory politics of memory, one that works through past traumas and injustices by way of adjudicating or "properly" forgetting them. Such a critical mode of historicity, as Nietzsche reminds us, does not imply a simple condemnation of past injustices, for to the extent that we are ourselves an effect of these injustices, we can never fully free ourselves from them. Nor does it entail a pious search for truth, since we cannot access the past without a certain degree of subjectivity which inevitably colors any truth claim about the past. What we can do, as Nietzsche suggests, is "confront our inherited and hereditary nature with our knowledge, and through a new, stern discipline combat our inborn heritage and implant in ourselves a new habit, a new instinct, a second nature, so that our first nature withers away" (76). Whereas monumental historiography unconsciously repeats the past through a mythologized form of recollection, the kind of critical historiography I have proposed here entails the double mechanism of narrating the past as past and inventing what Nietzsche calls a "past in which one would like to originate in opposition to that in which one did originate" (76). The aim of critical historiography, in short, is not the recollection of the past but its excision, in order to invent an alternative future.

Notes

1 "US Imperialism," in Schwarz and Ray, *A Companion to Postcolonial Studies*, 208.

2 It is worth noting here that unlike postcolonial theorists, some scholars in the field of American studies, like Pease, have begun to map the relationship between American culture and imperialism, demonstrating the importance of studying U.S. imperialism as a political, economic, and cultural process. See for example Kaplan and Pease, *Cultures of United States Imperialism*.

3 Appadurai, *Modernity at Large*, 169.

4 Bhabha, "The Third Space," 218.

5 As one anonymous reviewer insightfully pointed out, the term "liberalism," while frequently invoked generically, in fact has specific and often contradictory meanings in different historical periods. Throughout the text I use the term merely to signify the liberal tradition within immigration discourse, which is broadly characterized by an attitude of receptivity toward immigrants—i.e., xenophilia—and the attendant propagation of the myth of immigrant America. Such an attitude may of course be embraced by liberals and conservatives, Democrats as well as Republicans.

6 Boris's "The Racialized Gendered State" also offers useful analysis of the interstices of gender and race in the construction of national identity. In addition, the collected edition *Women-Nation-State* by Yuval-Davis and Anthias offers excellent historical studies of how gendered the immigration and citizenship laws are in Europe, Africa, and Asia. Similarly, the edited volume *Nationalisms and Sexualities* by Parker, Russo, Summer, and Yaeger contains many insightful essays on how discourses of sexuality and nationalism inform notions of identity and culture. And finally, Mosse's *Nationalism and Sexuality* provides an insightful study of the misogynist and heterosexist reproductive policies of European states.

7 My theoretical elaboration of immigration and cultural identity in this book has also been informed by such sociological works as *Immigrant America* by Portes and Rumbaut and *America's New Immigration Law* by Cornelius and Montoya.

8 Lipsitz, *The Possessive Investment in Whiteness*, 5.

Introduction: Nation and Immigration

1 Iacocca made this remark in response to an interviewer's question about why it is important to have a museum such as the Ellis Island Immigration Museum; Scott Smith, "A Leader for Liberty," 30.

2 The federal government assumed responsibility for immigration only in the late nineteenth century. Until then, states with large ports of entry, such as New York, Maryland, Massachusetts, and Pennsylvania, had the authority to legislate individually laws concerning the inspection, integration, recruiting, and welfare of their immigrants. But with the passage of the Immigration Act of 3 August 1882, the federal government established the administrative machinery to control immigration. Supported by the Supreme Court's ruling in *Henderson v. Mayor of New York* (1875), which declared unconstitutional individual states' laws regulating immigration, the act in effect transferred the authority of immigration control from states to the federal government, marking a crucial stage in the development of immigration as an important site for the state's regulatory practices in the United States. The federal government initially took charge of immigration by providing individual states with funds to cover immigrant welfare, while building the administrative machinery to regulate and control immigration. A few years later, with the passage of the Immigration Act of 1891, the Congress created the Office of Immigration, the predecessor to today's INS, to oversee the control of immigration. This investment in the Office of Immigration of the authority to supervise and control aliens, combined with Congress's active role in legislating new immigration laws, shifted the practice of regulating immigration from a regional and particular issue to a national and general one. As the federal government's role in regulating immigration increased, immigration was generalized as a national problem to be regulated and controlled by national apparatuses.

3 For an insightful history of Ellis Island see Pitkin, *Keepers of the Gate*.

4 On 1 March 2003 the responsibility for providing immigration and citizenship services was transferred from the INS to the U.S. Citizenship and Immigration Services (USCIS), a bureau of the Department of Homeland Security.

5 It is suggestive, given Ronald Reagan's zeal for anti-communism, that

the massive effort to transform the Ellis Island immigration center into a national museum was supported by and took place during his administration, because the idea for an immigration museum was conceived during the cold war when the country was looking for a national symbol. In the early 1950s the American Scenic and Historic Preservation Society campaigned to build a museum of immigration somewhere in the port of New York. William H. Baldwin, one of its trustees, reasoned that "the Cold War with the Soviet Union had produced a need for national unity . . . and such a museum would be a strong force to this end" (Pitkin, *Keepers of the Gate*, 181). In 1956 Congress passed a resolution approving the plan for a group of private citizens to finance and develop a museum of immigration at the base of the Statue of Liberty.

6 These words are used in various exhibitions in the museum and in the *Official Souvenir Guide of Ellis Island*.

7 In fact, the effort was so successful that according to Iacocca, "Ellis Island is the only unit in the National Park system that has generated an endowment that will prevent it from falling into disrepair ever again" (32). For a fee of $100, any visitor can put his or her ancestor's name on the Immigrant Wall of Honor: over $60 million has been raised in this fashion.

8 From the author's interview with a park ranger at the Ellis Island Museum of Immigration, May 1999.

9 Kirshenblatt-Gimblett, *Destination Culture*, 187.

10 I borrow the notion of "invented tradition" from Eric Hobsbawm, who defines it as "a set of practices, normally governed by overtly or tacitly accepted rules and of a ritual or symbolic nature, which seek to inculcate certain values and norms of behaviour by repetition, which automatically implies continuity with the past." See Hobsbawm and Ranger, *Invention of Tradition*, 1.

11 By "economics of immigration," I mean not only such economic issues as the need for labor, supply and demand, exploitation, and the production of both value and wealth, but also the political economy of immigration as a socio-legal phenomenon.

12 I borrow the notion of "retrospective illusion" from Étienne Balibar, who argues that the history of nations embodies an illusionary relation to the past to make the formation of national identity the fulfillment of a continuous project; see his "The Nation Form."

13 Throughout this book, I use the concept of nation, following Benedict Anderson, to mean "an imagined political community—and imagined as both inherently limited and sovereign"; *Imagined Communities*, 6.

14 The notion of forgetting through repression (*Verdrängung*) is the cornerstone of Freud's theory of psychoanalysis and appears throughout his work, from his discussion of screen memory in 1889 to his *The Interpreta-*

tion of Dreams (1905) and *Three Essays on the Theory of Sexuality* (1905), but the essays where he specifically elaborates his theory of amnesia are "Repression" (1915), "The Unconscious" (1915), and "Negation" (1925), all of which are included in his *General Psychological Theory.*

15 Steiner elaborates this distinction in two essays: "Turning a Blind Eye" and "The Retreat from Truth to Omnipotence in Sophocles' *Oedipus at Colonus.*"

16 Chambers uses the notion of denial to unpack the complex cultural and textual strategies of what he calls "an aftermath society," that is, a society "in which innocence is lost and regained regularly" as "collectively traumatic events are denied, and if necessary denied again." See his *Untimely Interventions,* xxi.

17 Renan, "What Is a Nation?"; see also Balibar and Wallerstein, *Race, Nation, Class.*

18 I am citing here Tocqueville's description of America's national origin in *Democracy in America* (15), but the idea that it conveys has been constantly reiterated by historians and politicians throughout the history of the nation.

19 Pease has made a similar point in his insightful essay "US Imperialism" by arguing that "the doctrine of exceptionalism regulated how citizens responded to the historical existence of US colonies by characterizing them as exceptions to its norms," 204.

20 Kohn, *American Nationalism,* 135.

21 *Congressional Quarterly,* 1980, p. 2066; quoted in Horowitz and Noirel, *Immigrants in Two Democracies,* 40.

22 Fuchs, "Thinking about Immigration and Ethnicity in the United States."

23 Cohen, *States of Denial,* 13.

24 I am using here Higham's definition of the term in his *Strangers in the Land,* 4.

25 Grant and Davison, *Founders of the Republic on Immigration, Naturalization, and Aliens,* 62, 70.

26 For an elaborate discussion of the differences between Hamiltonian (Federalist) and Jeffersonian (Republican) views of national citizenship see Roger M. Smith, *Civic Ideals,* 115–96.

27 Quoted in Gordon, "Assimilation in America," 268.

28 My claim about the importance of assimilation to the project of imagining a homogeneous nation does not deny the existence of dissenting and countervailing forces, for the very hegemonic effort to domesticate and assimilate all traces of difference engenders through its imaginative work rudiments of resistance and opposition. As I elaborate in the following section, however, the insoluble antinomies that characterize national imagining in the United States embody irreconcilable differences among competing perceptions of national identity; instead of undoing or undermining one an-

other, as some critics have suggested, these differences in practice coexist and reinforce each other through historical amnesia.

29 Lowe, *Immigrant Acts*, 30.

30 Honig, *Democracy and the Foreigner*, 75.

31 Fukuyama, "Immigrants and Family Values," 157.

32 The speech at the Republican National Convention in 2004 by Governor Arnold Schwarzenegger of California, in which he used the story of his life as a successful immigrant to claim that "there's no place, no country that is more compassionate, more generous, more accepting and more welcoming than the United States of America," provides a striking example of how prosperous immigrants are constantly mobilized to shore up national pride. "This Country Is Truly Open to You," *Los Angeles Times*, 1 September 2004, § A, p. 20.

33 See for example Omi and Winant, *Racial Formation in the United States*, 16, 19–21; Blauner, *Racial Oppression in America*, 89.

34 The argument that I am making here may apply in other national contexts. Indeed, there is a strong French tradition of treating immigration as hospitality—a tradition, some critics have shown, contradicted by the laws of hospitality that the French government has passed to limit immigration. For insightful discussions of (in)hospitality in France see Rosello, *Postcolonial Hospitality*, and the volume edited by Fassin, Morice, and Quiminal, *Les lois de l'inhospitalité*.

35 Derrida, "Step of Hospitality/No Hospitality," 77. Derrida also elaborates his notion of hospitality in *Adieu to Emmanuel Levinas*. Here he reads Levinas's *Totalité et infini* (1961) as a "treatise of *hospitality*," distinguishing an *ethics* of hospitality, which is unlimited, from a *politics* of hospitality, which implies laws that delimit the boundaries of hospitality.

36 Lipset and Raab, *The Politics of Unreason*, 20.

37 See Walzer, *What It Means to Be an American*.

38 See Roger M. Smith, *Civic Ideals*.

39 Hull, *Without Justice for All*, 7. See also Harwood, *In Liberty's Shadow*.

40 See their edited volume, *Mexican Migration to the United States*.

41 Michaels, *Our America*, 32.

42 Calavita, *Inside the State*, 8.

43 Lacey, "Toned Down Bill on Immigration Passes in House."

Chapter 1: Imagining America

1 *Basic Writings of Thomas Jefferson*, 341.

2 As Fuchs explains, there were three ideas about immigration and membership in colonial America: the Pennsylvania idea that "all white European settlers were welcomed into the colony on terms of equal rights"; the Massa-

chusetts idea that "welcomed only those newcomers who accepted the stringent beliefs and practices of that theocratic community"; and the Virginia idea that encouraged the importation of "workers as cheaply as it could get them, without necessarily welcoming them to membership in the community." *The American Kaleidoscope*, 7–8.

3 *The Papers of Alexander Hamilton*, 25:491, 493–94.

4 "An Act relative to German and Swiss Redemptioners," passed 16 February 1818, *Laws of Maryland*, 1818, chapter 226, cited in Abbott, *Historical Aspects of the Immigration Problem*, 213.

5 See Emery, *Alexander Hamilton*.

6 It must be acknowledged that Hamilton's personal negation is not unique, for it is often the case that recently naturalized immigrants embrace the most vociferous forms of anti-immigration sentiment. The most notorious case is that of Denis Kearney, an Irish immigrant who led the anti-Chinese agitation in California in the late nineteenth century.

7 For example see Said, "Reflections on Exile."

8 Hospitality and hostility, one may further argue, inevitably go together in that they are both boundary-making gestures that signify: "you are not one of us." There is, as Derrida has pointed out, "etymological" evidence of this entailment of hostility in hospitality in the two English words, which derive from *hospitium* and *hospes* (meaning guest) and *hostilis* and *hostis* (meaning enemy).

9 For an extensive biography of Crèvecoeur see Allen and Asselineau, *St. John de Crèvecoeur*.

10 For an illuminating discussion of the initial reception of the *Letters* see Rice, "Crèvecoeur and the Politics of Authorship in Republican America."

11 The boosterism of the book was so apparent and successful that the English critic Ayscough felt compelled to write a whole book — *Remarks on the Letters from an American Farmer* — arguing that it was a poisonously misleading narrative designed to lure Europeans to immigrate to America.

12 Crèvecoeur, *Letters from an American Farmer*, 40. References to the work will hereafter be given parenthetically in the text.

13 Beidler, "Franklin's and Crèvecoeur's 'Literary' Americans," 50.

14 See Lawrence, *The Symbolic Meanings*, 53–70, and Fender, *Sea Changes*, 12.

15 Ruttenburg, *Democratic Personality*, 278.

16 For an insightful discussion of Enlightenment philosophy in Crèvecoeur see Rucker, "Crèvecoeur's *Letters* and Enlightenment Doctrine." And for an extensive treatment of the romanticized notion of pastoral America in *Letters* see Marx, *The Machine in the Garden*, 107–16. More recently, Christine Holbo has shown the indebtedness of the *Letters* to Edmund Burke's theory of the sublime and beautiful and Abbé Raynal's theory of commerce; see

her "Imagination, Commerce, and the Politics of Associationism in Crèvecoeur's *Letters from an American Farmer.*"

17 For a discussion of the disillusionment with the American experiment
expressed in the *Letters*, see Mohr, "Calculated Disillusionment."

18 Ironically, or rather predictably, Crèvecoeur was a slave owner himself, a fact to which he turns an authorial blind eye to make his abolitionist
argument in *Letters*.

19 Bakhtin, *The Dialogic Imagination*.

Chapter 2: *Historicizing America*

1 Introduction, *Democracy in America*, xxxii.

2 Lacapra, *History and Reading*, 78.

3 Pease, "After the Tocqueville Revival," 95.

4 "Tocqueville, Territory, and Violence," in Shapiro and Alker, *Challenging Boundaries*, 141-64.

5 Lefort, *Democracy and Political Theory*, 177, 179.

6 Foucault uses the notion of governmentality to describe a new form
of government that emerged and developed in the eighteenth century, in
which population becomes the target of power, political economy its form
of knowledge, and apparatuses of security its technical means. See his "Governmentality."

7 Wolin, *Tocqueville between Two Worlds*, 202-3.

8 Lefort has also noted in passing: "The author of *Democracy in America*
replaces the notion of a power that can be localized, of a visible power whose
action depends upon those who are entrusted with it, with that of a diffuse,
invisible power, which is both internal and external to individuals; which is
produced by individuals and which subjugates individuals; which is imaginary as it is real, and which is imprinted on government, administration and
opinion alike" (174).

9 Darby, *View of the United States*; Humboldt and Bonpland, *Personal Narrative of Travel to the Equinoctial Regions of the New Continent during the Years
1799–1804*; Warden, *A Statistical, Political, and Historical Account of the United
States of North America*.

10 Tocqueville's emphasis on geography and natural elements was heavily
informed by Darby's view that the "physical arrangement" of the United
States had direct "moral and political effects" on Europeans who came to
inhabit it (132). Geography and climate, according to Darby, determined the
political and moral culture of the United States.

11 Even an admirer of Tocqueville such as Wolin admits that Tocqueville's last chapter on "the Indians and the Negroes" is a "lame" and "em-

barrassing" discussion that does not do justice to the incomplete project of democracy in America and the fact that the notion of democracy does not adequately "describe the political constitution of the United States." See his *Tocqueville between Two Worlds*, 266–68.

12 It is worth emphasizing that Tocqueville was not so much concerned about the truth or falsity of race theories as their "practical consequences" for mankind. In one of his letters to Gobineau, for example, he castigated his doctrine of racial inequality: "What purpose does it serve to persuade lesser peoples living in abject conditions of barbarism or slavery that, such being their racial nature, they can do nothing to better themselves, to change their habits, or to ameliorate their status? Don't you see how inherent in your doctrine are all the evils produced by permanent inequality: pride, violence, the scorn of one's fellow men, tyranny, and abjection in every one of their forms?" See his *"The European Revolution" and Correspondence with Gobineau*, 229.

13 Foucault, "Governmentality," 95.

14 Lipsitz uses this term figuratively and literally to argue that "white Americans are encouraged to invest in whiteness, to remain true to an identity that provides them with resources, power, and opportunity" (vii).

15 Arthur Mann, to cite an example, has argued, "American nationality is purely ideological," by which he means that principles of democracy and liberty are the foundation of nationality in the United States; see his *The One and the Many*, 47.

Chapter 3: Immigrant America

1 *The Poems of Emma Lazarus*, 202–3.

2 Bhabha, "The Other Question," 149.

3 Takaki, *Iron Cages*, 281.

4 Introduction, *A Historical Guide to Walt Whitman*.

5 Vance, "What They're Saying about Whitman."

6 Phillips, "Nineteenth-Century Racial Thought and Whitman's 'Democratic Ethnology of the Future,'" 290.

7 Molesworth, "Whitman's Political Vision," 100.

8 "Our Territory on the Pacific," in Whitman's *The Gathering of the Forces*, 247.

9 Pinsker, "Walt Whitman and Our Multicultural America," 721.

10 In focusing on the Preface, I do not contend that this text is an exemplar of Whitman's position on race or other matters, nor that it should be regarded as an accurate distillation of the position articulated in the main body of *Leaves of Grass*. Rather, I focus on this text because it can be—and in-

deed has been—read as a self-standing manifesto, one that is expressive of a certain view, prominent in the mid-nineteenth century, regarding America's relationship with diversity.

11 "Preface to Leaves of Grass, 1855," *The Portable Walt Whitman*, 5. All page numbers hereafter will be given parenthetically in the text.

12 "The Political Roots of *Leaves of Grass*," in Reynolds's *A Historical Guide to Walt Whitman*, 113.

13 As an example of the tendency to marginalize and obscure the horrors of slavery in Whitman, it is worth noting that the figure of Lucifer, a young male slave who appears in the 1855 edition of *Leaves of Grass*, vanishes in the final edition of 1881.

14 Nietzsche, *Untimely Meditations*, 69.

15 One example of Whitman's uncritical stance is that while he was against slavery, he also opposed equal rights for African Americans. Indeed, as Ed Folsom observes, Whitman "was more supportive of blacks during the period when the issue was slavery than during the period after emancipation, when the issue became the access of free blacks to the basic rights of citizenship, including the right to vote." "Lucifer and Ethiopia," 46.

16 Dana Phillips, for example, has argued that Whitman's "Starting from Paumanok" (1860) "neatly read 'the red aborigins' out of existence" (312). Ed Folsom also argues in his essay in *A Historical Guide to Walt Whitman* that "the poet creates no black characters, not a hint of a representation that offers a place or role for the freed slaves in reconstructed America" (52).

17 Graham, "Solving 'All the Problems of Freedom,'" 14.

18 Pinsker, "Walt Whitman and Our Multicultural America," 717.

19 Olsen, "Whitman's *Leaves of Grass*," 307.

20 Handlin, *The Uprooted*, 5. References to the book will hereafter be given parenthetically in the text.

21 Though it is difficult to determine Kennedy's motives in espousing such a position, one may speculate that his own identity as a Catholic outsider and the political exigencies of the cold war may have mediated his perception of immigrant America.

22 Liberal defenses of immigrants during this period can be divided into what one may call "ethnic pride" literature and criticisms of U.S. immigration policy; in both these literatures immigrants are viewed as marginalized in the American democratic polity and yet crucial to it.

23 See for example Balch, *Our Slavic Fellow Citizens*; Blegen, *Norwegian Migration to America*; Ford, *The Scotch-Irish in America*; Faust, *The German Element in the United States*; Hoglund, *Finnish Immigrants in America*; Hartmann, *Americans from Wales*; Sowell, *Ethnic America*.

24 See for example Mills's introductory chapter in *Arguing Immigration*, 16.

25   In this regard my argument differs from that made by Lowe: while I agree with her that the Asian American continues to "serve as a 'screen,' a phantasmatic site, on which the nation projects a series of condensed, complicated anxieties regarding external and internal threats to the mutable coherence of the national body," I do not agree that the Asian immigrant remains a threat by being figured as "the automaton whose inhuman efficiency will supersede American ingenuity"; see her *Immigrant Acts*, 18.

Chapter 4: *Discourses of Exclusion*

1   For a brief report of the controversy see "Wilson Ad Sparks Charges of Immigrant-Bashing," *Los Angeles Times*, 14 May 1994, § A, p. 1.

2   "Wilson Ad Sparks Charges of Immigrant-Bashing," 1.

3   See Cornelius, "America in the Era of Limits."

4   "Tensions on Hereford Drive," *Los Angeles Times*, 4 March 1996.

5   See for example Muller, "Nativism in the Mid-1990s," 106–9.

6   I am quoting Bruce Cain, a political scientist and the associate director of the Institute of Governmental Studies at the University of California, Berkeley, but the argument has been made by many economists, sociologists, political scientists, and immigrant-rights activists; "Hospitality Turns into Hostility," *Los Angeles Times*, 14 November 1993.

7   See Gordon, *Assimilation in American Life*, and Higham, *Strangers in the Land*.

8   This forgetfulness was revealed to me accidentally and anecdotally in an e-mail exchange with my graduate research assistant. In a hurriedly written note, I asked her to do a general search on the Know-Nothings, assuming that she knew something about them. She replied the next day, asking half apologetically and half embarrassedly, "Who/what were Know-Nothings?" Though her question worried me initially about my broaching such an "outdated" topic, it eventually proved useful in my thinking about the complementary relation between the nation's xenophobic and xenophilic tendencies, between its myth of immigrant asylum and its nativist isolation. That even a highly educated person in America knows almost nothing about its history of nativism speaks to the powerful ways in which the myth of immigrant America has dominated the discourse of nationalism in the United States, a myth that has made us forgetful of our nation's anti-immigrant tendencies.

9   *The Works of Alexander Hamilton*, 4:481.

10   Higham in *Strangers in the Land* traces the nation's anti-Catholicism to the early English colonizers' struggle against the two hostile Catholic empires of France and Spain in the New World; its anti-foreign and anti-

radical tradition to the late eighteenth century, when the French Revolution led to the stereotype of Europeans as "disloyal" and "revolutionary"; and the nativists' racism to the colonizers' ideology of Anglo-Saxon racial superiority.

11 Billington, *The Protestant Crusade*, 322.

12 Anbinder, *Nativism and Slavery*, 99.

13 Baker, *Ambivalent Americans*, xii.

14 Whitney, *A Defence of the American Policy*, vii. Page references will hereafter be given parenthetically in the text.

15 The quotation is from a lecture that John Adams delivered in 1798 to the inhabitants of Arlington and Sandgate, but the sentiment that it expresses was prevalent among the framers of the Constitution; Grant and Davidson, *The Founders of the Republic on Immigration, Naturalization and Aliens*, 6.

16 Powderly, "Immigration's Menace to the National Health," 60.

17 As will become clear from the development of my argument in the remaining pages of this chapter, I do not mean that this shift marked the end of nativist ideology and racism. Quite the contrary, my point is that the new form of nativism inaugurated an ideological (racist) conception of health.

18 Boston Committee of Internal Health, *Report of the Committee of Internal Health on the Asiatic Cholera*, 9–15, repr. in Abbott, *Historical Aspects of the Immigration Problem*, 594.

19 Given the shift in the national perception of immigrants, one may argue that the figured nation itself moves from a republic of ideas to a more embodied form.

20 See for example Kraut, *Silent Travelers*.

21 Yew, "Medical Inspection of the Immigrant at Ellis Island."

22 Analogously, in her insightful book *Abortion and the Politics of Motherhood*, Kristin Luker discusses how the nineteenth-century professionalization of medicine radically altered the perceptions of abortion in the United States, making it a scientific matter to be regulated by doctors and thus radically limiting women's choice in the matter.

23 Reed, "Immigration and the Public Health," 313. I will discuss Reed's essay in more detail later in this chapter.

24 The U.S. Marine Hospital Service was founded in 1789 to care for American merchant marine sailors. In 1903 its name was changed to the U.S. Public Health and Marine Hospital Service, a change that signaled the expansion of its task to care for the broader control of infectious diseases and the quarantine of those infected. In 1912 the service was again renamed by Congress, as the U.S. Public Health Service.

25 For an in-depth and illuminating account of the PHS see Mullan, *Plagues and Politics*.

26 It may be noted in passing that these doctors not only used their medical authority to advocate their nativist immigration policies but also took advantage of the arrival of new immigrants to concentrate and credentialize their authority as doctors. Given the context of new immigration, they could now claim to be uniquely situated to protect the nation.

27 The words are Reed's; see his "The Medical Side of Immigration," 392.

28 The first- and second-class passengers were checked cursorily by doctors aboard the vessels, and with few exceptions were saved a visit to Ellis Island. The disparate treatment of immigrants points to the association of poverty with illness, an association that was "justified" in environmental terms—e.g., the poor travel and live more closely together and therefore pose a greater health risk. The association of poverty with illness also suggests that the class component played a role in disciplining new immigrants.

29 As I will discuss in the following chapter, concerns about both "illegal" immigration and terrorism since 9/11 have functioned in a similar way, in that they have not only legitimized a broad range of disciplinary practices exercised over immigrants and foreigners but also subjected the average citizen to surveillance and vigilantism.

30 At the same time, of course, the embodied notion of national identity enabled the practice of medicine as a profession. In other words, while medical doctors took advantage of their "scientific" authority to call for more restrictive immigration policies, they utilized their crusade against lax immigration to consolidate and enhance their authority as physicians.

31 The historian Bernhard Knollenberg has even argued that the white settlers *intentionally* spread diseases such as smallpox among Native Americans as a way of clearing them from the land. See his "General Amherst and Germ Warfare."

32 For a balanced and insightful discussion of these earlier epidemics see Kraut, *Silent Travelers*, 11–49.

33 Reed, "Going through Ellis Island," 5–6.

34 Feagin, "Old Poison in New Bottles."

35 The dictionary constituted the fifth volume of the forty-two in *Reports of the Immigration Commission*.

36 As the historian Allan Chase has demonstrated, Albert Johnson, the chair of the House committee that drafted the Immigration Act of 1924, was closely associated with such racist scientists and intellectuals as Carl Brigham, Madison Grant, and Kenneth Roberts and followed their work; see Chase, *The Legacy of Malthus*, 270–90. Such an association, I may add, testifies to the formative role that nativism played not only in defining cultural identity in the United States but in crafting the nation's modern immigration policy.

37 I borrow these words from Perea, but the theoretical insight is that of

René Girard. See Perea's Introduction in *Immigrants Out!*, 1, and Girard's *Violence and the Sacred*.

38 Benjamin, *Illuminations*, 257.

Chapter 5: Practices of Exclusion

1 Every traveler entering the U.S. territory is inspected by a primary inspector who examines the traveler's entry documents—passport, resident alien card, etc. If the primary inspector suspects the traveler of being ineligible to enter, a secondary inspection follows that may involve anything from further standard questions about the person's intention in traveling to the United States to baggage and body searches.

2 The quotation is James Clifford's (see "Traveling Cultures," 109), but the idea is shared by many cultural and literary critics. For a critical discussion of travel as a privileged trope see my "Traveling to Teach," 40–41.

3 Gómez-Peña, "Death on the Border," 8.

4 Despite the Freedom of Information Act of 1966, certain crucial documents of the INS have been kept secret by the agency, and nondisclosure remains pervasive and prevalent. This attitude is consistent with the INS's disciplinary regime of power, one that relies on a hierarchical mode of observation in which there is no reciprocity between the observer and the observed. For a discussion of the INS's non-disclosure policy see Roland M. Kaplan, "The Secret Law of the Immigration and Naturalization Service," 140–51.

5 Miller, *The Novel and the Police*, 17.

6 Gilboy, "Deciding Who Gets In," 575.

7 The agent's discretionary power has been recently extended by the Immigration Act of 1996, which authorizes the expedited removal of refugees and other immigrants deemed "excludable" at the border by an inspector, as well as by the passage of the Patriot Act, which has allowed immigration officials to exercise authority with almost total impunity.

8 A discussion of how Asians have been stereotyped in western cultures is beyond the scope of this chapter. See Said, *Orientalism*, for an elaborate study of this issue.

9 I am paraphrasing here the words of an INS agent who is elaborating on how the knowledge of types helped him to be a better inspector. Gilboy, "Deciding Who Gets In," 581.

10 Quoted in Dwyer, *On the Line*, 109.

11 Foucault, *Discipline and Punish*, 139.

12 Vol. 23, no. 3 (summer 1992): 16–18. "Revenue nose," as the article explains, is "a term used by officers of Her Majesty's Customs Exercise to de-

scribe the sixth sense possessed by some Customs officers that gives them the ability to detect smugglers" (18).

13 Needless to say, lying in the application also puts the immigrant in violation of U.S. immigration law, and doing so can later be used to criminalize or deport him or her.

14 See U.S. Department of Justice, Immigration and Naturalization Service, "Building a Comprehensive Southwest Border Enforcement Strategy" (June 1996).

15 Although such high technology was initially deployed at the border between the United States and Mexico, since 9/11 the border with Canada and other ports of entry have been equipped with computer tracking networks and other surveillance systems to prevent the entry of suspected terrorists.

16 For examples of the nation's concern about the security of its border see Chaze, "Invasion from Mexico"; and Dowd, "Losing Control of the Borders." In his insightful *The Militarization of the U.S.-Mexico Border, 1978–1992*, Dunn elaborates how the government has turned the border into a military zone, using war strategies to guard against "alien invasion."

17 For a history of the Border Patrol see Perkins, *Border Patrol*.

18 The words are those of the INS commissioner Doris Meissner, in her foreword to *Meeting the Challenge through Innovation*.

19 Chavez, *Shadowed Lives*, 41.

20 Brinkley, "A Success at the Border Earned Only a Shrug."

21 The words are those of the agent Leo Aguirre of El Paso, Texas. Quoted in Chaze, "Invasion from Mexico," 37–38.

22 Chaze, "Invasion from Mexico," 37–38.

23 See *Hampton v. Mow Sun Wong*, 426 U.S. 88, 101–2 (1976). Needless to say, since 9/11, most courts have further empowered the federal government in imposing measures on aliens that raise serious questions of constitutionality. For a detailed study of such measures, see Cole, *Enemy Aliens*.

24 "Immigration Law after a Century of Plenary Power."

25 This view is echoed by a senior INS bureaucrat in Washington who cites one of his agents as saying, "You know we're here [at the border] playing a game. They [in Washington] don't want us to do our job. Illegal aliens come in and feed the economy and we're not allowed to do our job. It's a game." Quoted in Calavita, *Inside the State*, 164.

26 It is worth noting in passing that the idea of inconsequential retribution, or inadequate punishment, can also be extended to include ineffective employer sanctions. Even though the 1986 Immigration Reform and Control Act imposed for the first time sanctions against those who knowingly hire undocumented workers, the law maintains loopholes that effectively protect employers from prosecution. For a perceptive discussion of this issue, see *Inside the State*, 168–70.

27 See for example Portes, "Of Borders and States," in Cornelius and Montoya, *America's New Immigration Law*; and Lopez, "Undocumented Mexican Migration."

28 I am citing here the Dillingham Immigration Commission's report of 1911; see U.S. Congress, Senate Immigration Commission, 1911, 690–91. For a historical discussion of the Mexican immigrant as valuable laborer but undesirable citizen, see Reisler's "Always the Laborer, Never the Citizen," in Gutierrez, *Between Two Worlds: Mexican Immigrants in the United States.*

29 "Commodity-Migrants," in Ross's *Views across the Border*, 189.

30 Silverstein, "Job Market a Flash Point for Natives, Newcomers," 17.

31 See for example Maram, "Hispanic Workers in the Garment and Restaurant Industries in Los Angeles County."

32 "Economic Factors Influencing the International Migration of Workers," in Ross, 169.

33 Quoted in Stacy and Lutton, *The Immigration Time Bomb*, vii.

34 My discussion of the relation between state's command and national consensus is indebted to Antonio Negri's theory of "crisis-state." See, for example, his "Crisis of the Crisis-State," in *Revolution Retrieved*.

35 For a discussion of the duplicitous tendencies of the U.S. immigration policy see Calavita, "U.S. Immigration and Policy Responses," in Cornelius, Martin, and Hollifield, *Controlling Immigration*.

36 See Dwyer, *On the Line*, 100–120.

Conclusion: *Remembering 9/11*

1 Kakutani, "Vigilance and Memory," 14.

2 "Statement of U.S. Senator Russell Feingold on the Anti-terrorism Bill from the Senate Floor."

3 My argument here is indebted to Freud's insight about repetition as a form of disavowal. In this form of repression, he shows that "the patient does not *remember* anything of what he has forgotten and repressed, but *acts* it out" (150; emphasis in original). See his "Remembering, Repeating and Working-Through."

4 Žižek, *Welcome to the Desert of the Real*, 22.

Bibliography

Abbott, Edith, ed. *Historical Aspects of the Immigration Problem: Selected Documents*. Chicago: University of Chicago Press, 1926.

Allen, Gay Wilson, and Roger Asselineau. *St. John de Crèvecoeur: The Life of an American Farmer*. New York: Viking, 1987.

Anbinder, Tyler. *Nativism and Slavery: The Northern Know Nothings and the Politics of the 1850s*. Oxford: Oxford University Press, 1992.

Anderson, Benedict. *Imagined Communities: Reflections on the Origin and Spread of Nationalism*. London: Verso, 1992.

Anzaldúa, Gloria. *Borderlands/La Frontera: The New Mestiza*. San Francisco: Spinsters /Aunt Lute, 1987.

Appadurai, Arjun. *Modernity at Large: Cultural Dimensions of Globalization*. Minneapolis: University of Minnesota Press, 1996.

Ayscough, Samuel. *Remarks on the Letters from an American Farmer; or, a Detection of the Errors of Mr. Hector St. John; Pointing to the Pernicious Tendency of These Letters to Great Britain*. London: John Fielding, 1783.

Baker, Jean H. *Ambivalent Americans: The Know-Nothing Party in Maryland*. Baltimore: Johns Hopkins University Press, 1977.

Bakhtin, Mikhail. *The Dialogic Imagination*. Ed. Michael Holquist. Austin: University of Texas Press, 1981.

Balch, Emily G. *Our Slavic Fellow Citizens*. New York: Charities Publication Committee, 1910.

Balibar, Étienne. "The Nation Form: History and Ideology." *Review* 13 (1990): 329–61.

Balibar, Étienne, and Immanuel Wallerstein. *Race, Nation, Class: Ambiguous Identities*. London: Verso, 1991.

Behdad, Ali. *Belated Travelers: Orientalism in the Age of Colonial Dissolution*. Durham: Duke University Press, 1994.

———. "Traveling to Teach: Postcolonial Critics in the American Academy." *Race, Identity, and Representation in Education*. Ed. Cameron McCarthy and Warren Crichlow. New York: Routledge, 1993. 40–49.

Beidler, Philip D. "Franklin's and Crèvecoeur's 'Literary' Americans." *Early American Literature* 13, no. 1 (1978): 50–63.

Benjamin, Walter. *Illuminations*. New York: Schocken, 1969.

Bhabha, Homi. "The Other Question: Difference, Discrimination and the Discourse of Colonialism." *Literature, Politics, and Theory*. Ed. Francis Barker et al. London: Methuen, 1986. 148–72.

———. "The Third Space." *Identity, Community, Culture, Difference*. Ed. Jonathan Rutherford. London: Lawrence and Wishart, 1990. 207–21.

Billington, Ray Allen. *The Protestant Crusade, 1800–1860: A Study of the Origins of American Nativism*. New York: Macmillan, 1938.

Birkbeck, Morris. *Letters from Illinois*. Philadelphia: M. Carey, 1818.

Blauner, Robert. *Racial Oppression in America*. New York: Harper and Row, 1972.

Blegen, Theodore. *Norwegian Migration to America*. Northfield, Minn.: Norwegian-American Historical Association, 1931.

Boris, Eileen. "The Racialized Gendered State: Constructions of Citizenship in the United States." *Social Politics*, summer 1995, 160–80.

Boston Committee of Internal Health. *Report of the Committee of Internal Health on the Asiatic Cholera*. Boston City Documents 66, 1849. Repr. in Edith Abbott, ed. *Historical Aspects of the Immigration Problem: Select Documents*. Chicago: University of Chicago Press, 1926.

Brimelow, Peter. *Alien Nation: Common Sense about America's Immigration Disaster*. New York: Harper Perennial, 1995.

Brinkley, Joel. "A Success at the Border Earned Only a Shrug." *New York Times*, 14 September 1994.

Brooks, Nigel. "The Revenue Nose." *Customs Today* 27, no. 3 (1992): 16–18.

Brownstein, Ronald. "Hospitality Turns into Hostility." *Los Angeles Times*, 14 November 1993, § A, p. 1.

Bustamante, Jorge. "Commodity-Migrants: Structural Analysis of Mexican Immigration to the United States." *Views across the Border*. Ed. Stanley Ross. Albuquerque: University of New Mexico Press, 1978. 183–203.

Calavita, Kitty. *Inside the State: The Bracero Program, Immigration, and the INS*. New York: Routledge, 1992.

———. "U.S. Immigration and Policy Responses: The Limits of Legislation." *Controlling Immigration: A Global Perspective*. Ed. Wayne A. Cornelius, Philip L. Martin, and James F. Hollifield. Stanford: Stanford University Press, 1994. 55–82.

Chambers, Ross. *Untimely Interventions: AIDS Writing, Testimonial, and the Rhetoric of Haunting*. Ann Arbor: University of Michigan Press, 2004.

Chase, Allan. *The Legacy of Malthus: The Social Costs of the New Scientific Racism*. New York: Alfred A. Knopf, 1977.

Chateaubriand, François-René, Vicomte de. *Voyage en Amerique suivi des Natchez.* Paris: Lefèvre, 1838.

Chavez, Leo. *Shadowed Lives: Undocumented Immigrants in American Society.* Fort Worth: Harcourt Brace Jovanovich College Publishers, 1992.

Chaze, William. "Invasion from Mexico: It Just Keeps Growing." *U.S. News & World Report,* 7 March 1983.

Clifford, James. "Traveling Cultures." *Cultural Studies.* Ed. Lawrence Grossberg, Cary Nelson, and Paula Treichler. New York: Routledge, 1993. 96–111.

Cohen, Stanley. *States of Denial: Knowing about Atrocities and Suffering.* Cambridge: Polity, 2001.

Cole, David. *Enemy Aliens: Double Standards and Constitutional Freedoms in the War on Terrorism.* New York: New Press, 2003.

Cornelius, Wayne. "American in the Era of Limits: Nativist Reactions to the 'New Immigration.'" *Working Papers in U.S.-Mexico Studies* 3. San Diego: University of California, San Diego, 1982.

Cornelius, Wayne A., and Ricardo Anzaldua Montoya, eds. *America's New Immigration Law: Origins, Rationales, and Potential Consequences.* La Jolla: Center for U.S.-Mexican Studies, University of California, San Diego, 1983.

Cornelius, Wayne, and Jorge A. Bustamante, eds. *Mexican Migration to the United States: Origins, Consequences, and Policy Options.* La Jolla: Center for U.S.-Mexican Studies, University of California, San Diego, 1989.

Crèvecoeur, J. Hector St. John de. *Letters from an American Farmer.* Oxford: Oxford University Press, 1997.

Darby, William. *View of the United States.* Philadelphia: H. S. Tanner, 1828.

Davison, Stewart. *The Founders of the Republic on Immigration and Naturalization and Aliens.* New York: Charles Scribner's Sons, 1928.

Derrida, Jacques. *Adieu to Emmanuel Levinas.* Trans. Pascale-Anne Brault and Michael Naas. Stanford: Stanford University Press, 1999.

———. "Step of Hospitality/No Hospitality." *Of Hospitality: Anne Dufourmantelle Invites Jacques Derrida to Respond.* Trans. Rachel Bowlby. Stanford: Stanford University Press, 2000.

Dictionary of Races of Peoples: Reports of the Immigration Commission. Vol. 42. Washington: Government Printing Office, 1911.

Dillingham Immigration Commission's Report, 1911. U.S. Congress: Senate Immigration Commission, 1911.

Dowd, Maureen. "Losing Control of the Borders." *Time,* 13 June 1983.

Dunn, Timothy J. *The Militarization of the U.S.-Mexico Border, 1978–1992: Low-Intensity Conflict Doctrine Comes Home.* Austin: University of Texas Press, 1996.

Dwyer, Augusta. *On the Line: Life on the U.S.-Mexico Border.* London: Latin American Bureau, 1994.

Emery, Noemie. *Alexander Hamilton: An Intimate Portrait*. New York: G. P. Putnam's Sons, 1982.

Epstein, Joseph. Introduction to *Democracy in America*, by Alexis de Tocqueville. Trans. Henry Reeve. New York: Bantam, 2000.

Fassin, Didier, Alain Morice, and Catherine Quiminal, eds. *Les lois de l'inhospitalité: Les politiques de l'immigration à l'épreuve des sans-papiers*. Paris: La Découverte, 1997.

Faust, Albert B. *The German Element in the United States*. Boston: Houghton Mifflin, 1909.

Feagin, Joe. "Old Poison in New Bottles: The Deep Roots of Modern Nativism." *Immigrants Out! The New Nativism and the Anti-immigrant Impulse in the United States*. Ed. Juan F. Perea. New York: New York University Press, 1997. 13–43.

Fearon, Henry Bradshaw. *Sketches of America: A Narrative of a Journey of Five Thousand Miles through the Eastern and Western States of America*. London: Longman, Hurst, Rees, Orme, and Brown, 1818.

Fender, Stephen. *Sea Changes: British Emigration and American Literature*. Cambridge: Cambridge University Press, 1992.

Folsom, Ed. "Lucifer and Ethiopia: Whitman, Race, and Poetics before the Civil War and after." *A Historical Guide to Walt Whitman*. Ed. David S. Reynolds. Oxford: Oxford University Press, 2000. 52–96.

Ford, Henry Jones. *The Scotch-Irish in America*. Princeton: Princeton University Press, 1915.

Foucault, Michel. *Discipline and Punish: The Birth of the Prison*. Trans. Alan Sheridan. New York: Vintage, 1977.

———. "Governmentality." *The Foucault Effect: Studies in Governmentality*. Ed. Graham Burchell, Colin Gordon, and Peter Miller. London: Harvester, 1991. 87–104.

Freud, Sigmund. *General Psychological Theory: Papers on Metapsychology*. Ed. Philip Rieff. New York: Collier, 1963.

———. *The Interpretation of Dreams*. Ed. Harold Bloom. New York: Chelsea House, 1987.

———. "Remembering, Repeating and Working-Through." *The Standard Edition of the Complete Psychological Works of Sigmund Freud*. Trans. James Strachey. Vol. 12. London: Hogarth, 1958. 147–56.

———. *Three Essays on the Theory of Sexuality*. Ed. and trans. James Strachey. New York: Basic Books, 1975.

Fuchs, Lawrence H. *The American Kaleidoscope: Race, Ethnicity, and the Civic Culture*. Hanover: Wesleyan University Press, 1990.

———. "Thinking about Immigration and Ethnicity in the United States." *Immigrants in Two Democracies: French and American Experience*. Ed. Donald Horowitz and Gérard Noirel. New York: New York University Press, 1992. 39–65.

Fukuyama, Francis. "Immigrants and Family Values." *Arguing Immigration: The Debate over the Changing Face of America.* Ed. Nicolaus Mills. New York: Simon and Schuster, 1994. 151–68.

Gilboy, Janet. "Deciding Who Gets In: Decisionmaking by Immigration Inspectors." *Law and Society Review* 25, no. 3 (1991): 571–600.

Girard, René. *Violence and the Sacred.* Baltimore: Johns Hopkins University Press, 1977.

Gómez-Peña, Guillermo. "Death on the Border: A Eulogy to Border Art." *High Performance* 12 (1991): 8–9.

Gordon, Milton. *Assimilation in American Life: The Role of Race, Religion, and National Origin.* New York: Oxford University Press, 1964.

————. "Assimilation in America: Theory and Reality." *Daedalus* 90 (1961): 263–85.

Graham, Rosemary. "Solving 'All the Problems of Freedom': The Case of the 1860 *Leaves of Grass.*" *ATQ* 7, no. 1 (March 1993): 5–23.

Grant, Madison, and Charles Stewart Davidson, eds. *The Founders of the Republic on Immigration, Naturalization and Aliens.* New York: Charles Scribner's Sons, 1928.

Hamilton, Alexander. "The Examination." *The Papers of Alexander Hamilton.* Ed. Harold C. Syrett. Vol. 25. New York: Columbia University Press, 1977.

————. *The Works of Alexander Hamilton.* Ed. Henry Cabot Lodge. Vol. 4. Washington: Federal Edition, 1904.

Hampton vs. Mow Sun Wong, 426 U.S. 88 (1976).

Handlin, Oscar. *The Uprooted: The Epic Story of the Great Migrations That Made the American People.* Boston: Little, Brown, 1951.

————. "We Need More Immigrants." *Atlantic* 191, no. 5 (1953): 27–31.

Hartmann, Edward G. *Americans from Wales.* Boston: Christopher, 1967.

Harwood, Edwin. *In Liberty's Shadow: Illegal Aliens and Immigration Law Enforcement.* Stanford: Hoover Institution Press, 1986.

Higham, John. *Strangers in the Land: Patterns of American Nativism, 1860–1925.* New York: Atheneum, 1973.

Hobsbawm, Eric, and Terence Ranger, eds. *Invention of Tradition.* Cambridge: Cambridge University Press, 1992.

Hoglund, A. William. *Finnish Immigrants in America, 1880–1920.* Madison: University of Wisconsin Press, 1960.

Holbo, Christine. "Imagination, Commerce, and the Politics of Associationism in Crèvecoeur's *Letters from an American Farmer.*" *Early American Literature* 32 (1997): 20–65.

Honig, Bonnie. *Democracy and the Foreigner.* Princeton: Princeton University Press, 2001.

hooks, bell. "Representing Whiteness in the Black Imagination." *Cultural*

Studies. Ed. Lawrence Grossberg, Cary Nelson, and Paula Treichler. New York: Routledge, 1993. 338–46.

Horowitz, Donald, and Gérard Noirel, eds. *Immigrants in Two Democracies: French and American Experience*. New York: New York University Press, 1992.

Hull, Elizabeth. *Without Justice for All: The Constitutional Rights of Aliens*. Westport, Conn.: Greenwood, 1985.

Humboldt, Alexander von, and Aimé Bonpland. *Personal Narrative of Travel to the Equinoctial Regions of the New Continent during the Years 1799–1804*. Trans. Helen Maria Williams. Philadelphia: M. Carey, 1815.

Jefferson, Thomas. "First Annual Message to Congress." *Basic Writings of Thomas Jefferson*. Ed. Philip S. Foner. New York: Wiley, 1944.

Kakutani, Michiko. "Vigilance and Memory." *New York Times*, 12 September 2002.

Kaplan, Amy, and Donald E. Pease, eds. *Cultures of United States Imperialism*. Durham: Duke University Press, 1993.

Kaplan, Roland M. "The Secret Law of the Immigration and Naturalization Service." *Iowa Law Review* 56, no. 1 (1970): 140–51.

Kennedy, John F. *A Nation of Immigrants*. New York: Harper and Row, 1964.

Kirshenblatt-Gimblett, Barbara. *Destination Culture: Tourism, Museums, and Heritage*. Berkeley: University of California Press, 1998.

Knollenberg, Bernhard. "General Amherst and Germ Warfare." *Journal of American History* 41 (1954): 762–63.

Kohn, Hans. *American Nationalism: An Interpretative Essay*. New York: Macmillan, 1957.

Kraut, Alan M. *Silent Travelers: Germs, Genes, and the "Immigrant Menace."* New York: Basic Books, 1994.

Lacapra, Dominick. *History and Reading: Tocqueville, Foucault, French Studies*. Toronto: University of Toronto Press, 2000.

Lacey, Marc. "Toned Down Bill on Immigration Passes in House." *Los Angeles Times*, 19 September 1996, § A, p. 20.

Lawrence, D. H. *The Symbolic Meanings: The Uncollected Versions of Studies in Classic American Literature*. Ed. Armin Arnold. London: Centaur, 1962.

Lazarus, Emma. *The Poems of Emma Lazarus*. Boston: Houghton, Mifflin, 1889.

Lefort, Claude. *Democracy and Political Theory*. Trans. David Macey. Cambridge: Polity, 1988.

Lipset, Seymour Martin, and Earl Raab. *The Politics of Unreason: Right-Wing Extremism in America, 1790–1970*. New York: Harper and Row, 1970.

Lipsitz, George. *The Possessive Investment in Whiteness: How White People Profit from Identity Politics.* Philadelphia: Temple University Press, 1998.

Locke, John. *Two Treatises of Government.* Ed. Peter Laslett. Cambridge: Cambridge University Press, 1967.

Lopez, Gerald. "Undocumented Mexican Migration: In Search of a Just Immigration Law and Policy." *UCLA Law Review* 28 (1981): 615–714.

Loving, Jerome. "The Political Roots of *Leaves of Grass.*" *A Historical Guide to Walt Whitman.* Ed. David S. Reynolds. Oxford: Oxford University Press, 2000. 97–119.

Lowe, Lisa. *Immigrant Acts: On Asian American Cultural Politics.* Durham: Duke University Press, 1996.

Luker, Kristin. *Abortion and the Politics of Motherhood.* Berkeley: University of California Press, 1984.

Mann, Arthur. *The One and the Many: Reflections on the American Identity.* Chicago: University of Chicago Press, 1979.

Maram, Sheldon L. "Hispanic Workers in the Garment and Restaurant Industries in Los Angeles County." *Working Papers in U.S.-Mexico Studies.* San Diego: University of California, San Diego, 1980.

Marshall, F. Ray. "Economic Factors Influencing the International Migration of Workers." *Views across the Border.* Ed. Stanley Ross. Albuquerque: University of New Mexico Press, 1978. 163–82.

Marx, Leo. *The Machine in the Garden: Technology and the Pastoral Idea in America.* Oxford: Oxford University Press, 1968.

Meissner, Doris. Foreword. *Meeting the Challenge through Innovation.* Washington: Immigration and Naturalization Service, 1996.

Michaels, Walter Benn. *Our America: Nativism, Modernism, and Pluralism.* Durham: Duke University Press, 1997.

Miller, D. A. *The Novel and the Police.* Berkeley: University of California Press, 1988.

Millman, Joel. *The Other Americans: How Immigrants Renew Our Country, Our Economy, and Our Values.* New York: Viking, 1997.

Mills, Nicolaus. Introduction. *Arguing Immigration: The Debate over the Changing Face of America.* Ed. Nicolaus Mills. New York: Simon and Schuster, 1994.

Mohr, James C. "Calculated Disillusionment: Crèvecoeur's *Letters* Reconsidered." *South Atlantic Quarterly* 69 (1970): 354–63.

Molesworth, Charles. "Whitman's Political Vision." *Raritan* 12, no. 1 (1992): 98–112.

Morton, Nathaniel. *New England's Memorial.* 6th ed. Boston: Congregational Board of Publication, 1854.

Mosse, George. *Nationalism and Sexuality: Respectability and Abnormal Sexuality in Modern Europe.* New York: H. Fertig, 1985.

Motomura, Hiroshi. "Immigration Law after a Century of Plenary Power: Phantom Constitutional Norms and Statutory Interpretation." *Yale Law Review* 100, no. 3 (1990): 545.

Mouffe, Chantal, ed. *Dimensions of Radical Democracy: Pluralism, Citizenship, Community*. London: Verso, 1992.

———. *The Return of the Political*. London: Verso, 1993.

Mullan, Fitzhugh. *Plagues and Politics: The Story of the United States Public Health Service*. New York: Basic Books, 1989.

Muller, Thomas. "Nativism in the Mid-1990s: Why Now?" *Immigrants Out! The New Nativism and the Anti-immigrant Impulse in the United States*. Ed. Juan F. Perea. New York: New York University Press, 1997. 105–18.

Nazario, Sonia. "Natives, Newcomers at Odds in East L.A.; Hereford Drive Offers a Window into Tensions between Mexican Americans, New Arrivals." *Los Angeles Times*, 4 March 1996, § A, p. 1.

Negri, Antonio. "Crisis of the Crisis-State." *Revolution Retrieved: Selected Writings on Marx, Keynes, Capitalist Crisis and New Social Subjects, 1967–1983*. London: Red Notes, 1988.

Nietzsche, Friedrich. *Untimely Meditations*. Ed. Daniel Breazeale. Trans. R. J. Hollingdale. Cambridge: Cambridge University Press, 1997.

Nisbet, Robert. "Many Tocquevilles." *American Scholar* 46, no. 1 (1977): 59–75.

Olsen, Robert. "Whitman's *Leaves of Grass*: Poetry and the Founding of a 'New World' Culture." *University of Toronto Quarterly* 64, no. 2 (1995) 305–23.

Omi, Michael, and Howard Winant. *Racial Formation in the United States: From the 1960s to the 1990s*. New York: Routledge, 1994.

Parker, Andrew, Mary Russo, Doris Summers, and Patricia Yaeger. *Nationalisms and Sexualities*. New York: Routledge, 1992.

Pease, Donald E. "After the Tocqueville Revival; or, The Return of the Political." *boundary 2* 26, no. 3 (1999): 87–114.

———. "US Imperialism: Global Dominance without Colonies." *A Companion to Postcolonial Studies*. Ed. Henry Schwarz and Sangeeta Ray. London: Basil Blackwell, 2000. 203–20.

Perea, Juan F. Introduction. *Immigrants Out! The New Nativism and the Anti-immigrant Impulse in the United States*. Ed. Juan F. Perea. New York: New York University Press, 1997. 1–10.

Perkins, Clifford Alan. *Border Patrol: With the U.S. Immigration Service on the Mexican Boundary, 1910–1954*. El Paso: Texas Western Press, 1978.

Phillips, Dana. "Nineteenth-Century Racial Thought and Whitman's 'Democratic Ethnology of the Future.'" *Nineteenth-Century Literature* 49, no. 3 (1994): 289–320.

Pinsker, Sanford. "Walt Whitman and Our Multicultural America." *Virginia Quarterly Review* 75, no. 4 (1999): 716–22.

Pitkin, Thomas N. *Keepers of the Gate: A History of Ellis Island.* New York: New York University Press, 1975.

Portes, Alejandro. "Of Borders and States: A Skeptical Note on the Legislative Control of Immigration." *America's New Immigration Law: Origins, Rationales and Potential Consequences.* Ed. Wayne A Cornelius and Ricardo Anzaldua Montoya. San Diego: Center for U.S.-Mexico Studies, 1983. 17–32.

Portes, Alejandro, and Rubén G. Rumbaut. *Immigrant America: A Portrait.* Berkeley: University of California Press, 1990.

Powderly, Terence. "Immigration's Menace to the National Health." *North American Review* 175 (1902): 53–60.

Reed, Alfred C. "Going through Ellis Island." *Popular Science Monthly* 82 (January 1913): 5–18.

———. "Immigration and the Public Health." *Popular Science Monthly* 83 (October 1913): 313–38.

———. "The Medical Side of Immigration." *Popular Science Monthly* 80 (April 1912): 384–90.

Reisler, Mark. "Always the Laborer, Never the Citizen." *Between Two Worlds: Mexican Immigrants in the United States.* Ed. David D. Gutierrez. Wilmington, Del.: Scholarly Resources, 1996. 23–44.

Renan, Ernest. "What Is a Nation?" Trans. Martin Thom. *Nation and Narration.* Ed. Homi K. Bhabha. London: Routledge, 1990. 8–22.

Reynolds, David S. Introduction. *A Historical Guide to Walt Whitman.* Ed. David S. Reynolds. Oxford: Oxford University Press, 2000. 3–14.

Rice, Grantland S. "Crèvecoeur and the Politics of Authorship in Republican America." *Early American Literature* 28 (1993): 91–119.

Rosello, Mireille. *Postcolonial Hospitality: The Immigrant as Guest.* Stanford: Stanford University Press, 2001.

Rucker, Mary E. "Crèvecoeur's *Letters* and Enlightenment Doctrine." *Early American Literature* 13 (1978): 193–212.

Ruttenburg, Nancy. *Democratic Personality: Popular Voice and the Trial of American Authorship.* Stanford: Stanford University Press, 1998.

Said, Edward. *Orientalism.* New York: Vintage, 1978.

———. "Reflections on Exile." *Granta* 13 (1984): 159–72.

Shapiro, Michael J., and Hayward R. Alker, eds. *Challenging Boundaries.* Minneapolis: University of Minnesota Press, 1996.

Silverstein, Stuart. "Job Market a Flash Point for Natives, Newcomers." *Los Angeles Times*, 15 November 1993, § A, p. 17.

Smith, Roger M. *Civic Ideals: Conflicting Visions of Citizenship in U.S. History.* New Haven: Yale University Press, 1997.

Smith, Scott. "A Leader for Liberty." *Hemisphere Magazine*, December 2000, 29–32.

Sowell, Thomas. *Ethnic America: A History*. New York: Basic Books, 1981.

Stacy, G. Palmer, III, and Wayne Lutton. *The Immigration Time Bomb*. Alexandria, Va.: American Immigration Control Foundation, 1985.

"Statement of U.S. Senator Russell Feingold on the Anti-terrorism Bill from the Senate Floor," 25 October 2001.

Steiner, John. "The Retreat from Truth to Omnipotence in Sophocles' *Oedipus at Colonus*." *International Review of Psycho-Analysis* 17 (1990): 227–37.

———. "Turning a Blind Eye: The Cover Up for Oedipus." *International Review of Psycho-Analysis* 12 (1985): 161–72.

Stevens, Jacqueline. *Reproducing the State*. Princeton: Princeton University Press, 1999.

Takaki, Roland. *Iron Cages: Race and Culture in Nineteenth-Century America*. New York: Alfred A. Knopf, 1979.

———, ed. *Debating Diversity: Clashing Perspectives on Race and Ethnicity in America*. Oxford: Oxford University Press, 2002.

"This Country Is Truly Open to You." *Los Angeles Times*, 1 September 2004, § A, p. 20.

Tocqueville, Alexis de. *Democracy in America*. Trans. Henry Reeve. New York: Bantam Classic, 2000.

———. *"The European Revolution" and Correspondence with Gobineau*. Ed. John Lukacs. Gloucester, Mass.: Peter Smith, 1968.

U.S. Department of Justice, Immigration and Naturalization Service. *Building a Comprehensive Southwest Border Enforcement Strategy*. Washington: Immigration and Naturalization Service, 1996.

———. *Guide for the Inspection and Processing of Citizens and Aliens by Officers Designated as Immigration Officers*. Washington: Immigration and Naturalization Service, 1986.

———. *Immigration Detention Officer Handbook*. Washington: Immigration and Naturalization Service, 1987.

———. *Meeting the Challenge through Innovation*. Washington: Immigration and Naturalization Service, 1996.

Vance, William. "What They're Saying about Whitman." *Raritan* 16 (1997): 127–51.

Volney, Constantin François Chasseboeuf, Comte de. *Tableau du climat et du sol des États-Unis d'Amérique*. Trans. C. B. Brown. New York: Hafner, 1968 (1804).

Walzer, Michael. *What It Means to Be an American*. New York: Marsilio, 1992.

Warden, David Bailie. *A Statistical, Political, and Historical Account of the*

United States of North America; from the Period of their First Colonization to the Present Day. Edinburgh: A Constable, 1819.

Weintraub, Daniel M. "Wilson Ad Sparks Charges of Immigrant-Bashing." *Los Angeles Times,* 14 May 1994, § A, p. 22.

Whitman, Walt. *The Gathering of the Forces.* Ed. Cleveland Rodgers and John Black. New York: Putnam, 1920.

———. Preface to *Leaves of Grass. The Portable Walt Whitman.* Ed. Mark Van Doren. New York: Penguin, 1945.

———. "Song of Myself." *Complete Poetry and Selected Prose of Walt Whitman.* Boston: Houghton Mifflin, 1959.

Whitney, Thomas R. *A Defence of the American Policy, as Opposed to the Encroachments of Foreign Influence, and Especially to the Interference of the Papacy in the Political Interests and Affairs of the United States.* New York: DeWitt & Davenport, 1856.

Wolin, Sheldon. *Tocqueville between Two Worlds: The Making of a Political and Theoretical Life.* Princeton: Princeton University Press, 2001.

Yew, Elizabeth. "Medical Inspection of the Immigrant at Ellis Island, 1891–1924." *Bulletin of the New York Academy of Medicine* 56 (1980): 488–510.

Yuval-Davis, Nira, and Floya Anthias, eds. *Women-Nation-State.* London: Macmillan, 1989.

Žižek, Slavoj. *Welcome to the Desert of the Real.* London: Verso, 2002.

Index

Ali Behdad is a professor of English

and comparative literature at the University

of California, Los Angeles.

Library of Congress
Cataloging-in-Publication Data

Behdad, Ali, 1961–
A forgetful nation : on immigration and
cultural identity in the United States /
Ali Behdad.
p. cm.
Includes bibliographical references and index.
ISBN 0-8223-3606-5 (cloth : alk. paper)
ISBN 0-8223-3619-7 (pbk. : alk. paper)
1. United States—Ethnic relations. 2. United States
—Race relations. 3. National characteristics, American.
4. United States—Emigration and immigration—Political as-
pects—History. 5. Amnesia—Political aspects—United States—
History. 6. Nativism—History. 7. Xenophobia—
Political aspects—United States—History. 8. Pluralism
(Social sciences)—United States—History. 9. National
characteristics, American, in literature. 10. Emigration
and immigration in literature.
I. Title. E184.A1B34 2005
305.8′00973—dc22   2005009528